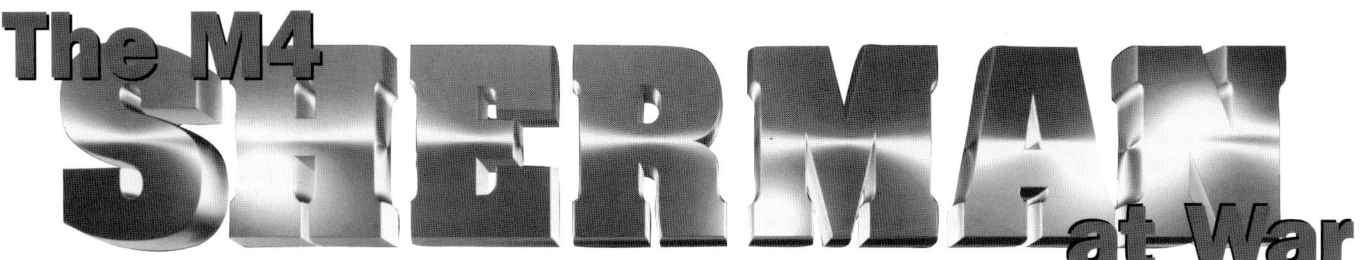

The M4 SHERMAN at War

The European Theatre 1942-1945

Steven J. Zaloga

CONCORD
PUBLICATIONS COMPANY

M4 Development

The US Army was a relative late-comer to the tank business in World War 2. The US tank force on the eve of war in Europe in 1939 was that of second-rate power; indeed the US Army had fewer tanks than armies like Italy or Poland. The neglect of the US armored force was caused by a complicated set of conditions including the economic stagnation of the Great Depression, and the tendency towards isolationism in US foreign policy. By 1940, President Franklin Roosevelt had begun to commit the US Army to a major rebuilding due to the perception that the United States would eventually be dragged into war. An important element in this effort was the considerable expansion of the US defense industry, to supply Lend Lease needs as well as the growing US Army.

The clearest evidence of the stagnation of American tank design was the US Army's first medium tank, the dreadful M2A1 medium tank which was manufactured from December 1940 through August 1941. This embarrassing design was manufactured simply because no other types were available. It is a grim curiosity that the M2A1 entered production at exactly the same time that the T-34 medium tank entered production in the Soviet Union. Although US tank design had suffered from a lack of funding, the US Ordnance Corps had wisely chosen to invest its scanty budget in tank components, such as guns, transmissions, and suspensions. So when new tanks were demanded, the Ordnance Corps could respond reasonably quickly, as occured in 1940.

The first modern US medium tank was the M3, later called the Lee by the British Army. This tank used an obsolete configuration patterned after the French Char B-1 bis with the main 75mm gun in a hull mounting with limited traverse, and a secondary 37mm gun in a small turret. This design was selected because US industrial facilities were not yet ready to manufacture cast turrets large enough to accomodate the 75mm gun that was desired. Production of the M3 Lee began at the American Locomotive Works and Baldwin Locomotive Works in June 1941, the same month that German invaded the Soviet Union. Production continued until December 1942 by which time 6,258 had been built. Of these, 70% were exported, including 2,887 to Britain and 1,386 to the Soviet Union. The M3 Lee, and the modified M3 Grant medium tanks, were first used by Britain in the Western Desert Campaign in 1941. They were appreciated for their firepower and automotive reliability, but the outdated configuration was regarded as deficient. The M3 Lee was used by the US Army for training the new armored divisions. Ultimately, few were used by the US Army in combat, mainly during the early stages of the 1942 Tunisian campaign.

Design of the M4 tank was started in February 1941 and the first T-6 prototype was ready by September 1941. The M4 used essentially the same chassis as the M3 Lee. The superstructure was modified to permit use of a conventional turret, armed with a 75mm dual-purpose gun. US Army doctrine stressed the need for a dual-purpose weapon, capable of firing both armor piercing and high explosive ammunition. This was based in part on the advice of US liaison officers serving with the British Army in the desert fighting who noted the problems that British tanks were having when armed with weapons like the 2 pounder gun that only fired armor piercing (AP) ammunition.

The T-6 prototype was subjected to numerous modifications, and the first production M4A1 medium tank emerged in February 1942 at the Lima Locomotive Works in Ohio, two months after the US had entered the war. The first production model was the M4A1. This employed a cast-hull which became the characteristic feature of this version. A welded hull version was also planned which was identical automotively, sharing the same Whirlwind radial aircraft engine. The first M4 was manufactured at the Pressed Steel Car Company in July 1942. One of the main production problems facing the US war industry was the lack of suitable engines. The Whirlwind radial engine was in widespread demand by the aviation industry for warplanes, so alternative engines had to be found. The GM 6-71 diesel bus engine was adapted but mounting two together, and this resulted in the M4A2. The M4A2 used a welded hull like the M4, but had a different engine deck configuration due to differences in the engine cooling system. The M4A2 actually entered production before the M4, with the first being built by the Grand Blanc Tank Arsenal in April 1942. The US Army was opposed to using diesel powered tanks due to the problems this created with fuel supply in the field. As a result, the M4A2 was not regularly used in combat by the US Army. It was principally shipped to the Soviet Union, which preferred diesel tanks anyways, and many were also supplied to the Free French and Polish armored units through Lend Lease. The only American forces to regularly use the M4A2 in combat was the US Marine Corps, which preferred diesels since they shared the fuel used by amphibious landing craft.

The most popular version of the M4 in US Army service was the M4A3 which employed a Ford GAA gasoline engine. Production of these began in June 1942, and except for small numbers of trials vehicles and howitzer tanks shipped through Lend Lease, nearly all were earmarked for the US Army. The last major M4 variant was the M4A4 which was powered by the unusual Chrysler A-91, an engine created by mating four automobile engines together. The M4A4 entered production in July 1942, and most were supplied to Britain. They were used stateside by some US units for training, but there is no evidence that any were issued to US units in combat. The M4A5 designation was reserved for the Canadian Ram tank. The M4A6 was a minor type using a new engine and composite cast/welded hull, but none were used in combat.

Improved M4 Medium Tanks

All of these M4 variants underwent continual evolution. Many of the evolutionary changes in the M4 series are mentioned in the captions.

Generally, changes introduced on one model carried through all versions. One of the earliest changes was the substitution of a new suspension bogie for the M-3 type, sometimes called a heavy-duty bogie, which had the return roller mounted on a trailing arm instead of over the main assembly.

The welded hull M4 versions (M4, M4A2, M4A3) were improved with a new uparmored hull with a simplified glacis plate at a 47⁰ angle that entered production in 1944; a similar improvement was introduced on the M4A1 cast hull version around the same time. This change was accompanied by improved ammunition racks with water-filled cavities to reduce the risk of ammunition fires if a tank was hit. Sometimes, these tanks had the designation "W" (for "Wet") added to their names, such as M4A3(75)W, or they were called M4 (75mm, wet); the former style is used in this book.

One of the most important changes was the decision to up-gun the M4 medium tank with a 76mm M1 gun mounted in an enlarged T-23 turret. These entered production as the M4A1(76)W in January 1944, the M4A2(76)W in May 1942, the M4A3(76)W in March 1944. Neither the M4 nor the M4A4 were built with the 76mm gun.

During combat, it was found that it would be useful to have a support tank version of the M4 armed with a howitzer to fire larger high explosive rounds. These were built on the M4 and M4A3 chassis, primarily for use by the US Army. These entered production in February 1944, and used the improved hull, but without wet stowage. One of the rare versions of the Sherman to see combat was the M4A3E2 Jumbo tank. This was a special assault tank with much heavier armor on the front and sides. Only 254 were built beginning in May 1944, and they were issued in small numbers to most US armored divisions starting in the autumn of 1944. Although originally armed with the normal 75mm gun, most were rearmed with the 76mm gun before seeing combat.

The final major evolutionary change in the M4 series was HVSS (Horizontal Volute Spring Suspension).

The M4 had long been criticised for its poor performance in mud, snow, sand and other poor soil conditions. This was due to the fact that its tracks were very narrow. Expedient solutions, such as "duckbill" extended end-connectors could ameliorate the situation, but a new suspension spaced further out from the hull was needed to use a wider track. In August 1944, production of the first M4A3(76)W HVSS tanks began. These are sometimes called M4A3E8 after the prototype with this suspension, but this was not an official designation for the production types. The HVSS suspension was added to M4 105mm howitzer tanks produced from September 1944 and M4A3 105mm howitzer tanks starting in August 1944. The first tanks with HVSS suspension began entering combat in December 1944. HVSS suspension was not fitted to any other M4 variant during the war, though after the war, some other variants were rebuilt with this feature.

In total, 46,732 M4 medium tanks were built through June 1945, of which 22,098 (47%) were provided to allied armies through Lend Lease. By way of comparison, the Germans built only 18,870 tanks during the same period from 1942 to 1945. The only tank manufactured in larger numbers during the war was the Soviet T-34 with 64,550 built through 1945.

The M4 chassis also served as the basis for a wide range of other armored vehicles. The M10 76mm tank destroyer and M36 90mm tank destroyer were counterparts of the M4 intended specifically for anti-tank missions. The M7 105mm Howitzer Motor Carriage, M12 and M40 155mm Gun Motor Carriage were the principal self-propelled artillery weapons of the US Army in World War 2. Specialized types like the M32 armored recovery vehicle were also manufactured. In total, over 15,000 armored vehicles derived from the M4 were also built during the war, of which over 10,000 were the M10 and M36 tank destroyers.

The M-4 in Combat

The 2nd Armored Division was the first US Army unit to receive the M4A1 medium tank in large numbers in the summer of 1942. This advantage was shortlived, as the division was ordered to transfer its tanks to Britain for use in the forthcoming offensive at El Alamein which took place in late October 1942. A total of 318 M4A1 and M4A2 medium tanks were shipped through the middle of September where they were called the Sherman II and Sherman III. The British Army had adopted the policy of naming American tanks after US Civil War generals, and the M4 was known, appropriately enough, as the Sherman. This name was never officially adopted by the US Army, but the M4 subsequently became better known in the popular mind as the Sherman. However, the M4 tank was seldom, if ever, referred to as a Sherman by US tankers during World War 2.

The Sherman was first used in combat on 24 October 1942 during the battle for El Alamein with British armored units. The Sherman was immediately popular in British service. The layout was more modern than the M3 Grant and Lee, and the Sherman had better firepower than any contemporary British tank. It was the only tank in British service during the offensive that compared favorably to the German Pz.Kpfw. III or Pz.Kpfw. IV tanks of the period.

The US Army's 2nd Armored Division was reequipped with M4 and M4A1 tanks in the early autumn of 1942 in preparation for Operation Torch, the invasion of French North Africa. The 1st Armored Division at the time was already equipped with the M3 medium tank, but M4 and M4A1 medium tanks were provided to the 2nd and 3rd Battalions, 1st Armored Regiment of the 1st Armored Division before it was shipped to Tunisia in December 1942.

The combat debut of the M4 in US service took place on 6 December 1942 when a platoon from the 66th Armored Regiment, 2nd Armored Division was sent into action against entrenched German anti-tank guns near Djebel bou Aoukar in Tunisia. Manned by inexperienced crews, most were quickly knocked out. The M4s unhappy debut in US Army service foreshadowed the grim battles that were to follow. In Februrary 1943, the 1st Armored Regiment of the 1st

Armored Division was sent into action near Sid bou Zid in Tunisia to defend against a major Afrika Korps offensive codenamed Operation Fruhlingswind (Spring Wind), the opening phase of what would become known as the battle for Kasserine Pass. The German offensive contained the most experienced Afrika Korps tank units as well as the highly prized sPzAbt 501 with its new Tiger I tanks. The inexperienced American tankers were outnumbered and severely beaten by the veteran German tankers losing 44 M4 and M4A1s on 14 February and about as many during a failed counterattack the next day. Nevertheless, the US tanks managed to knock out about 19 German tanks before succumbing. More training was needed. M4 and M4A1 medium tanks were used through the conclusion of the Tunisian campaign.

In general, the US tankers were pleased with the M4's performance, especially as compared to the M3 medium tank and the M3 "Stuart" light tank. American tankers felt that they could hold their own against German PzKpfw III and Pzkpfw IV tanks. The real problem was the M3 medium tank, which suffered from limited main gun traverse and was too large a target. The M3A1 light tank was roundly criticized as being completely unsuited for modern tank combat due to its thin armor and puny 37mm gun. It was acknowledged that the M4 could not tangle with the thickly armored Tiger heavy tank, but these were encountered in very small numbers. The US Army had its own heavy tanks in developement that were expected to be able to deal with this threat. The Tunisian campaign showed serious problems in the configuration of early US armored divisions, notably too many light tanks, and they were reorganized in 1943 with the M4 medium tanks predominating.

The next major campaign for the M4 and M4A1 tanks was Operation Husky, the invasion of Sicily. Sicily was very mountainous and not suited to tank warfare. As a result, there were fewer armored units committed to the invasion than to the Tunisian campaign. The 70th Light Tank Battalion was equipped entirely with M5 light tanks and the 753rd Tank Battalion was equipped with the M4A1 medium tank. The 2nd Armored Division, reorganized and reequipped after the Tunisian fighting, was the largest US armor unit deployed on Sicily. Axis armor forces on Sicily consisted mainly of the Hermann Goering Panzer Division, the sPzAbt 504 Tiger regiment and the Italian 131 Reggimento Carristi equipped with obsolete French Renault 35.R infantry tanks.

The hilly terrain of Sicily did not favor tank actions, and the initial tank skirmishes were confused and indecisive. The 753rd Tank Bn. knocked out three Tigers for the loss of 4 M4A1s near Piano Lupo on 11 July 1943, and several more were lost during a firefight with 2nd Armored Division. Most of the Italian Renault 35.R tanks were destroyed by US infantry. The US forces enjoyed the advantage of naval gunfire support, and several German tank attacks were stopped in their tracks. By 16 July 1943, the German attempts to stamp out the Gela beach-head had failed, costing 30 PzKpfw III and IV tanks and 14 of the 17 Tigers of 2./sPzAbt 504. There was little tank fighting later in the campaign.

Gen. George S. Patton, commanding the US forces in the Sicily campaign, ordered the 2nd Armored Division to consolidate its forces for a new mission. Patton decided that the division had been improperly used, chopped up into small sub-units to support the infantry. Instead, he used it to spearhead a rapid assault to clear out western Sicily and capture Palermo. This was the type of exploitation mission for which the US armored division had been designed, and the 2nd Armored Division served admirably in this role. This mission took advantage of the M4's excellent automotive performance and reliability, characteristics which separated it from most other tanks of the period. The M4's excellent dual-purpose 75mm gun was very effective in routing out anti-tank gun positions, machine gun nests and similar targets. In general, Patton and the US Army were very happy with the performance of the 2nd Armored Division and the M4 medium tank in Sicily and saw no major need for a change.

The British Army had a different viewpoint. The experience of the North African desert campaign had convinced British tankers of the need to continually increase the anti-tank performance of their tank guns. British tanks in the desert fighting had gone from the machine gun armament of the Light Tank Mk. VI in 1940, to the 2 pdr. on the Matilda and Valentine of 1941, to the 6 pdr. and 75mm gun in 1942. British tank design was being pushed along by the threat of new German tanks and tank guns. German tank firepower was being pushed along by Soviet tank design.

The appearance of the Tiger I tank in Tunisia, and later in Sicily, convinced the British Army that something beyond the 6 pdr. and 75mm gun would be needed for the invasion of Europe in 1944. They decided to adapt the new towed 17 pdr. anti-tank gun as a tank weapon. The question remained as to which tank should be armed with it. British tank design during World War II was an embarrassment. Britain concentrated its industrial efforts on aircraft and ship design, and the army was left with the scraps. A new tank had been introduced in the final phase of the North Africa battles, the sluggish, but well armored Churchill tank. It was adequate for infantry support. But a new cruiser tank to replace the arthritic, thinly armored and undergunned Crusader was delayed until 1944. Fortunately, the US was able to supply large numbers of M4A4 Sherman tanks to fill the gap. The turret of the Sherman was barely able to accomodate the big 17 pdr. gun inside, so a bustle had to be added to the rear to reposition the radio. Nevertheless, the 17 pdr. conversion worked, and the new type became known as the Firefly. It was undoubtedly the best version of the Sherman for tank fighting to appear during the war.

Britain offered the 17 pdr. to the US Army, expecting the American to adopt it just as they had adopted the 6 pdr. for the US Army the 57mm anti-tank gun. Instead, the US Army refused. There were many reasons for the lack of US interest in the 17 pdr. To begin with, there was a lack of foresight about future German tank developments. The heavy Tiger had been encountered and overcome in Tunisia and Sicily without any major problems. US liaison teams in Moscow were shown a new Panther tank captured in the summer 1943 Kursk battle. But it was not as well armed or as well armored as the Tiger I and appeared to be a curiosity more than a threat. What the US Army failed to appreciate was that the Panther was intended for a different role than the Tiger I. The Tiger I was built in very limited numbers for special heavy tank regiments. The Panther was intended as a medium tank for regular German panzer divisions and would be built in large numbers (by German standards). Instead of encountering handfuls of Tigers, by the time of the Normandy invasion, half of all German tanks in France were the deadly Panther.

The second problem was US Army doctrine. The US Army viewed the principal role for its armored divisions to be exploitation. The infantry and artillery would secure a breach in enemy lines, and the armored divisions would rush through into the enemy rear. It was classic Blitzkrieg doctrine based on the US interpretations of Germany's 1940-41 campaigns. Unfortunately, this doctrine was no longer working for Germany and had been significantly modified by the new tactics and technology being developed on the Eastern Front. Panzer divisions could not avoid confronting enemy tank units and had to have the firepower to overwhelm them as was so clearly shown in the encounters with the new Soviet T-34. The Germans quickly adapted to the changing nature of armored warfare, but this was not very apparent to US planners.

The US Army in 1943-44 still had an outdated doctrine which did not favor the use of tanks for tank-vs.-tank combat. Indeed, the US Army had formed a special branch, the Tank Destroyer Force, specifically aimed at combating enemy tanks. The tank destroyers were given the specialized guns for destroying enemy tanks. At the time the M4 medium tank was armed with a short 75mm dual-prupose gun, its counterpart tank-destroyer, the M10, was armed with a long 76mm gun with superior anti-armor performance. If any vehicle would receive a new anti-tank gun to deal with the new German heavy tanks, it would be the tank destroyers.

The 17 pdr. was viewed as unsuitable for this role mainly because of the logisitical burden it would impose. The US Army already had too many calibers of ammunition in production and couldn't afford another one. Britain did not have the industrial capacity to supply both its own forces and the US Army with 17 pdr. ammunition. The US Army did not spurn the 17 pdr. on its technical merits, but mainly because of logistical and manufacturing concerns.

This attitude was not limited to stateside engineers isolated from the war zone. In 1944, the Ordnance Corps planned to begin slowly replacing the 75mm gun on the M4 with the new M1 76mm gun. This gun had better anti-armor performance than the 75mm gun, and used ammunition already in the pipeline for the tank destroyers. US tank commanders, when first shown the new M4A3(76)W in Britain in 1944, didn't want the new tank. Most of them, including George Patton, argued that the new 76mm gun did not have an adequate high explosive projectile, which they felt was more important in armored warfare than the improved anti-tank projectile since tank-vs. tank fighting was so rare.

In May 1944, the 1st Armored Division encountered its first Panther tanks during the breakout from the Anzio beach-head in Italy. It was too late to have any impact on the tank gun debate.

The M4 Medium Tank in Normandy

Four battalions of M4 tanks were scheduled to land with the first wave of troops at Normandy, two per beach. Two additional battalions were held in reserve. Britain had devised an amphibious version of the M4 called the DD tank, for Duplex Drive. Enough of these were supplied to the US Army for Operation Overlord. Utah Beach was the objective for the 70th and 746th Tank Battalions. The 70th had two companies of DD tanks, and one company of normal M4s fitted with wading trunks (its other company of M5A1 light tanks was left in England). The 746th Tank Bn. was equipped with normal M4 tanks fitted with deep water wading trunks which would allow them to drive ashore after being let off in shallow water from LCT assault craft. During the landing operation on 6 June 1944, both of these battalions put their tanks ashore without major difficulty, losing only a few tanks in tidal depressions.

The situation at Omaha beach was far worse. The water conditions off Omaha beach were much choppier than off Utah beach. Like the 70th Tank Battalion, both the 741st and 743rd Tank Bns. had two companies of DD tanks and one of normal tanks with wading trunks. Of the 32 DD tanks in the 741st, 27 sank after encountering high swells, 3 became stuck on their LCT landing craft and could not be launched, and only 2 swam in to shore. The 743rd didn't even attempt to put their DD tanks into the water, and simply landed them ashore. Aside from 8 tanks from the 743rd lost when their LCTs were sunk by German shore guns, all the others were landed. In total, 96 tanks were landed at Omaha beach within the first hour of the landing. The US tank units did not have the specialized mine clearing or combat engineer "Funnies" of the British Army, and beach obstructions caused bloody delays at Omaha. Nevertheless, by the day's end, the Normandy beach-head was firmly in Allied hands.

The Germans held their armor forces away from the beaches to lessen their vulnerability to Allied naval bombardment as had occured at Sicily and Anzio. They had expected that the invasion would come to the north on the Pas de Calais, and so had their forces improperly concentrated. During the first week of the Normandy fighting, they began moving their armor southward, especially towards the key town of Caen which controlled the road junctions leading away from the beach-head. Caen was in the British sector, and the British Army bore the brunt of the German tank attacks during the first several weeks of fighting.

Normandy was not well suited to tank fighting, as the fields were criss-crossed with bocage, a deep hedgegrow developed over the centuries by Normandy farmers to limit soil erosion from the harsh coastal winds. These formed natural tank traps, and most of the figting in the US sector was conducted by infantry with small numbers of tanks for fire support. The June fighting led US tankers to devise novel solutions to the bocage problem, notably the Cullin hedgegrow cutters, named after their inventor. They were also called Cullin prongs or Rhino devices. Tankers had found that when they tried to crash through the bocage, they could not build up enough speed to plow through. Instead, the tanks simply climbed the hedgegrows, thereby exposing the thin belly armor to German anti-tank teams in the neighboring hedges. The Cullin device was simply an array of girders attached to the transmission housing. When the tank struck the hedgegrow with the Cullin device, it stuck in the roots of the hedge, and allowed the tank to bulldoze through. Although widely celebrated at the time, some tankers interviewed by the author state that it didn't work as well as advertised and was not as widely used as the popular myths would suggest.

What did work in Normandy was air attack. German tank forces in Normandy had already been severely weakened by constant allied air attack. Contrary to the popular myths of Tornados and Thunderbolts blasting tanks with rockets and machine gun fire, in fact very few German tanks were actually destroyed from the air. Rather, the Anglo-American tactical air forces managed to shoot up the logisitical support such as trucks and repair vehicles which were essential to keep the panzer divisions operational. In addition, the Panther tanks were not capable of sustained road marches, and the air attacks managed to shatter the railroad network on which the Germans depended for moving their tank units. With the Germans fixated on the British 21st Army around Caen, and relatively immobile due to air attack, the US Army prepared to crash out of the bridge-head towards

Brittany on 25 July 1944 in Operation Cobra.

Cobra was preceded by a massive carpet bombing that devastated what German tank forces were present in front of the US positions, and helped eliminate the tenacious German infantry anti-tank teams that had proven such as threat in the earlier Normandy fighting. Cobra was a roaring success, and by early August, the 2nd, 3rd, 4th and 6th Armored Divisions were charging forward. With their defenses unhinged, the Germans tried to stem the American tide with a panzer attack at Mortain, including the excellent 2nd Panzer Division, as well as 1st and 2nd SS Panzer, and 116th Panzer divisions. The panzers gave the US infantry a rough time, but bolstered by omnipresent air support and the 2nd and 3rd Armored Division, the German assault was held. With British, Canadian and Polish armored thrusts from the north, and American from the south, the German army in Normandy was about to be encircled and trapped east of Falaise in an enormous debacle.

The performance of the M4 tank in the Normandy campaign campaign was acceptable, but the number of Panther tanks came as a surprise. The fine grained terrain characteristic of the coastal area did not allow the Germans to take maximum advantage of the firepower advantage enjoyed by the Panther. Nevertheless, the main concern to Shermans about the Panther was not its main gun. Indeed, either the PzKpfw IV or the Panther could penetrate the Sherman frontally from normal combat ranges of 1,000 yards. The Panther was a problem because of its thick, well sloped armor. A 75mm armed Sherman could not penetrate the armor of a Panther frontally except for a fluke shot, such as one ricocheting off the lower gun mantlet and into the thin roof armor over the driver. The 76mm gun on the new M4A1(76)W and M4A3(76)W could penetrate the Panther (theoretically) at 600 yards using the normal M62 armor piercing round. A far better alternative was the new tungsten-carbide core T4 HVAP round, sometimes called souped-up AP or hyper-shot by US tankers. This

could penetrate a Panther frontally at most normal combat ranges, but most tanks had only two or three rounds of this ammunition at any one time and it remained scarce until 1945.

The thin armor and mediocre firepower of the M4 compared to the Panther was a source of bitter complaint by US tankers. The initial resistance towards the 76mm tanks was quickly forgotten, and battalion commanders were soon pleading for more 76mm tank and more hyper-shot. However, the technical disparity between US and German tanks did not have a significant impact on the course of the fighting in 1944, although it did lead to higher US losses. The reasons for this were many. Although the Germans had a tough reputation after the bloody nose suffered by US tank units in Tunisia, by 1944, the quality of German tankers was decreasing and the quality of US tankers was increasing. The reason was training. US tankers in 1944 were far better trained in combined-arms tactics than their 1942 counterparts, and in many cases they were better trained than their German counterparts. No doubt there were many veteran German tank crews in Normandy in 1944, but there were also many green crews to fill the enormous gaps caused by Germany's long years of war. New German tankers got very little field training before entering combat due to fuel shortages. While the Gemans may have had more exceptional veteran crews in June 1944, on average, the American tankers were better trained.

The situation for the German panzer forces continued to decline as the war progressed. During the Lorraine campaign in September 1944, the German 5th Panzer Corps massed the largest concentration of German tanks seen since the battles at Caen and Mortain in July 1944. This counterattack force included over 300 tanks, with the majority being new Panther tanks. Unfortunately for the Wehrmacht, the crews and commanders were as new as their tanks. Their opponent was the 4th Armored Division, known as "Patton's Best", a well trained, well-led division which had become battle hardened since the fighting for Coutances in July

1944. From 19 to 22 September 1944, the 4th Armored Division broke the back of the German counteroffensive near Arracourt, destroying 107 tanks and 30 assault guns for the loss of only 14 M4 tanks and 7 M5A1 light tanks. Two of the new panzer brigades were wiped out in the fighting, and by the end of the fighting for Arracourt, the 4th Armored Division had destroyed 285 German tanks and armored vehicles for a loss of 25 medium tanks and 7 tank destoyers. At the same time, the veteran French 2e Division Blindee smashed another panzer brigade putting an end to the largest German armor operation in the West until the Battle of the Bulge.

The M4 had performed well in these battles due to the quality of its crews, and inspite of the technical shortcomings of the tank. The German tankers did not know how to exploit terrain to their best advantage because during training they simply didn't have enough fuel to practice field formations. In contrast, the 4th Armored Division had developed tactics to approach closely and hit the Panthers on their sides where they could be penetrated by 75mm guns. The M4 would fire smoke rounds at the Panthers to blind them, and then use the terrain to close on the Panthers before the smoke would dissapate. Some M4 tankers recall that the German crews were so inexperienced that they would abandon their tanks after being hit by 75mm high explosive rounds which did not penetrate.

Meeting engagements of the type seen at Arracourt were relatively uncommon in France. More often, small German armor formations would wait in ambush to hit unsuspecting M4 tanks and scoot away before they could be engaged. In these ambushes, many M4s were lost, their thin armor providing inadequate protection for their crews. On average, one crewman was lost every time an M4 was put out of action; the new vehicles with "wet" stowage being less susceptible to deadly ammunition fires than the older M4 tanks. Tank and anti-tank guns were the most common cause in Normandy, but after the summer of 1944, German infantry panzerfaust rocket grenade launchers became the predominent source of losses.

Battle of the Bulge

The last major tank-vs.tank encounters on the Western Front in World War II came in December 1944-January 1945 during the Battle of the Bulge. The Germans obtained a strategic surprise and threw their last reserve of panzer forces against US infantry units in the Ardennes region of Belgium. Several infantry divisions were crushed, but by the third week of December, the US Army was rushing substantial tank forces into Belgium to stem the German offensive. These tank battles were often fought under appalling weather conditions and at very close ranges. Both sides suffered very heavy losses in men and tanks. The critical difference was that the US had plenty of tanks and trained crews and Germany did not. There were no major encounters with German panzer forces after the Ardennes fighting as Germany was obliged to shift its surviving panzer divisions to the east in a hopeless atttempt to hold back the massive Soviet January offensive.

While the ultimate outcome of the war was no longer in doubt after the German defeat in the Ardennes, the war was far from over. The Wehrmacht continued to resist, particularly once the US Army reached German soil. The character of the fighting changed, with brutal street-by-street fighting taking part in many German towns. The changing style of fighting is reflected in the photos in this book. The US tank crew began more deliberate efforts to reinforce the M4's inadequate armor. Two approaches were taken. The most common technique was to load sandbags on the hull front, and sometimes on the hull sides as well. This was intended to offer a measure of stand-off protection against the panzerfaust rocket grenades. Sometimes the sandbags were filled with sand, sometimes with concrete. Officially, it was discouraged, since it added a great deal of weight leading to more frequent breakdowns and armor specialists argued that it did not offer significant additional protection anyways. Whether the protection was only psychological or not, the practice was popular in many units. The other approach was to layer on more steel armor. This was far less common, since steel armor was far more difficult to obtain than sandbags and concrete. Some of the armor came from knocked out US and German tanks, other armor was prepared by ordnance depots. Tanks with added armor were sometimes used in the role of assault tanks, leading columns into areas likely to be protected by panzerfausts or anti-tank guns. This was the role for which the M4A3E2 Jumbo was designed, but there were seldom enough of these available. Another improvised method was to use tanks fitted with bulldozer blades, with their blades elevated to offer a shield.

The M4 Sherman will win few nominations for the category of the best tank of World War 2. It was not as innovative as the Soviet T-34 or as well armored/armed as the Panther or Tiger I. Yet it deserves consideration in other categories. Automotively, it was one of the most dependable and rugged tanks of World War 2. A tank is just a chunk of useless steel if it is broken down with a bum transmission or engine as was so often the case with German heavy tanks. It was also well suited for mass production. German military writers often note that the Wehrmacht was overwhelmed in the west by larger numbers of tanks and other weapons. They have seldom acknowledged that this was possible because the US stuck to a proven, inexpensive design instead of producing small numbers of superbly crafted, but expensive heavy tanks like the Panther and Tiger.

Photo Sources

Unless otherwise noted, all photos in this book are official US Army Signal Corps photographs. These have been collected by the author at several archives including the Defense Audio Visual Agency offices formerly at the Pentagon and the DAVA Still Records Depository at the Anacostia Navy Yards. This collection is now maintained by the US National Archives. Other photos have come from personal collections, unit records, and the photo collections of other services such as the US Navy.

The North African Campaign

When it first went into combat in North Africa in the autumn of 1942, the 1st Armored Division was still partly equipped with the older M3 Lee medium tank. This is a M3 medium tank of E Company, 13th Arm'd. Regt., 1st Armored Division at Souk el Arba, Tunisia on 26 November 1942 at rest following combat the day before in support of British infantry of the 36 Brigade Group. The 1st Armored Division used a complicated pattern of geometric signs to identify its component units; the insignia of E Company can be seen on the hull side between the two crewmen on the right.

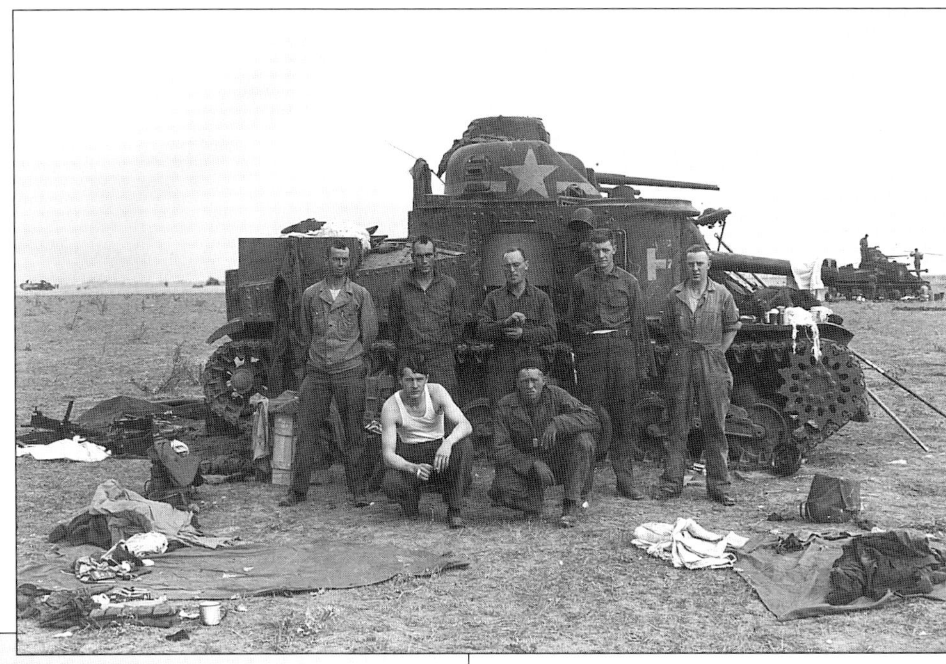

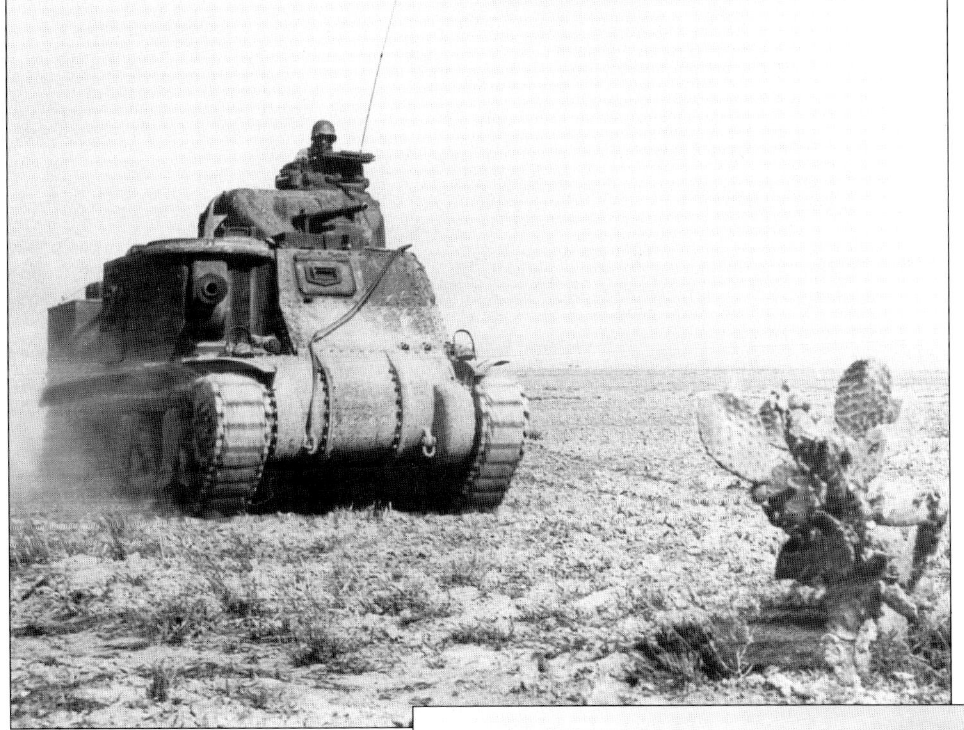

By the end of 1942, the M3 Lee medium tank was obsolete when compared to German tanks of the period. This M3 Lee of the 13th Arm'd. Regt., 1st Armored Div. is seen advancing near Souk el Khemis, Tunisia on 25 November 1942 during the battles by the Eastern Task Force to capture Tunis.

An M4A1 medium tank of G Co., 1st Arm'd. Regt., 1st Armored Div. crosses a dried out river bed near Sidi bou Zid, Tunisia on 14 Feb 1943. Most of this unit was knocked out later in the day during fighting with the German 21.Panzer Division. The German offensive, codenamed Fruhlingswind, nearly wiped out the 3rd Battalion, 1st Arm'd. Regt. About 15 of the 44 M4 and M4A1s lost were knocked out by Tigers of the sPzAbt. 501, the only Tiger unit in North Africa.

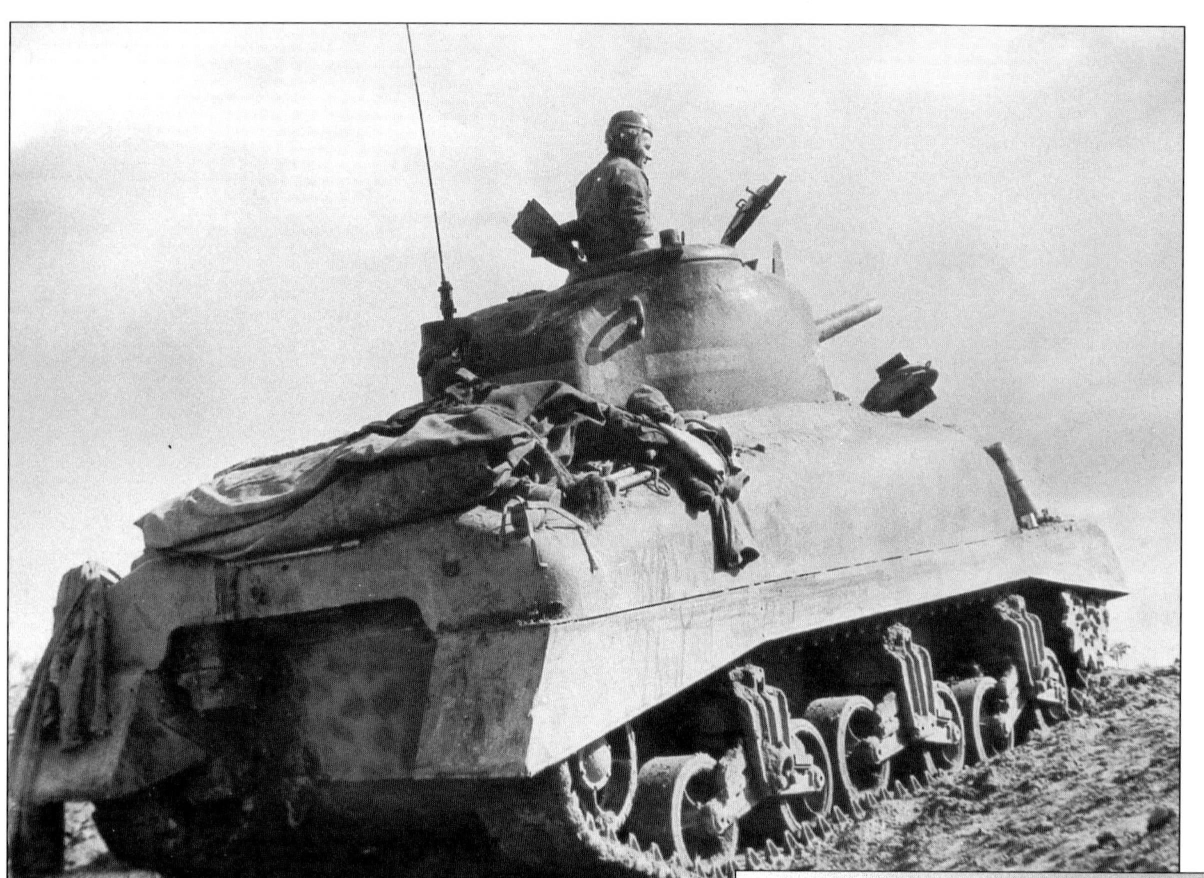

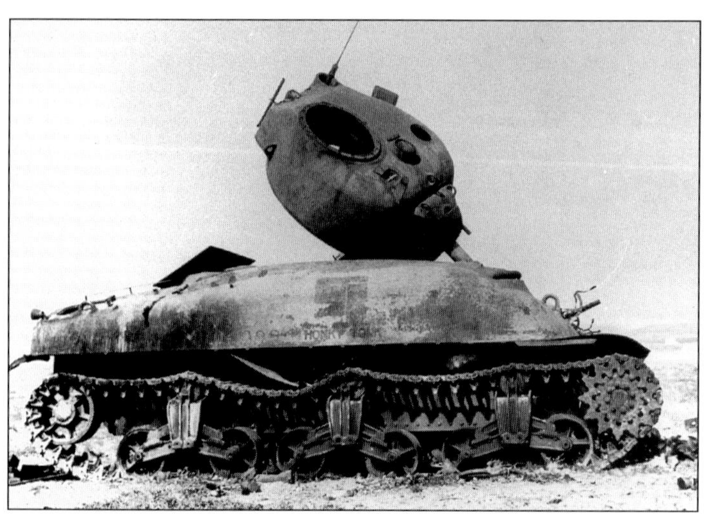

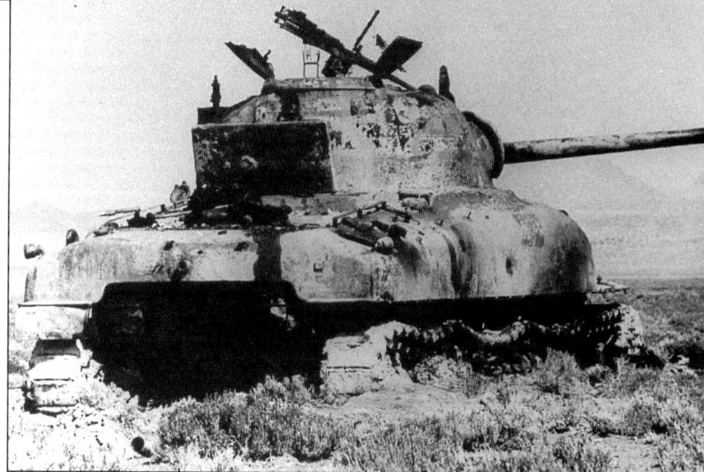

One of the M4A1 medium tanks lost at the battle for Sidi bou Zid from the 3rd Battalion, 1st Arm'd. Regt., 1st Armored Division. A number of these tanks were knocked out at long range by 88mm anti-aircraft guns supporting the German attack.

"Honky-Tonk", a M4A1 medium tank of H Co., 1st Arm'd. Regt. which has suffered a catastrophic ammunition fire, blowing off its turret during the fighting at Sidi bou Zid on 14-15 February 1943. A total of over 80 M4 and M4A1 tanks were lost during the fighting where an American force was overwhelmed by much larger and more experienced elements of Rommel's Afrika Korps. This is an early production M4A1 as is evident from the early M3 style of suspension.

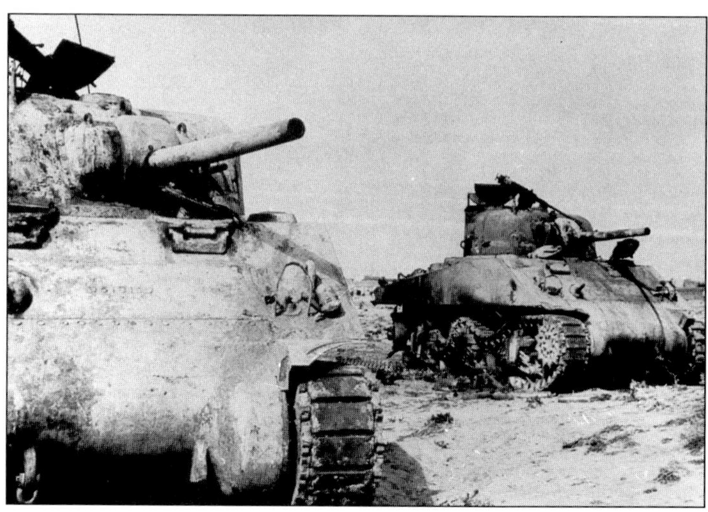

A pair of M4 medium tanks of F Company, 1st Arm'd. Regt., knocked out during the 15 February counterattack by Combat Command C southwest of Sidi Salem. This company was virtually wiped out in a short engagement with Pz.Kpfw. III and Pz.Kpfw.IV tanks with the tank in the foreground, #19, knocked out by a 75mm round from a Pz.Kpfw IV, and the tank in the background, #3, knocked out by a 50mm round from a Pz.Kpfw III. These are early production M4 tanks with the early suspension, early pattern armored visors for the driver and co-driver, and the early gun mantlet without the armored collars.

The M4A1 tank "Henry III" of Lt.Col. Henry Gardiner, commander of the 2nd Battalion, 13th Armored Regiment, 1st Armored Division. Gardiner lost two previous M4 medium tanks, including "Henry II" on 17 February at Sbeitla, but Rommel had called his battalion's defense of Sbeitla "clever and hard fought". The geometric design on the forward hull side is the tactical sign of the HQ Company of 2nd Battalion. (Col. Henry Gardiner)

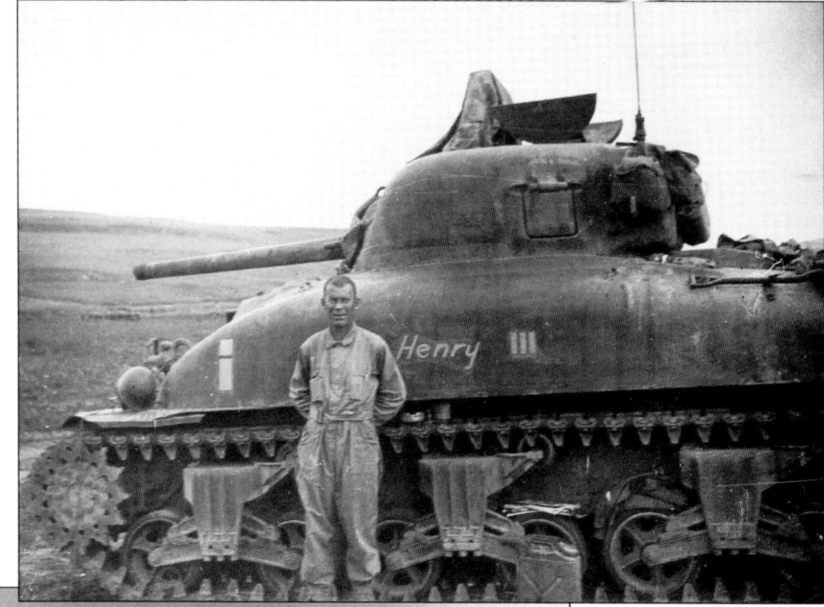

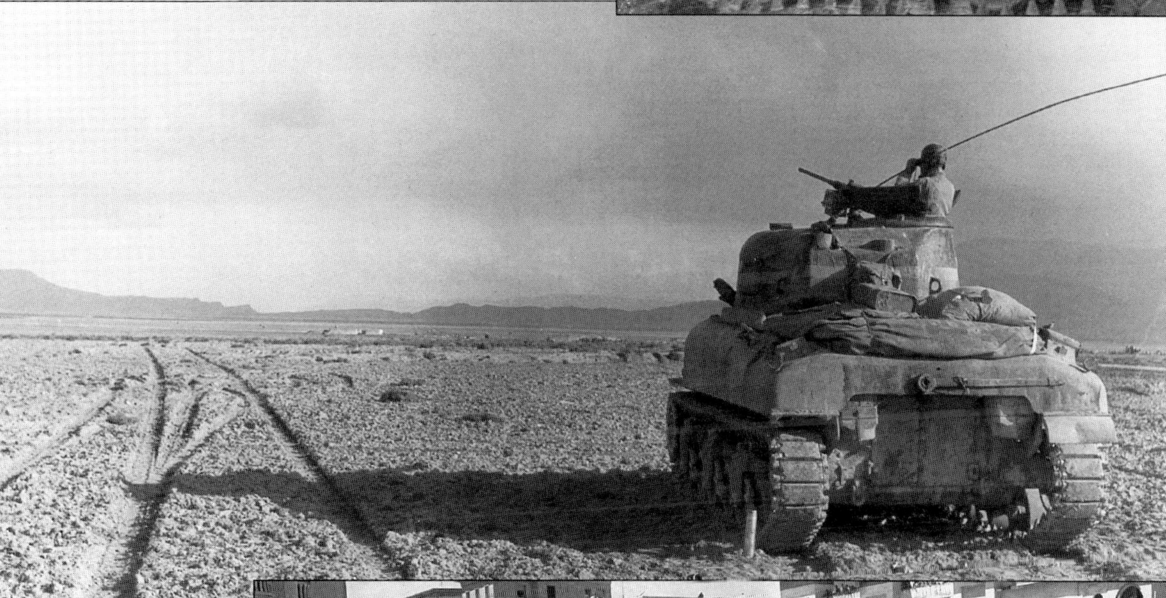

A M4A1 medium tank of Capt. G. W. Meade, commander of I Co., 1st Arm'd. Regt., 1st Armored Div. on the approaches to Kasserine Pass, Tunisia on 24 Feb 1943 shortly after the Allies had finally stopped the German and Italian advance. By this time, the 1st Armored Division had suffered very heavy tank casualties and had very few Shermans left in service.

The Allied victory in North Africa is celebrated on 4 July 1943 in Rabat, Morocco with a pair of camouflaged M7 105mm howitzer motor carriages in the lead. The M7 was a self-propelled artillery vehicle based on the M4 tank chassis. The sand camouflage on the M7s and the T-30 75mm howitzer motor carriages behind them was probably applied for the parade and does not follow the standard pattern.

The Italian Campaign

A M4A1 medium tank of the 2nd Armored Division on the beaches of Sicily on 10 July 1943. This tank belonged to "E" Company as is evident by its name. The small geometric signs below the name Eternity are the tactical signs of the 2nd Armored Division on Sicily, which have still not been deciphered completely. The white circle painted around the US star was adopted at the time of the Sicily invasion due to experiences in North Africa where it was found that the star could be mistaken for a German cross at long ranges.

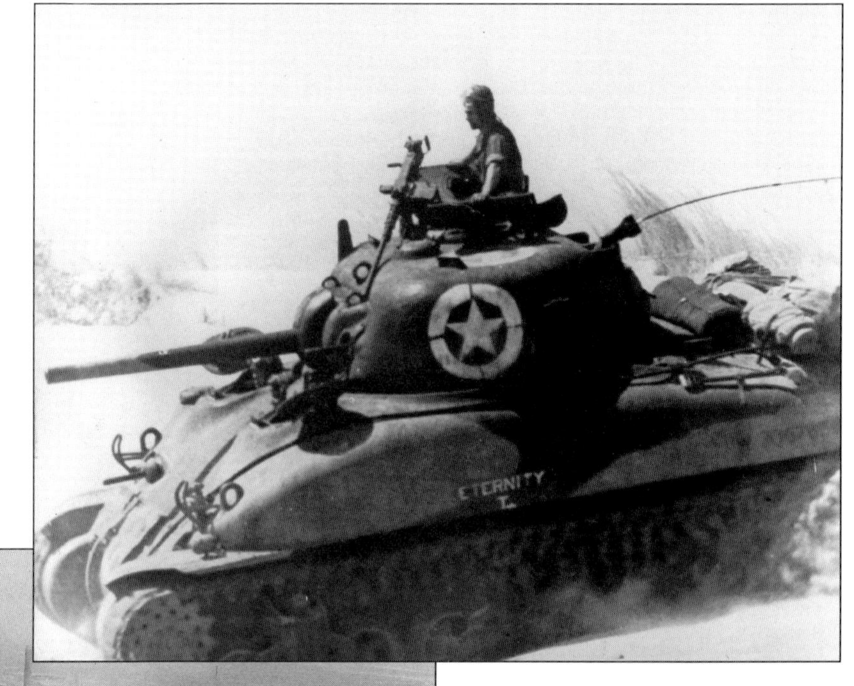

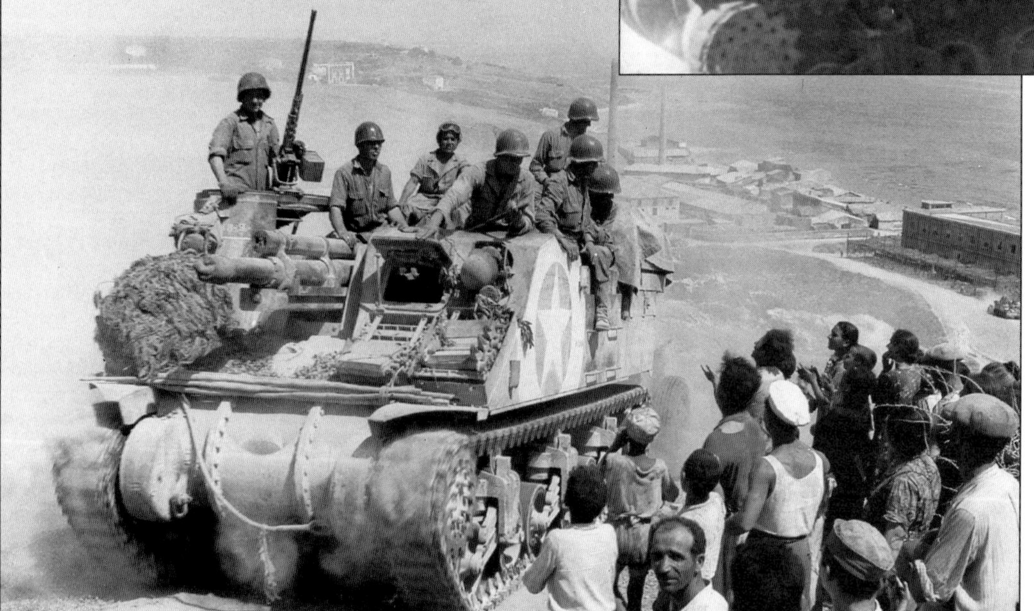

A M7 105mm howitzer motor carriage of the 2nd Armored Division in the outskirts of Sciacca, Sicily on 20 July 1943. This is an early production vehicle using the older M3 medium tank suspension. The large circle added to the US star insignia seems too large to fit the superstructure side.

A M7 105mm howitzer motor carriage named "Anna" of A Battery, 69th Armored Field Artillery of the 1st Armored Division near Nettuno, Italy on 2 February 1944, eleven days after the Anzio landing. This particular howitzer provided extensive fire support for the VI Corps offensive on the previous several days as is evident from the large number of cardboard ammunition packing cases littered around the weapon.

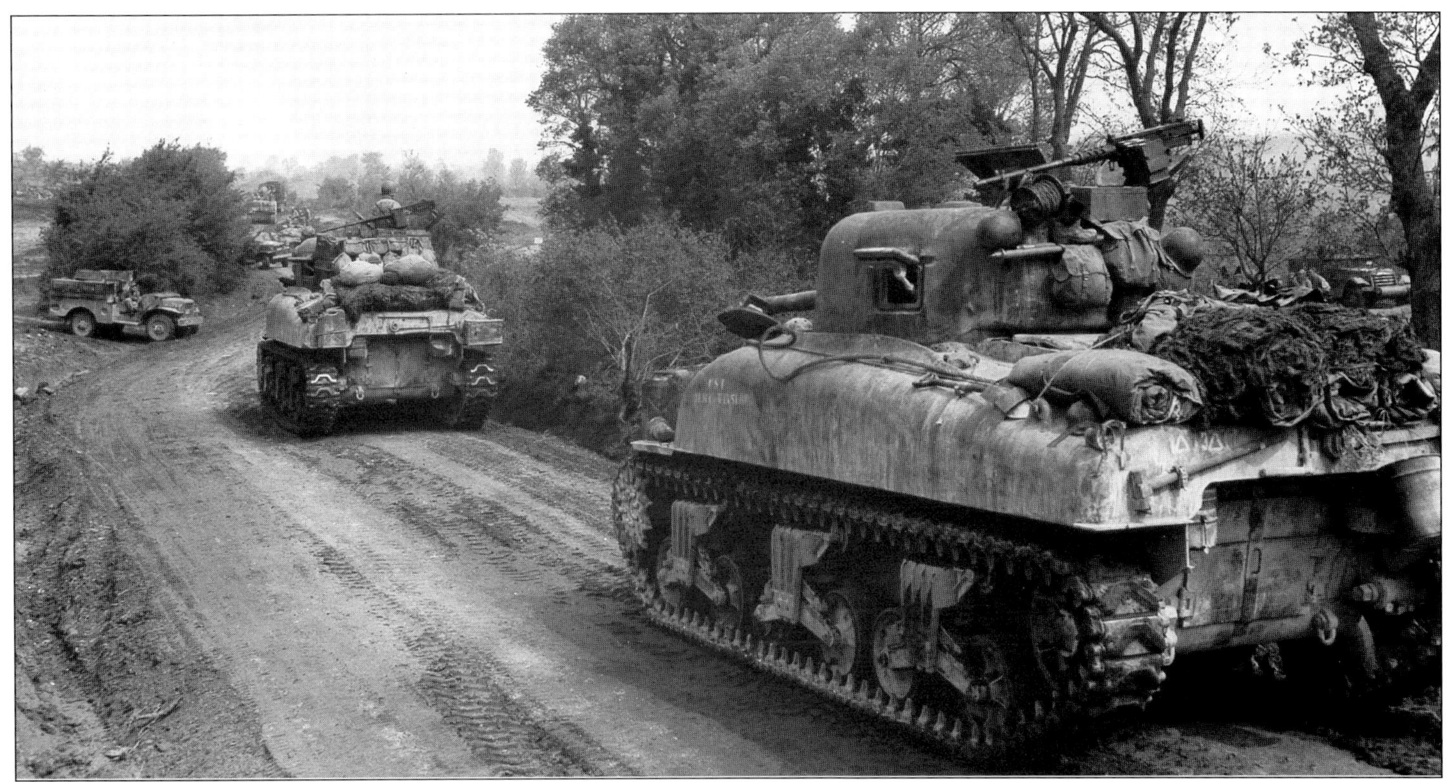

A column of M4A1 medium tanks of the 13th Arm'd. Regt., 1st Armored Division on 27 April 1944 during preparations leading to the final breakout from the Anzio beach-head in May 1944. During the Italian campaign, the 1st Armored Division did not employ the elaborate geometric tactical insignia used in North Africa.

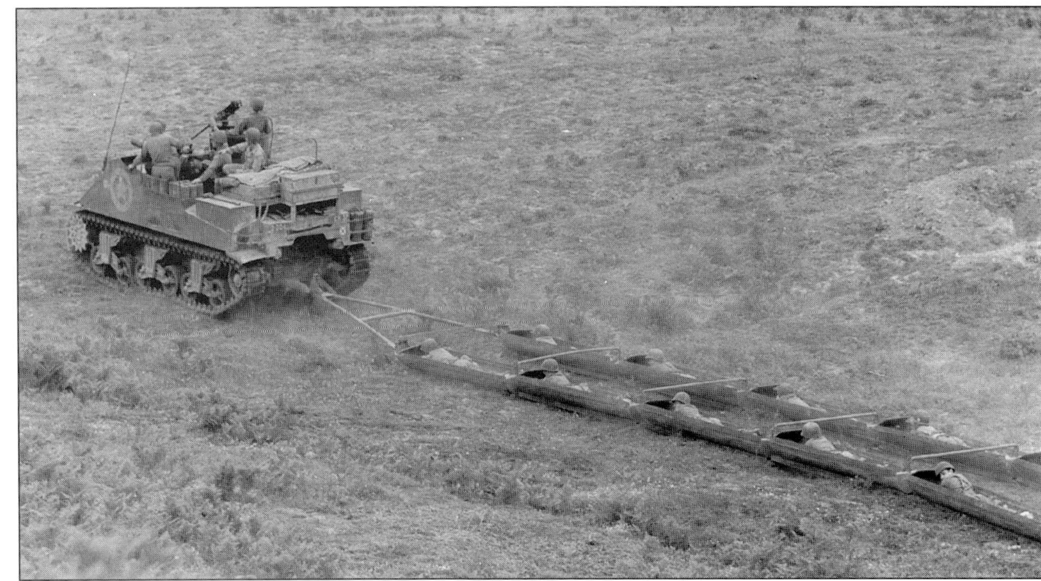

The US Army experimented with several unusual devices prior to the breakout from Anzio in May 1944, including this "Battle Sled" being towed behind a M7 HMC developed by Brig. Gen. John O'Daniel, commander of the 3rd Infantry Division. The idea was that it would provide protection to the infantry when attacking pillboxes or other defended objectives. It isn't known if it was ever used in combat.

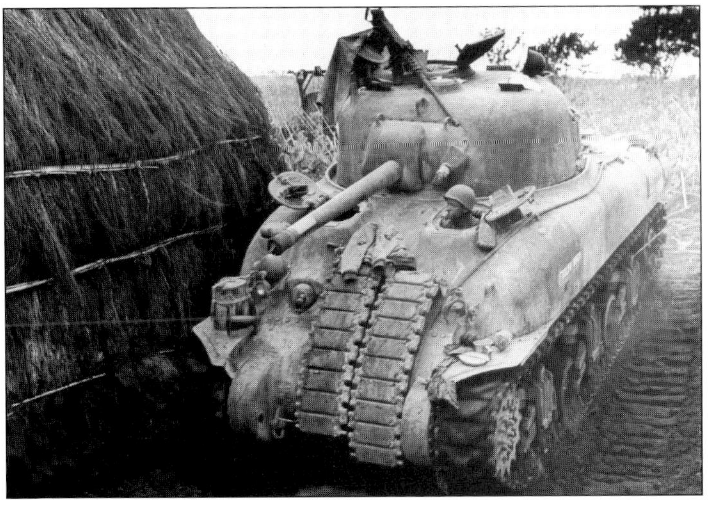

A M4A1 "Foolish Fella" of the HQ of F. Co, 13th Arm'd. Regt., 1st Armored Division in the Anzio beach-head on 27 April 1944. The double row of spare track links was a standard feature of 1st Armored Division tanks to improve their protection against German anti-tank guns. The 1st Armored Division used simplified tactical markings in Italy, consisting of bands painted around the gun barrel, repeated on the rear sides of the turret. The half-band on the forward barrel of this tank identifies it as a headquarters tank.

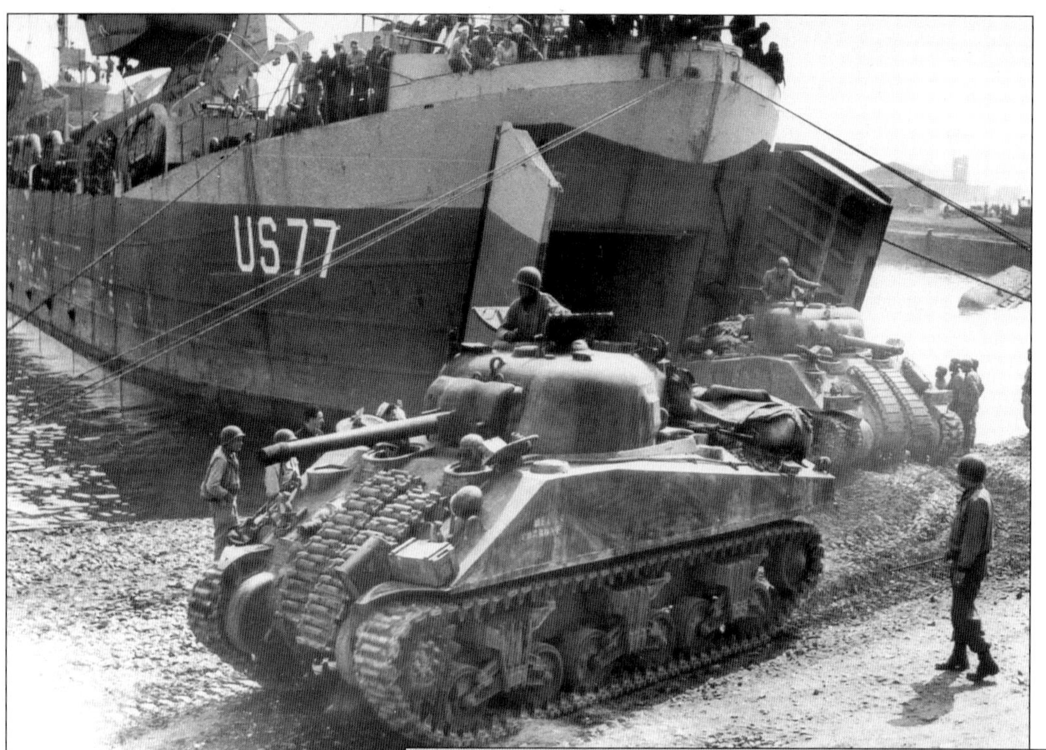

More M4 tanks pour ashore from an LST at Anzio on 23 May 1944 in support of the drive on Rome. The 1st Armored Division was the only armored division committed to this theatre after Sicily, but it had the separate 191st and 751st Tank Bns. attached.

"Weenie One", a camouflaged M4A1 of 1st Armored Division near Cisterna on 25 May 1944 during "Operation Buffalo", the attack towards Rome. By now the division was battle-hardened, and the Germans lost 15 Tiger I tanks during the fighting that day. Two days later, the division would encounter the first German Panther tanks in this theatre during the fighting near Velletri.

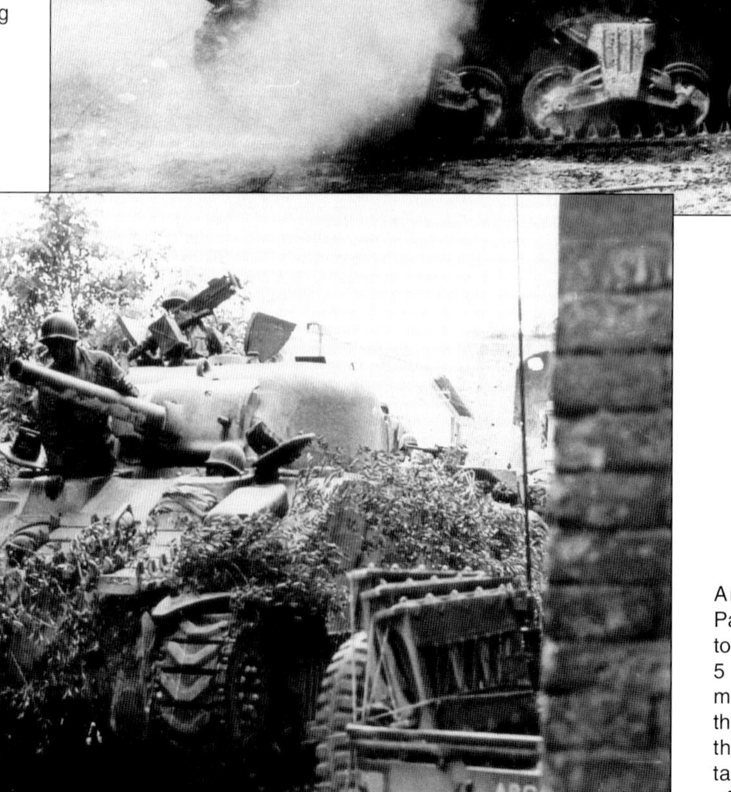

A M4 medium tank of the 1st Armored Division in the town of Paganico outside Rome. The division took part in the capture of Rome on 4-5 June 1944, and then proceeded to move against German forces north of the city towards the Arno River. Notice the white countershading under the tank's gun barrel, a rare use of this official US engineer camouflage technique.

A M4 medium tank of an independent tank battalion attached to 5th Army passes through Rome on 5 June 1944. The white Allied star with a circle was the standard US insignia at this stage of the war. Many units, including the 1st Armored Division, painted it out since it made too clear an aiming point for German anti-tank guns.

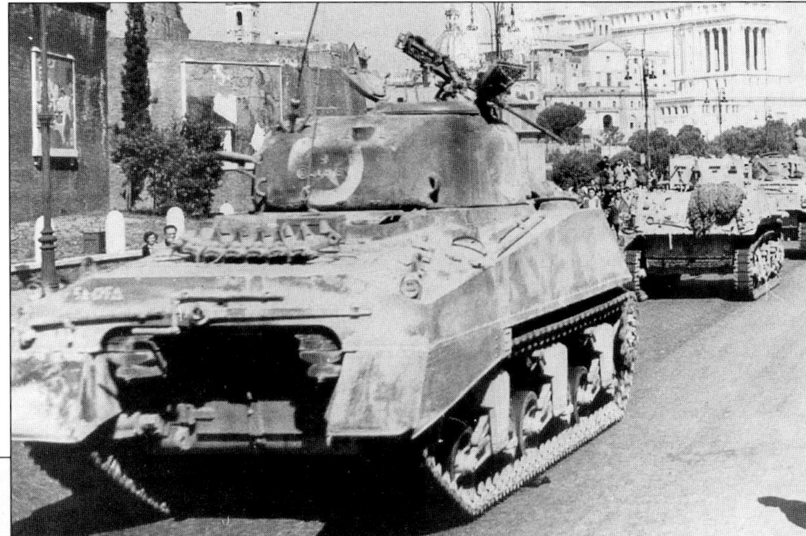

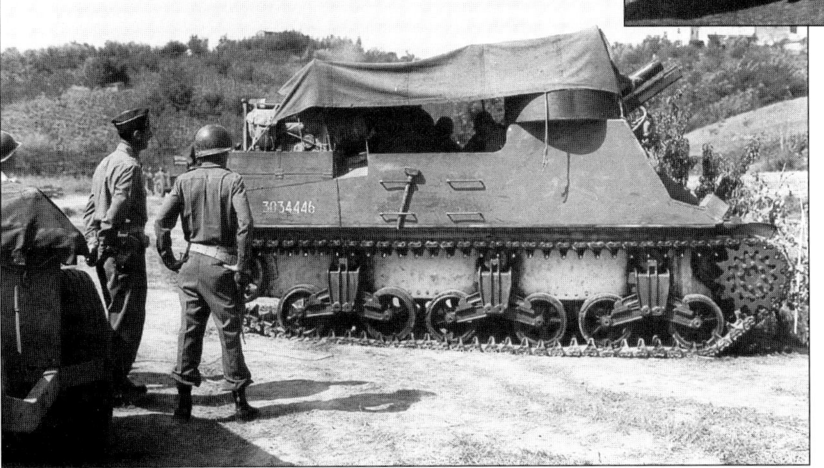

A M7 105mm howitzer motor carriage of the 91st Armored Field Artillery Battalion conducting a fire support mission on 24 August 1944 while the commander of the US 5th Army in Italy, Lt. Gen. Mark C. Clark looks on. This is an early production M7 HMC evident from its M3 pattern suspension. Interestingly enough, the lower hull sides are painted white, an engineer camouflage practice intended to break-up the apparent shape of the M7 by reducing the contrast between the hull and suspension.

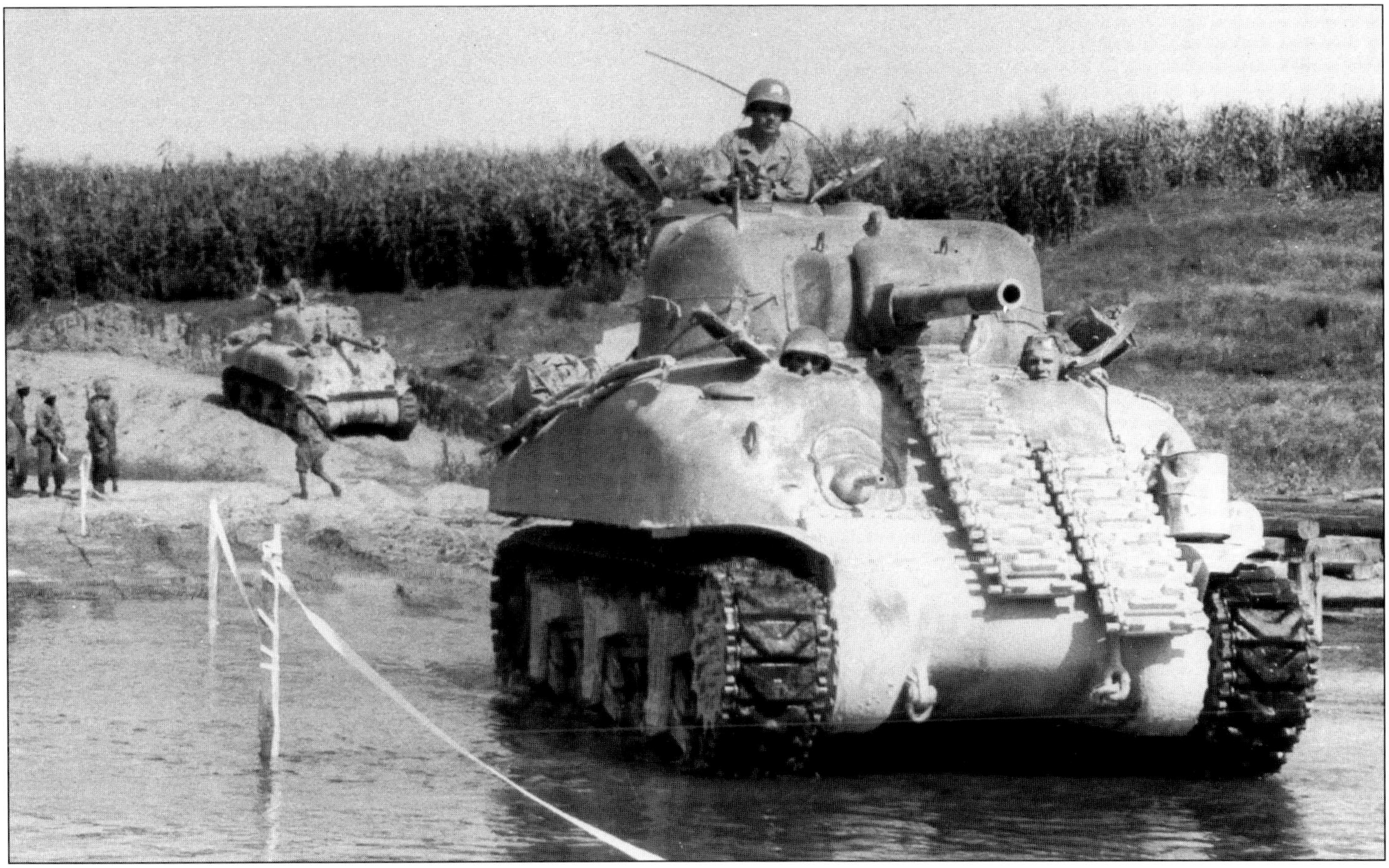

A M4A1 tank of the 1st Tank Battalion, 1st Armored Division crosses the Arno river at a ford near Casoina, Italy on 1 August 1944. The division was reorganized from its former "heavy" configuration on 20 July 1944, one of the last armored divisions to do so.

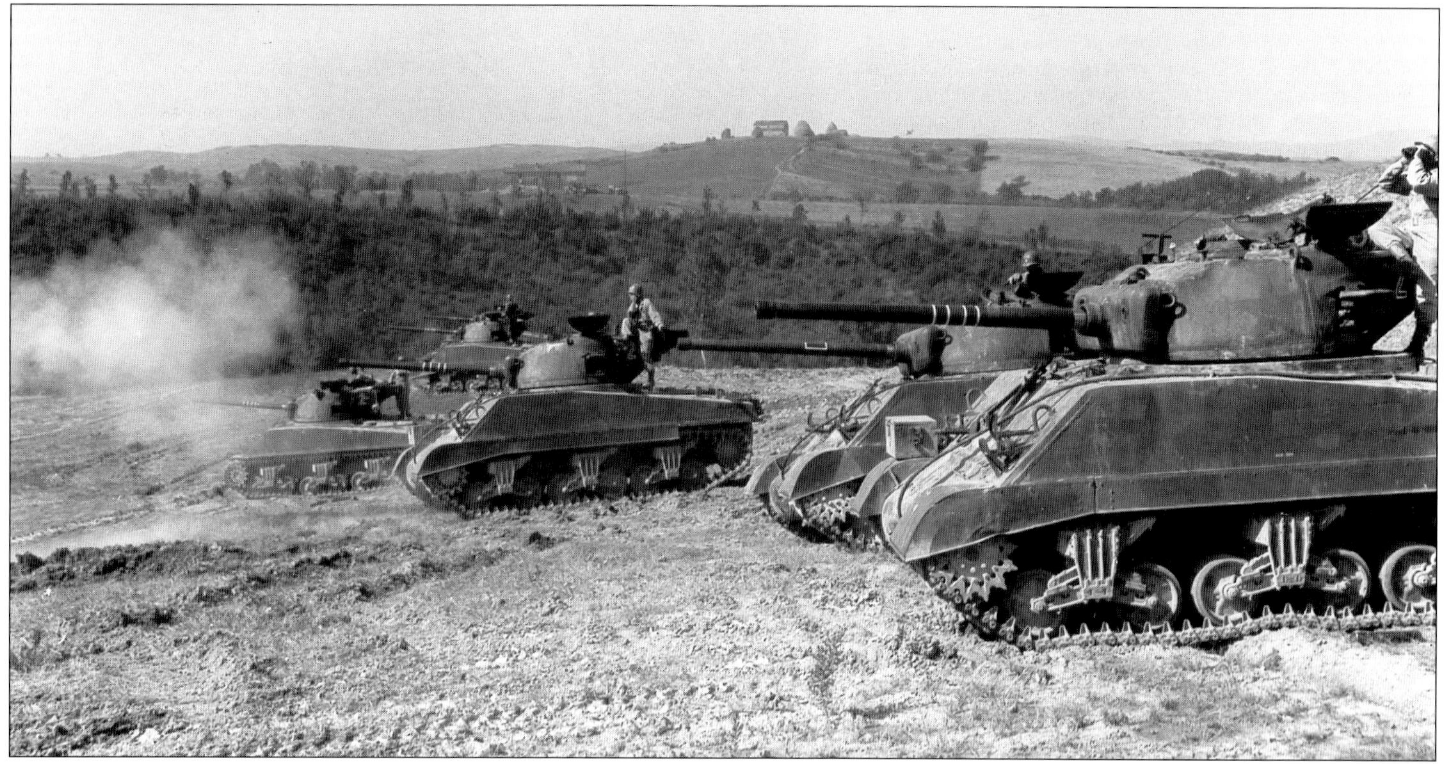

In August 1944, some battalions of the 1st Armored Division began to receive their first M4A3(76)W, armed with the long 76mm gun. Here, the 2nd Platoon, A Co., 13th Tank Battalion try out their new weapons at a firing range near Lorenzana, Italy on 19 August 1944.

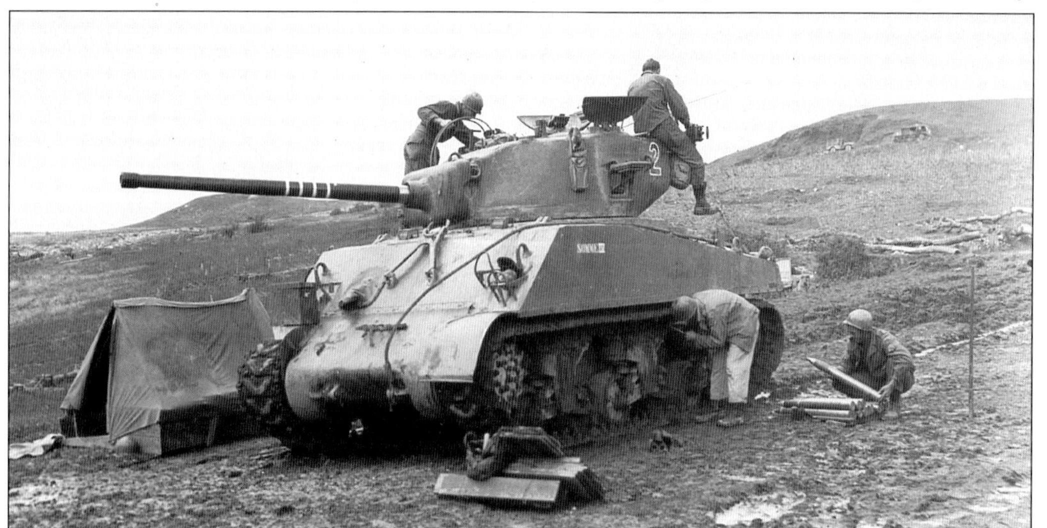

The crew of a M4A3(76)W of the 4th Tank Battalion, 1st Armored Division at St. Lucia, Italy prepare and load ammunition into their tank named Somme IV prior to the attack on Bologna on 19 October 1944. The crew has added a set of ciruclar steel rod hoops over an improvised artillery sight mounted in front of the gunner's station on the right turret roof. By this stage of the Italian campaign, few German tanks were encountered and the M4 tanks were frequently used to provide indirect fire support.

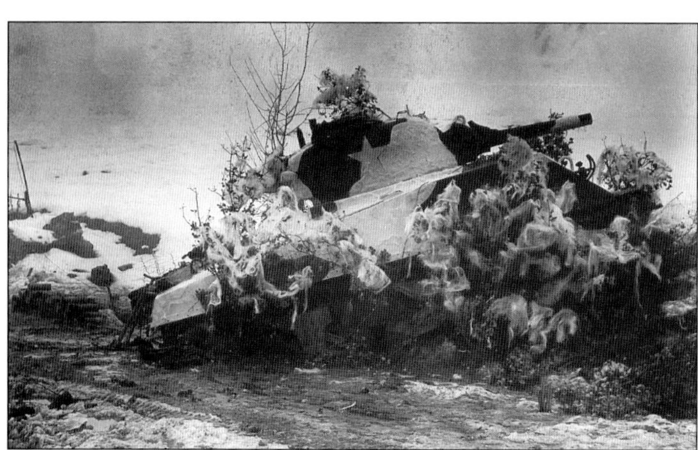

Tanks were often used for indirect fire support in the later phases of the Italian campaign, so the crews became adapted at camouflage when firing from static positions. This M4A3(75)W of the 751st Tank Bn. has been camouflaged with white paint and spun glass obtained from a local factory near Poretta, Italy on 1 February 1945.

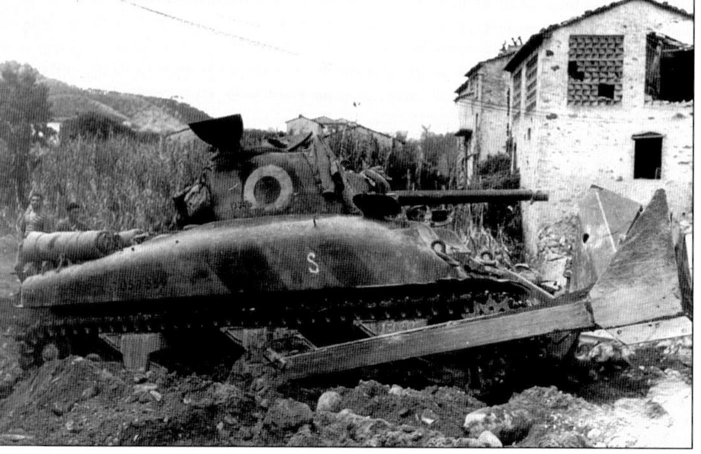

The 1st Armored Division suffered frequent losses to German mines and anti-tank traps during the fighting in Italy and so showed more enthusiasm for combat engineer tanks than most other US armored units. Here, an M4A1 fitted with an M-1 bulldozer blade is used to clean up battle damage in a town in Italy on 12 September 1944. The significance of the circle insignia on the turret is not known.

The Normandy Campaign

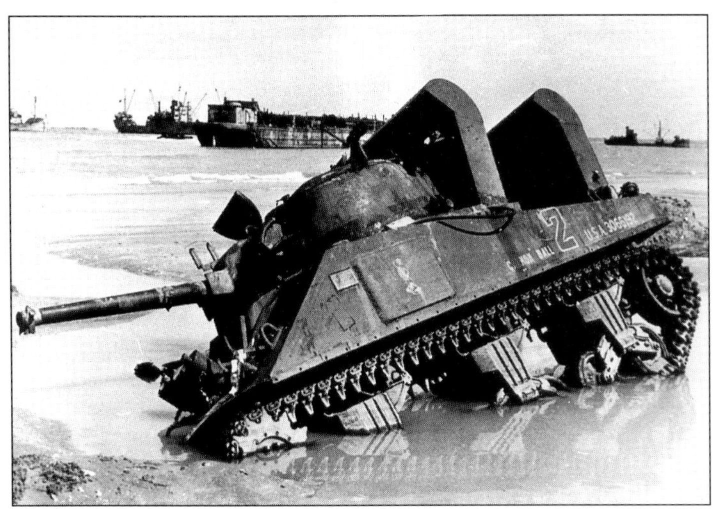

There are no known photos of US tanks during the D-Day landing at Normandy on 6 June 1944. This photo, taken a day after the landing at Utah Beach, shows a M4 medium tank, named Cannon Ball, probably of C Co., 70th Tank Bn. that became trapped in a tidal pool while wading in from an LCT. It is fitted with two deep water fording trunks, but these were obviously not sufficient due to the depth of the water. The other two companies of the 70th Tank Bn. were equipped with amphibious Duplex Drive M4s, and were the only US unit to have any success with this type of tank at Normandy due to the calmer ocean conditions at Utah Beach. The 741st Tank Bn. at Omaha Beach lost 27 of its 32 DD tanks due to strong wave conditions. (US Navy)

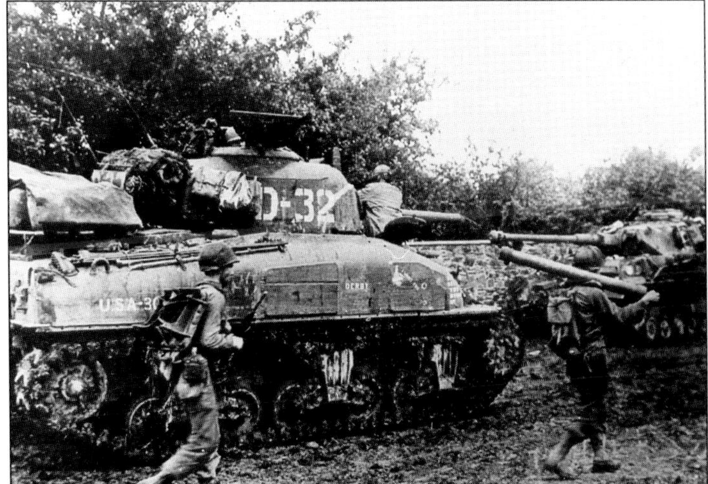

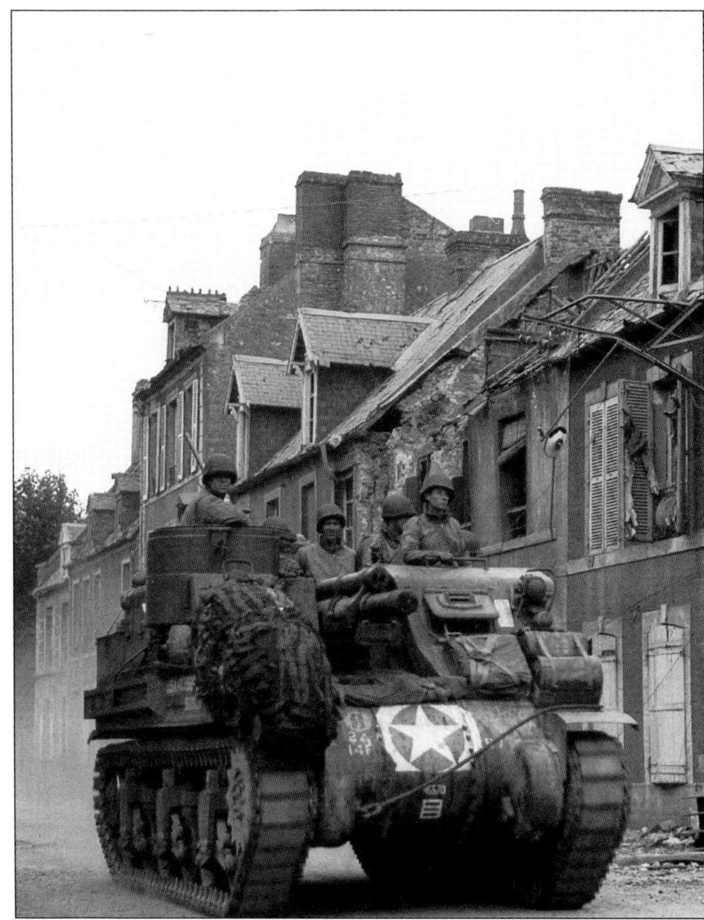

A M7 HMC of the 14th Field Artillery Bn., 2nd Armored Division passing through the town of Carentan on 18 June 1944 during the drive towards the seaport of Brest. This M7 has had a mine storage rack added to the hull side, a feature not normally seen on artillery vehicles.

A M4A1 medium tank named "Derby" of the 2nd Armored Division passes a disabled German PzKpfw IV tank during the fighting south-east of Coutances in July 1944 while an 81mm mortar team walks alongside. By this stage of the war, most early production Sherman tanks in US service had been upgraded by adding applique armor on the hull sides over their ammunition storage bins, as well as in the front of the gunner's station on the right side of the turret.

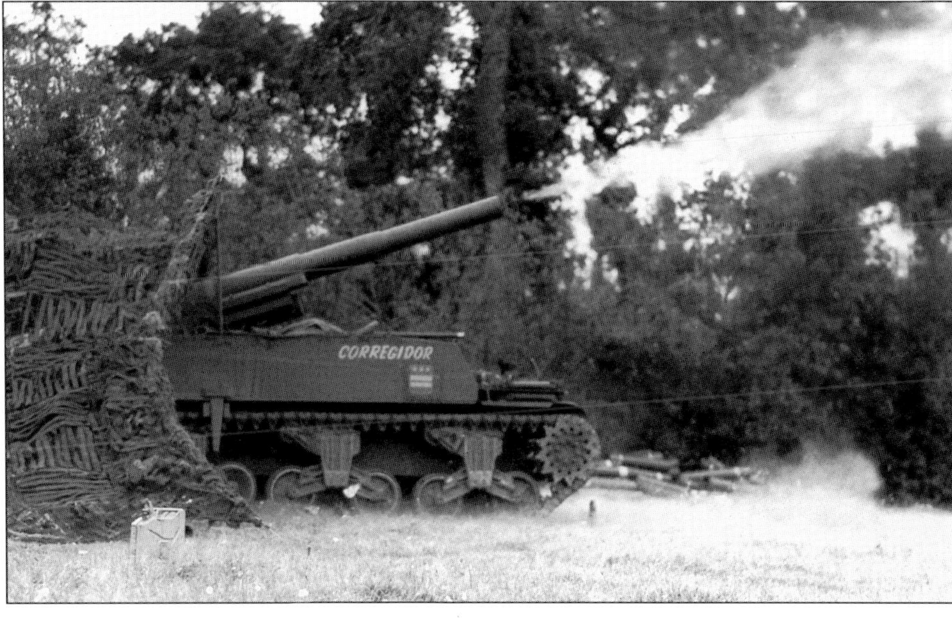

"Corregidor", a M-12 155mm Gun Motor Carriage (GMC) fires in support of the US adavnce near St. Lo on 16 July 1944. The M-12 was based on the M4 tank chassis. Operation Cobra culminated in the British and American armies trapping most of the German forces in Normandy in the Falaise pocket in August.

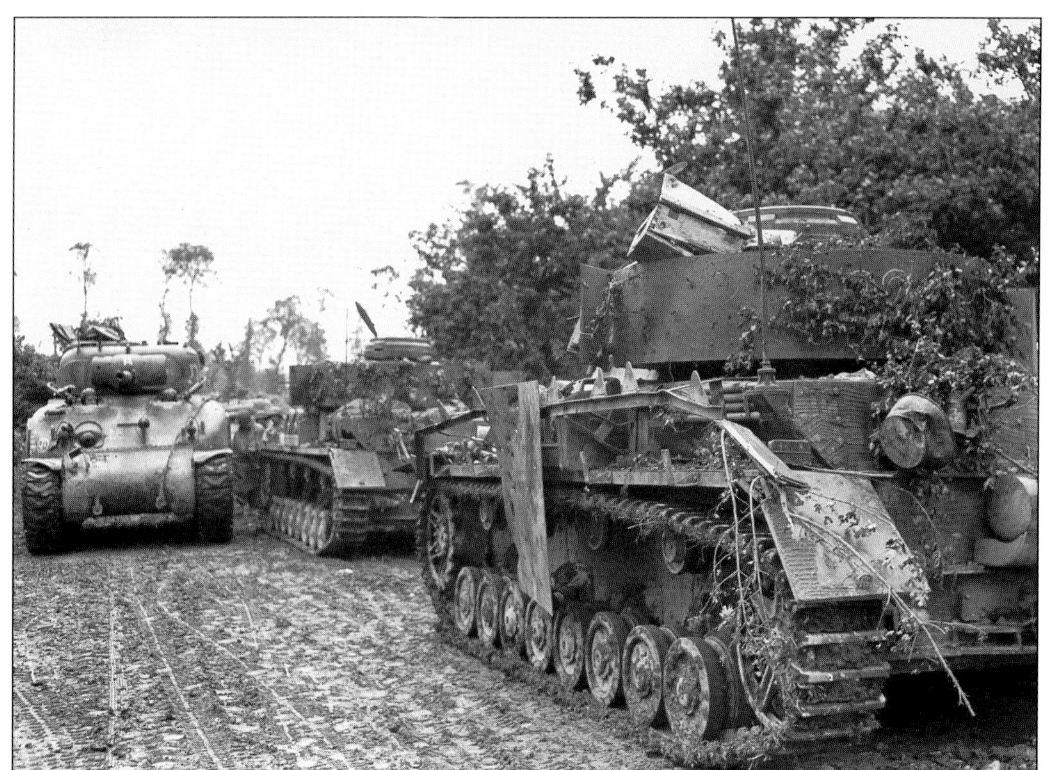

A M4A1 supporting the 30th Infantry Division passes down a column of knocked out German Pz.Kpfw IV tanks near St. Lo on 9 July 1944. Operation Cobra, the breakout from St. Lo, was preceded by a massive carpet bombing of German positions which took a heavy toll of German panzer divisions.

The crew of an M4 medium tank set up camp for the night near St. Paul de Verney on 17 July 1944. The tank name "Inez" and letter I on the turret indicate a tank from I Company, probably of either 2nd or 3rd Armored Division which was active in the St. Lo campaign at this time. Notice that the US white stars have already been painted out, a lesson quickly learned in the bocage terrain of Normandy with its roads channeled by hedgegrows.

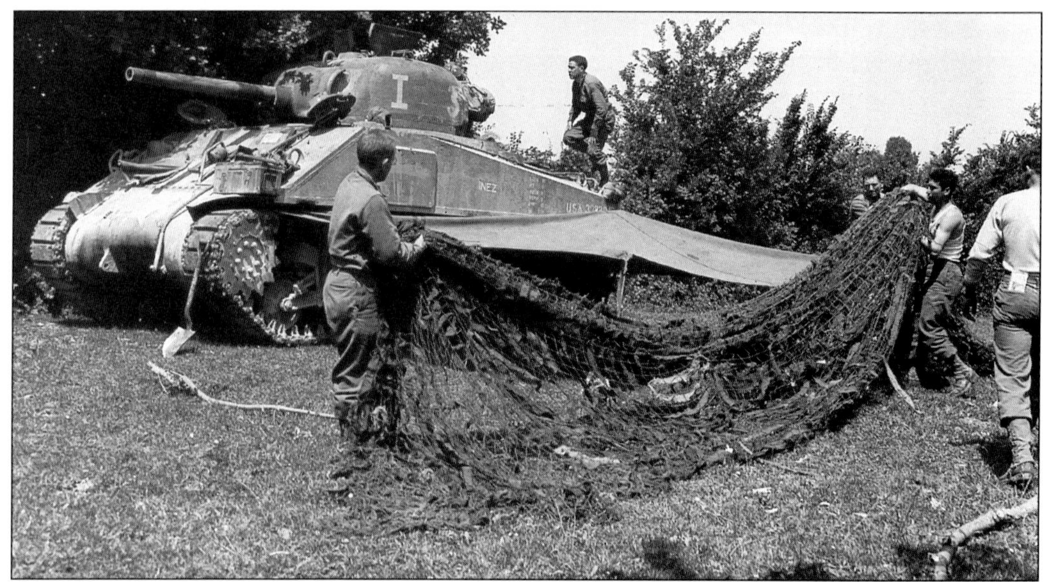

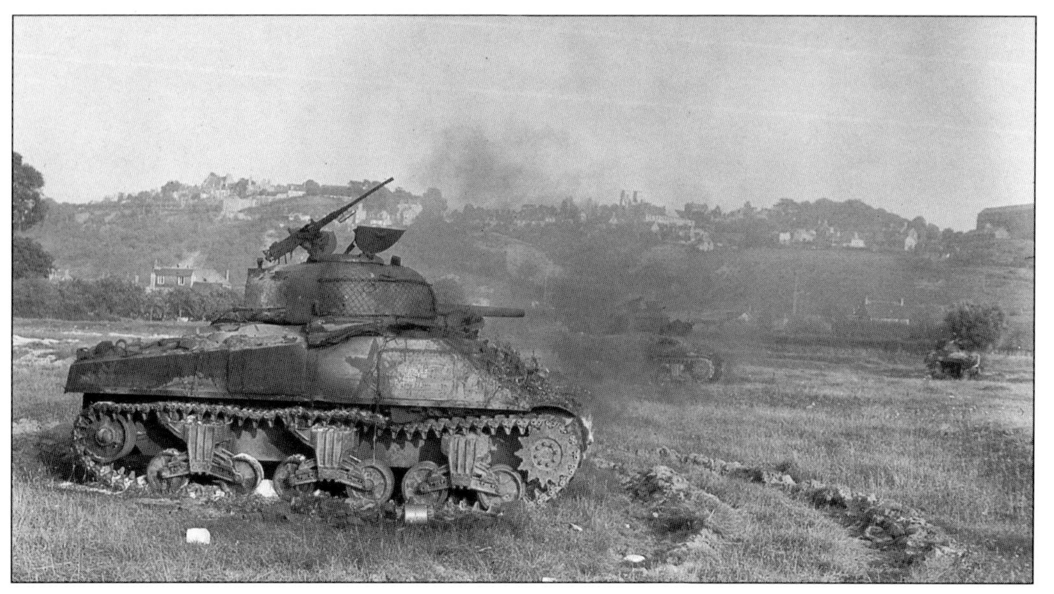

Several M4 medium tanks from the 4th Armored Division burn in a field outside Avranches, France during fighting there on 31 July 1944. The tank in the foreground has suffered an ammunition explosion in the right sponson which has blown the sponson floor down onto the upper run of track. Although the gasoline powered versions of the Sherman tank were notorious for their tendency to burn after hit, in fact these early Shermans without the wet ammunition stowage were a greater hazard to the crew as ammunition fires led to catastrophic internal fires.

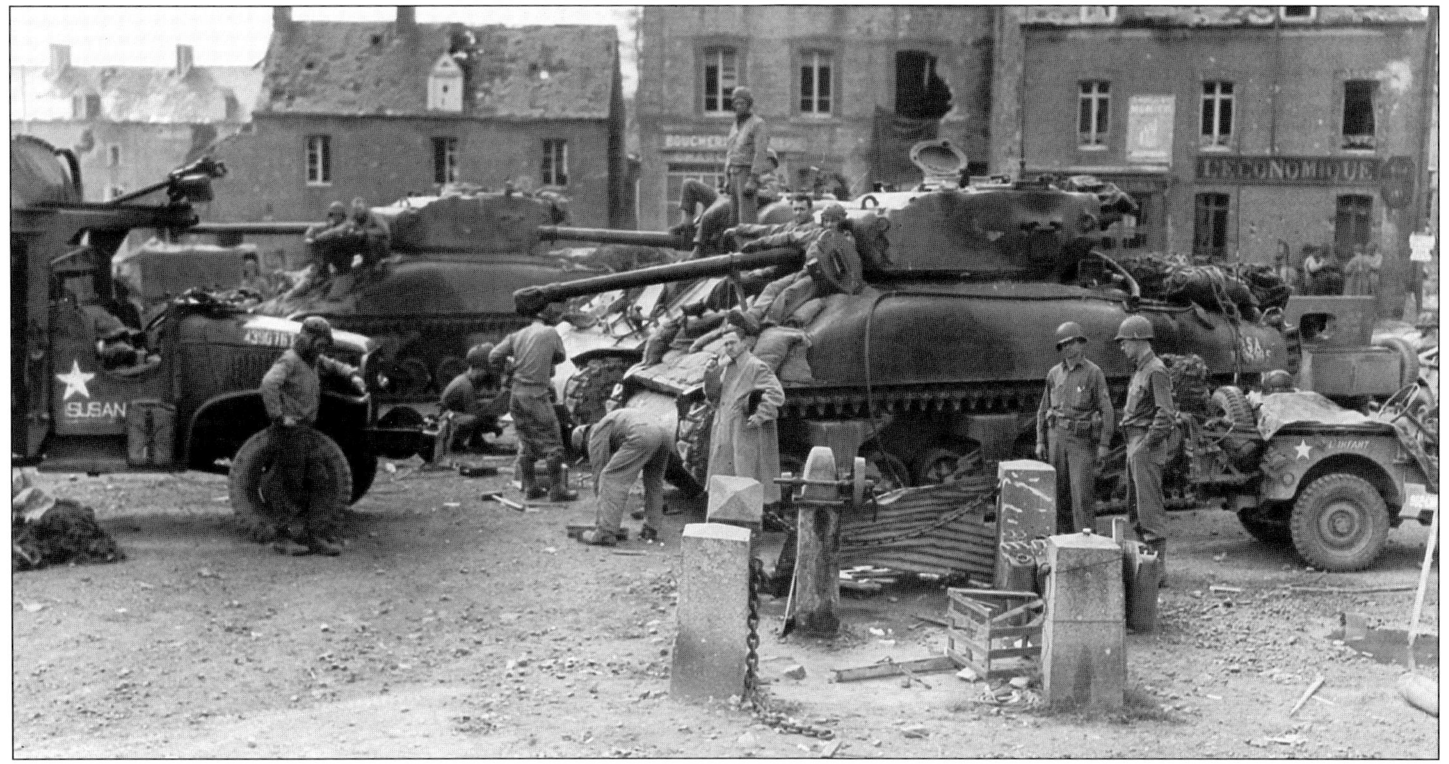

A platoon of M4A1(76)W tanks, probably from the 2nd Armored Division, undergo repairs in the town square of St. Jean de Daye on 26 July 1944. The new 76mm gun was not well received when first issued to US tank units as its high-explosive projectile was not as effective as the type available with the 75mm gun. The 76mm gun was better appreciated in July when US tank units began encountering the thickly armored German Panther tank in greater numbers.

A pair of M4 tanks of the 8th Tank Bn., 4th Armored Division pass through Coutances, France in pursuit of retreating German forces on 31 July 1944. The 8th Tank Battalion heavily camouflaged its tanks with mud and foliage prior to the breakout efforts near Coutances.

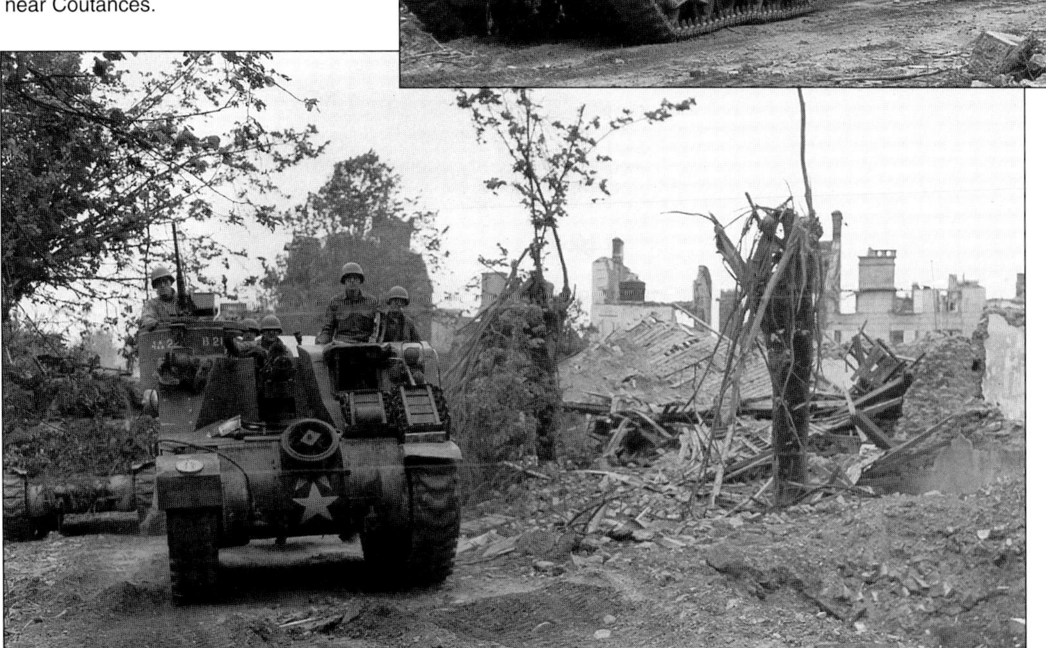

A M7 HMC of the 4th Armored Division advances through Coutances, France on 31 July 1944. The town of Coutances was shattered by repeated Allied bomber attacks and artillery barrages since it controlled Route N171, the main coastal road south out of Normandy and into Brittany.

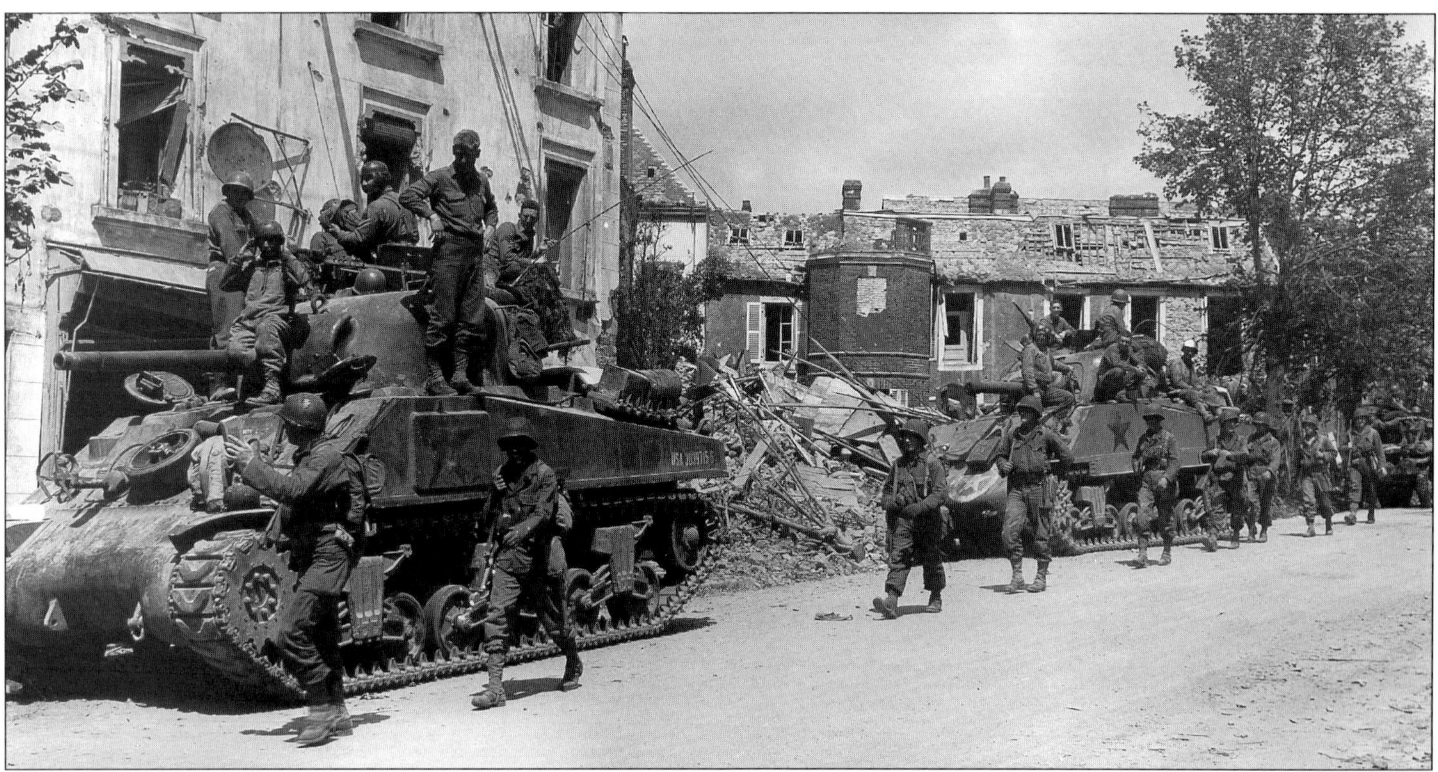

An infantry column marches past a pair of M4 Sherman tanks in the ruins of Coutances after the US Army had gained control of the town in late July 1944. The tank to the left is a new M4 105mm howitzer tank with the new 47° hull. These entered production in February 1944. These howitzer tanks were usually deployed in the HQ of tank battalions to provide added fire support.

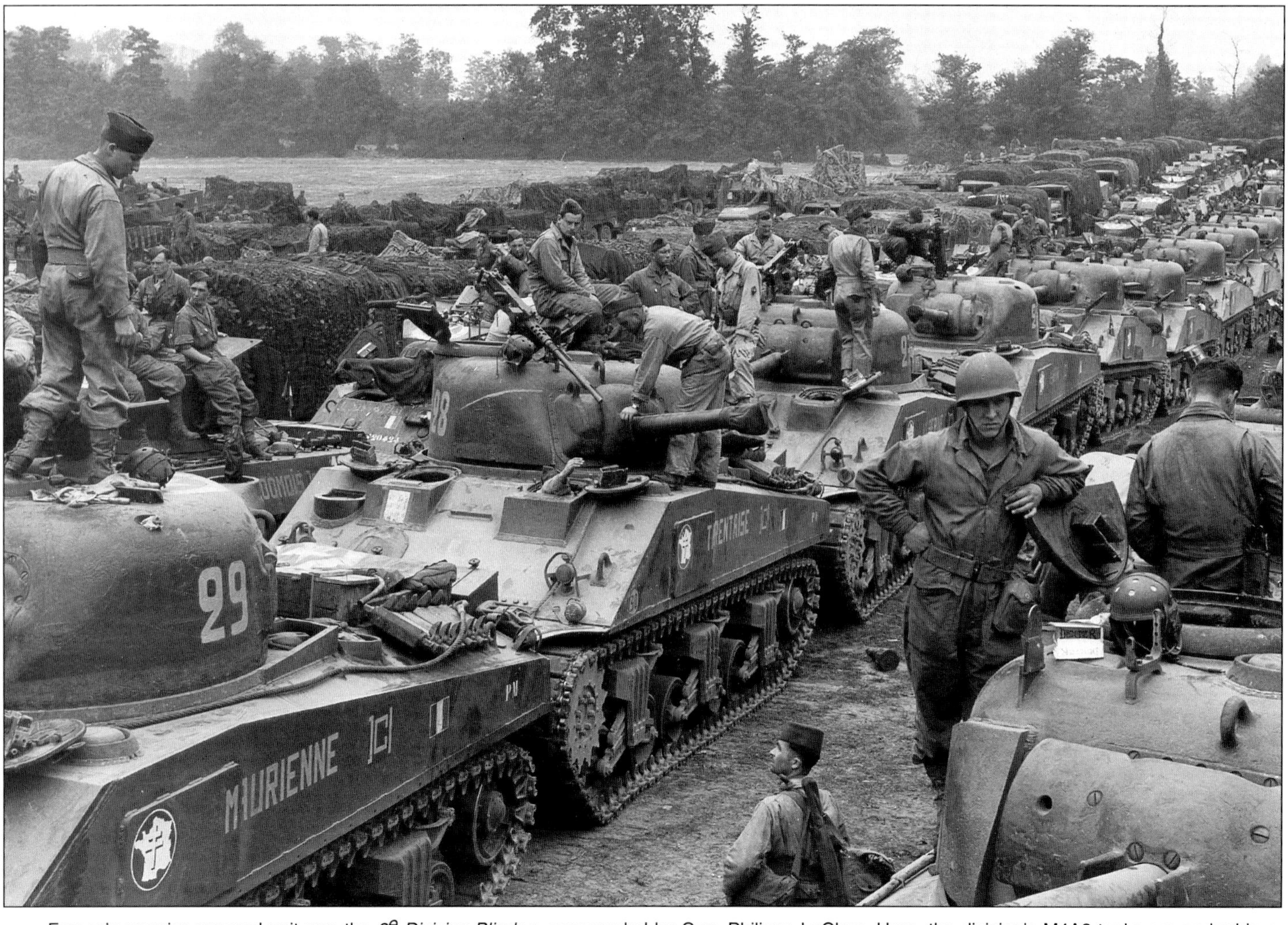

France's premier armored unit was the *2e Division Blindee*, commanded by Gen. Philippe LeClerc. Here, the division's M4A2 tanks are parked in a field near Utah Beach in Normandy, shortly after the division had been landed from England on 2 August 1944. The markings on the hull side of the M4A2s reveal them to belong to the *12e Regiment de Chasseurs d'Afrique*.

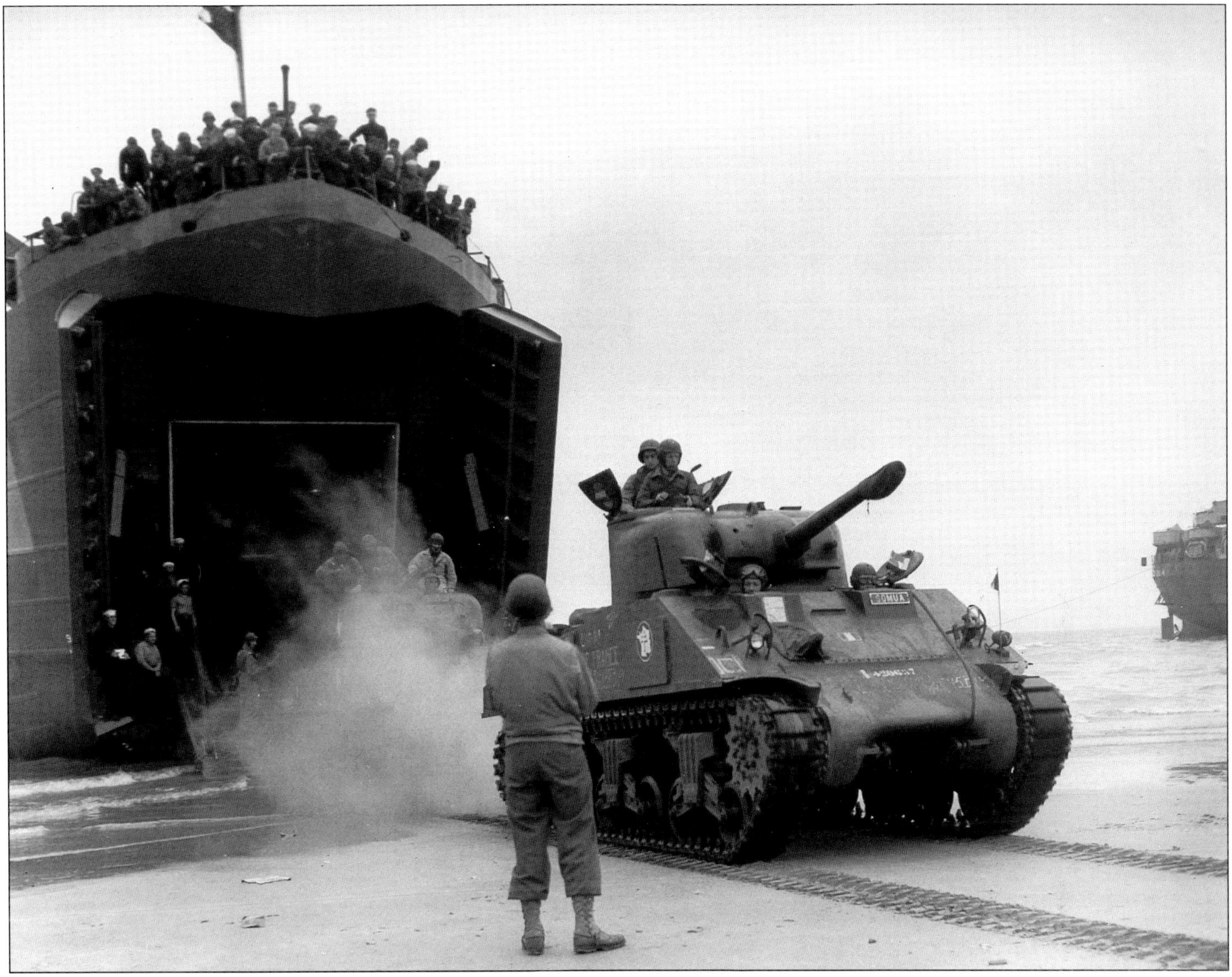

Another M4A2 of the *12^e RCC, 2^e Division Blindee,* lands from an LST at Utah Beach on 2 August 1944. Shortly after landing, the division was committed in the drive to liberate Paris. Notice the SOMUA name plate on the hull, probably an indication that one of the crew had previously served on 35.S SOMUA cavalry tanks. Today's new French main battle tank, the AMX LeClerc, is named after the legendary commander of this division.

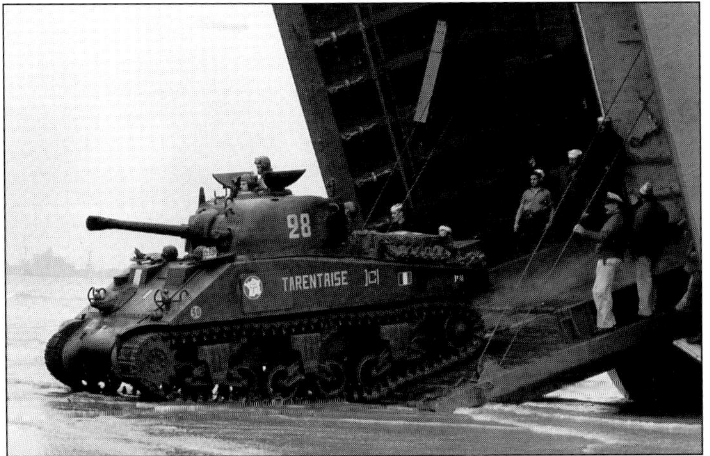

"Tarentaise," a French M4A2 of *12^e RCC, 2^e Division Blindee,* comes ashore from an LST at Utah Beach on 2 August. The M4A2 was a diesel powered version of the Sherman tank and was not regularly used by the US Army. It was mainly produced for Lend-Lease supply to the Soviet Union, but it was also used by the US Marine Corps in the Pacific.

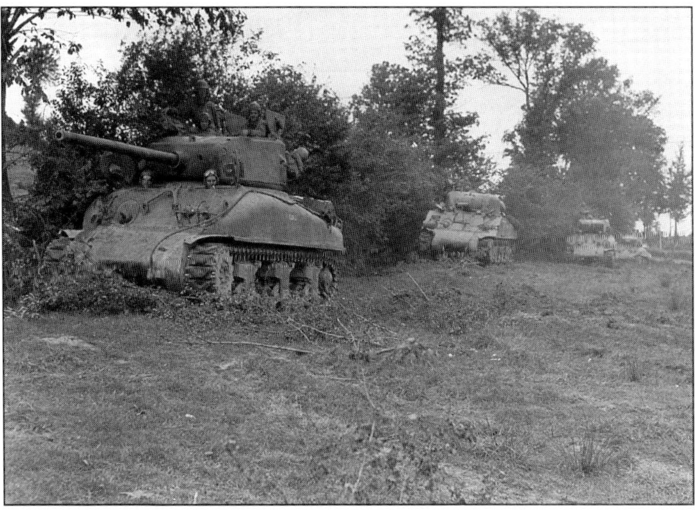

A column of tanks from E Company, 2nd Armored Division use the cover of a tree line near Champ du Bouet while awaiting orders. The lead tank is one of the new M4A1(76)W, and judging from the vehicle number, E-1, is probably the company commander's tank.

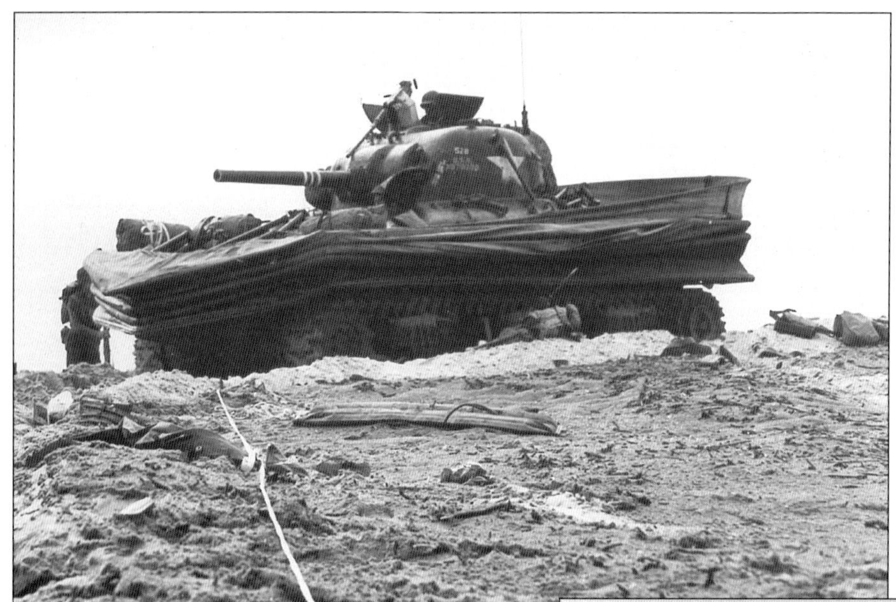

A M4A1 Duplex Drive tank at Alpha Yellow Beach near the resort town of St. Tropez on 15 August 1944 during Operation Dragoon, the invasion of southern France. The DD Shermans had an erectable screen to enable them to float, and two propellors at the rear (hence the name "duplex drive"). They were used with mixed results at Normandy due to rough sea conditions, but had fewer problems in the Mediterranean due to the calm summer waters.

A pair of M4A1 Duplex Drive tanks on the beach in front of an LST during the invasion of southern France on 15 August 1944. This amphibious operation is less well known than the D-Day landings at Normandy as it was not as violently contested by the Germans who were quite weak on the southern French Mediterranean coast between Toulon and Cannes.

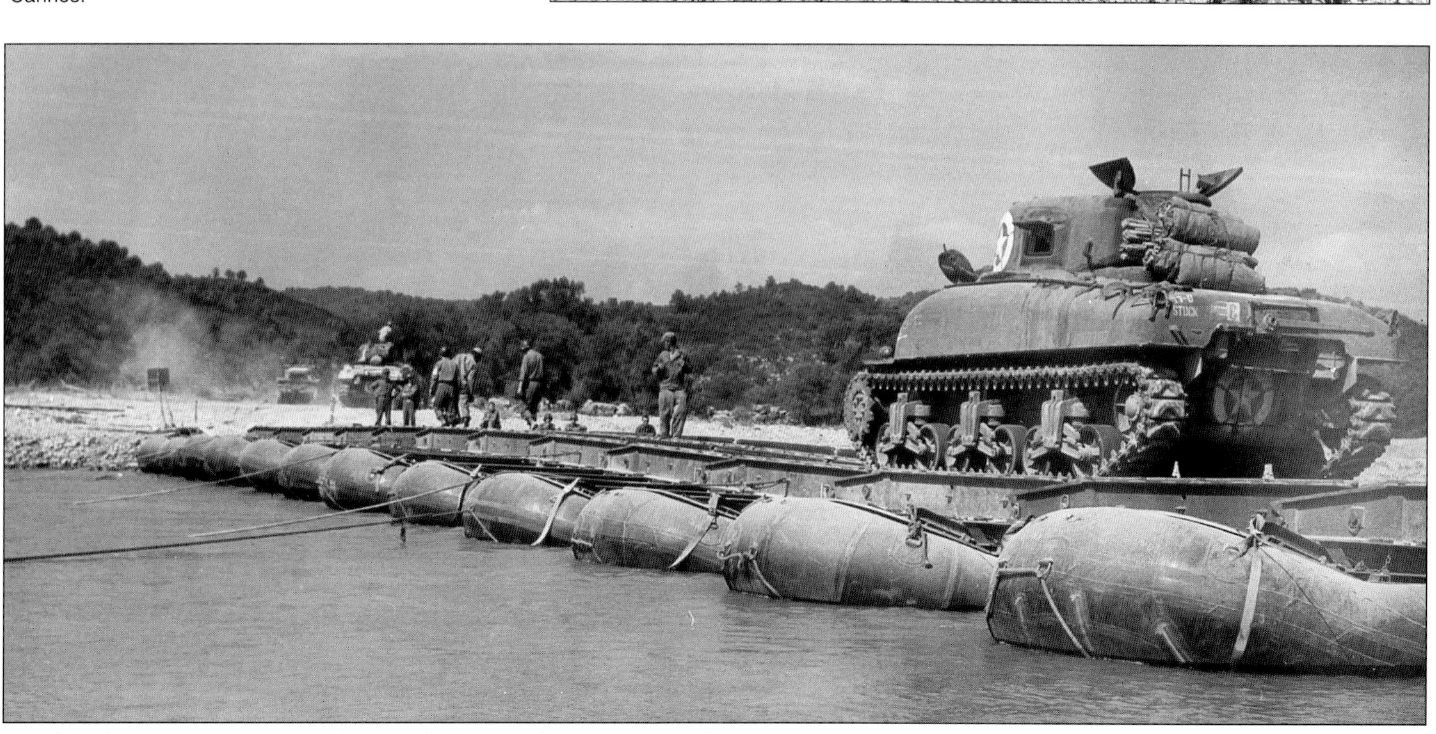

A M4A1 crosses a pontoon bridge over the Durance River in southern France on 25 August 1944 as the Operation Dragoon forces spread out from the beach-head. This is an early production M4A1 as is evident from the M3 style bogies. The forces employed in southern France drew on units from the Mediterranean theatre where the tanks were more dated than reserves in Britain used during the Normandy invasion.

A 10-ton wrecker lifts the Wright-Continental R-975 Whirlwind radial engine from the engine compartment of a M4 medium tank of the 2nd Armored Division in a repair yard near Le Teilleul, France on 16 August 1944. As is evident in this view, the 2nd Armored Division usually camouflage painted its tanks at this stage of the war. Although the division painted the company letter on the turret during the opening stages of the Normandy fighting, by August most units had painted this marking out as being too much of an attraction for German anti-tank gunners.

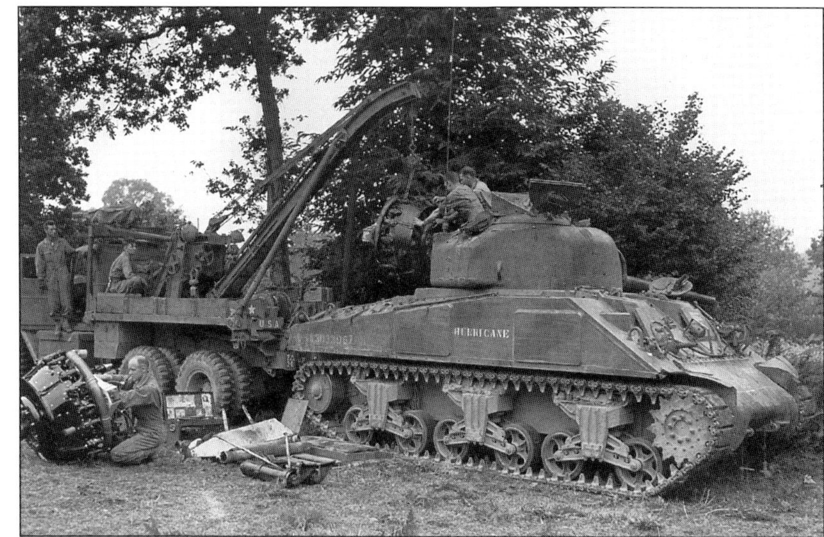

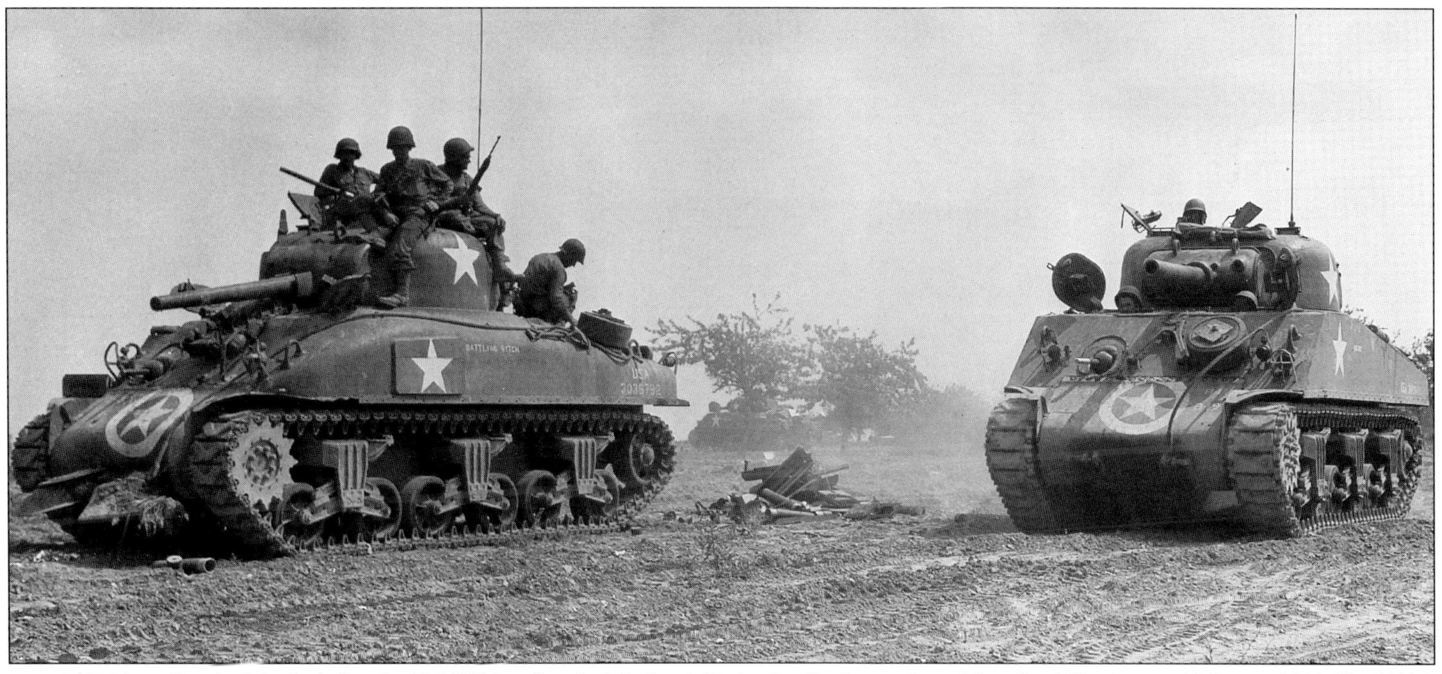

A M4A1 medium tank to the left and a M4(105) howitzer tank to the right shortly after the capture of the city of Chartres on 16 August 1944. The M4A1 is fitted with a Cullin hedgegrow cutter, an improvised set of welded prongs attached to the transmission housing to help tanks plow through the thick bocage (hedgegrows) characteristic of the Normandy and Brittany coastal area.

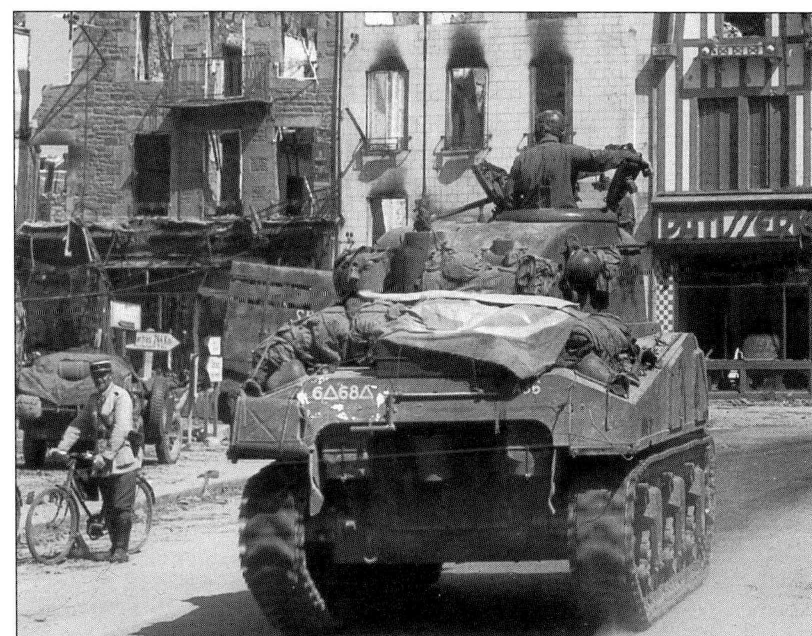

A M4 of the 68th Tank Bn., 6th Armored Division passes through the heavily damaged town of Avranches on 4 August 1944 during the Operation Cobra breakout. Barely evident on the rear deck is an orange recognition panel, used to prevent Allied fighter bombers from attacking friendly tanks. There were three different colors available, and they could be switched periodically for security reasons.

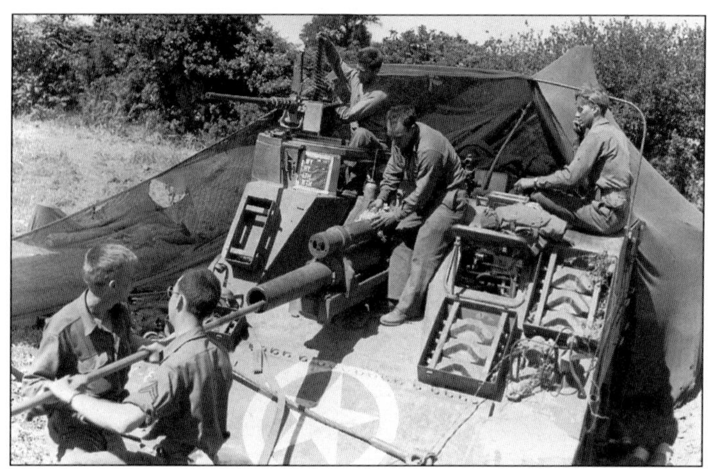

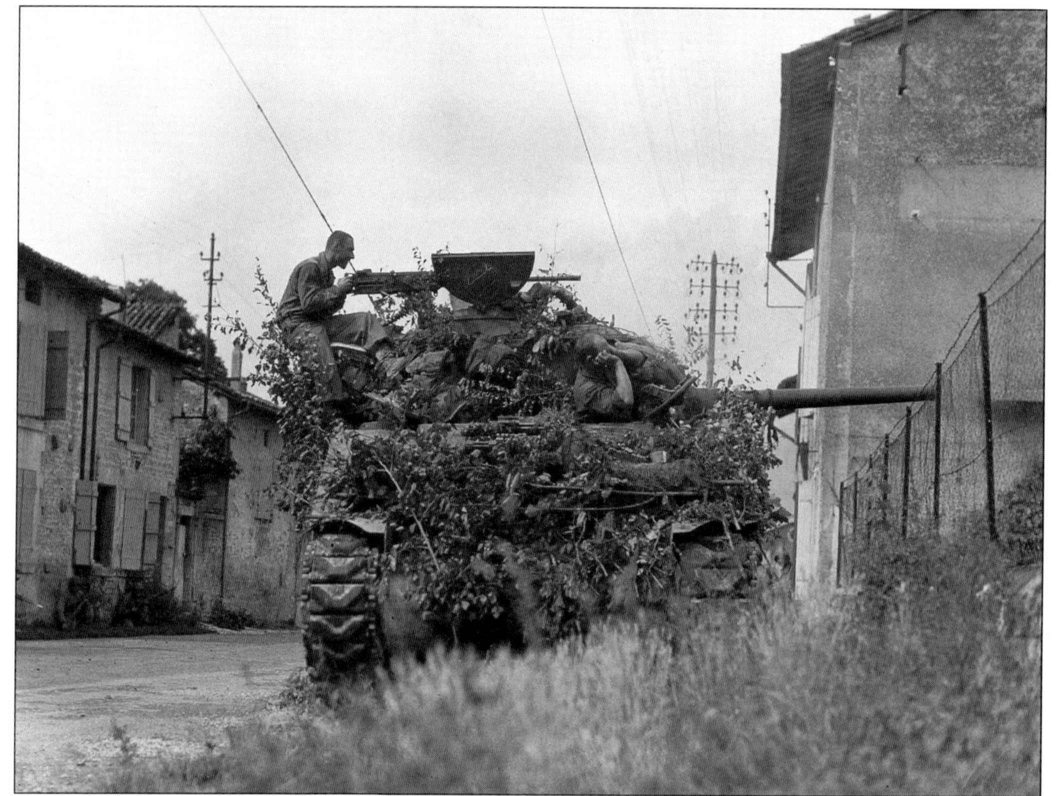

The crew of an M7 105mm HMC of the 83rd Field Artillery, 6th Armroed Division, clean the tube of their weapon during a lull in the fighting at Brest on 13 August 1944. Most self-propelled guns carried a large camouflage net to provide cover when used from static positions for long periods of time. The seaport at Brest was the main headquarters of the German Atlantic fleet and had been heavily fortified to prevent its capture by Allied forces.

The tank commander of a M4 medium tank of the 8th Tank Battalion, 4th Armored Division blasts away with a Browning .50 cal HB machine gun at German pioneer troops trying to dynamite a bridge over the Marne river on 21 August 1944. This machine was mainly intended for anti-aircraft protection but was more often used to attack unarmored targets and enemy troops.

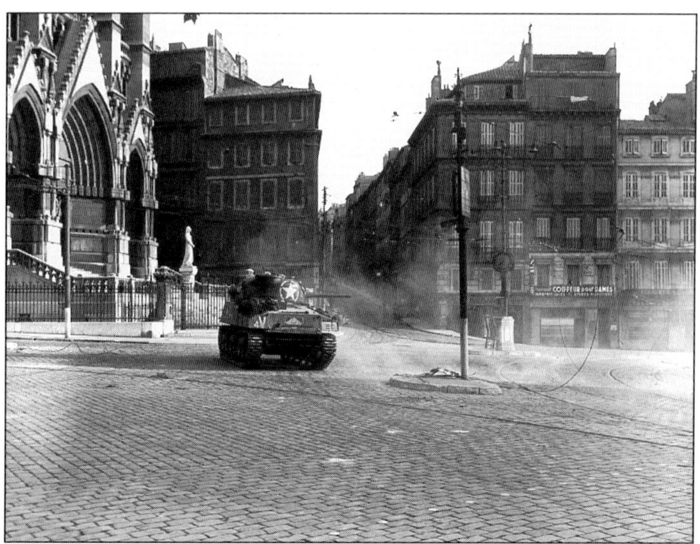

A M4A2 tank, named Vesoul, of the French *1ᵉ Division Blindee* in front of the St. Vincent de Paul church in the La Canebiere section of Marseilles fires at German forces in the old port section on 25 August 1944 during the fighting for the famous port city.

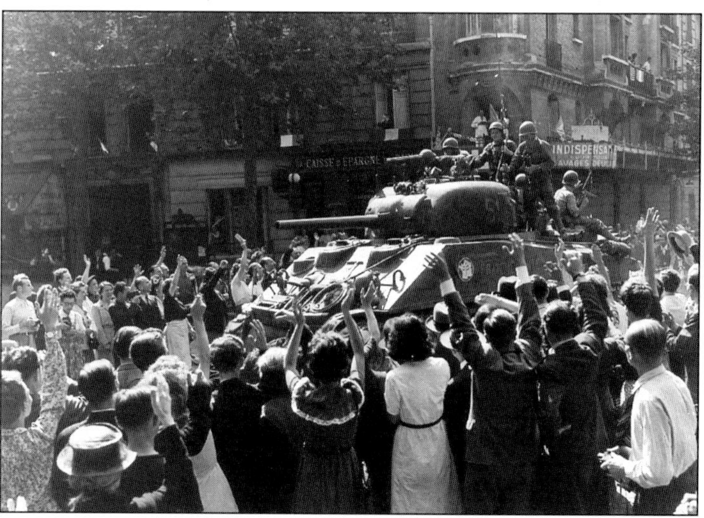

A dramatic moment as M4A2 tanks of LeClerc's *2ᵉ Division Blindee* enter Paris along Avenue Victor Hugo on 25 August 1944. Although the division's role in the liberation of Paris was its most famous moment, its superb combat capabilities were revealed in the fighting in the Lorraine in September 1944 against German tank units.

A member of the French resistance and several tank crews take cover behind a M4 medium tank of 8th Tank Battalion, 4th Armored Division on 31 August 1944 while the tank tries to stop German troops from destroying a bridge over the Marne near Rashecourt.

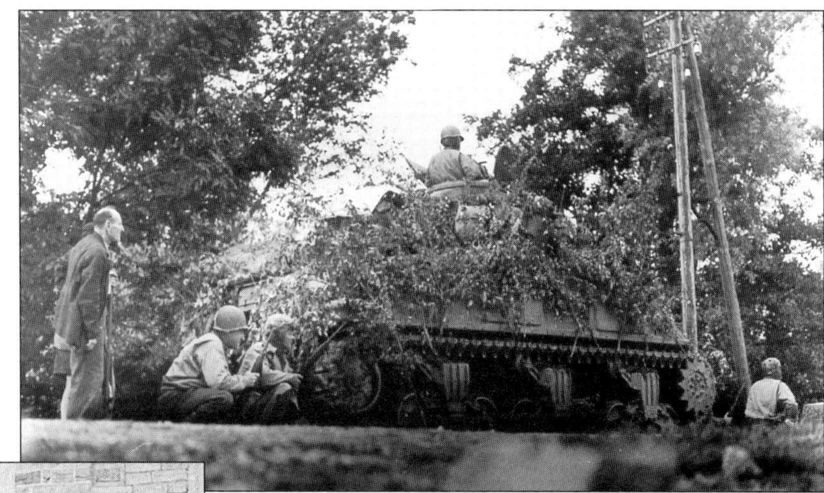

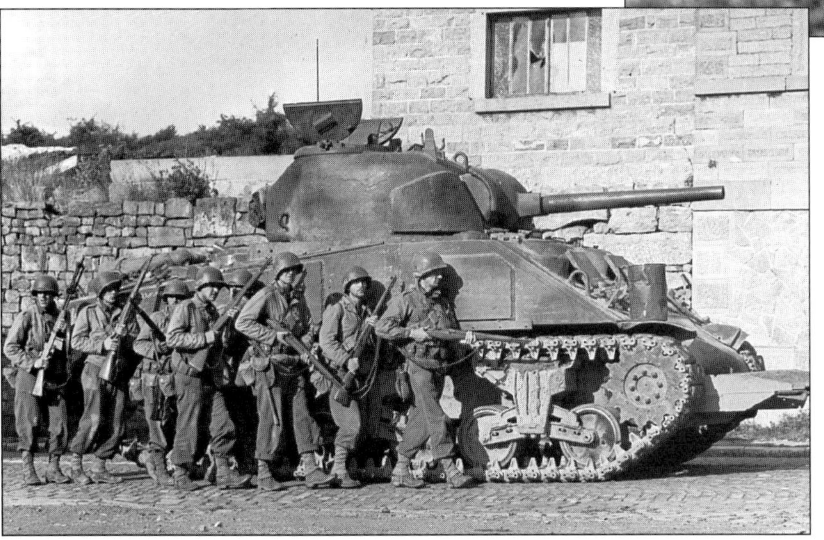

A M4 tank supports the infantry of I Co., 60th Rgt., 9th Infantry Division during fighting near the Belgian border on 9 September 1944. This tank still has a Cullin hedgegrow device on its bow. It was the usual US Army practice to attach a separate tank battalion to infantry divisions in combat.

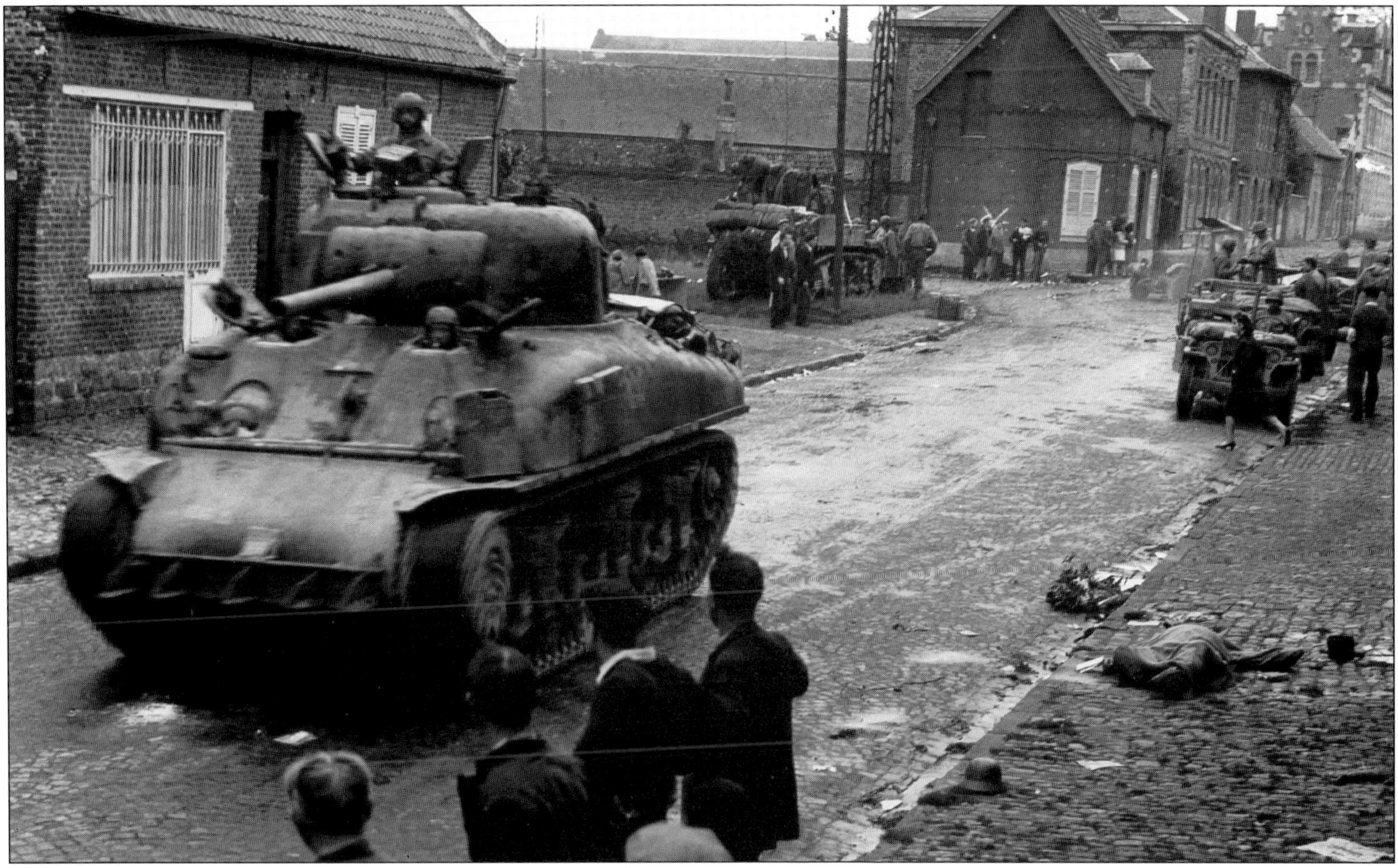

A M4A1 medium tank, fitted with a Cullin hedgerow cutter on the bow, passes through Aubencheil-Aubac near the French-Beligan border on 2 September 1944. The town had been captured only hours before, and a dead German soldier still lies on the pavement.

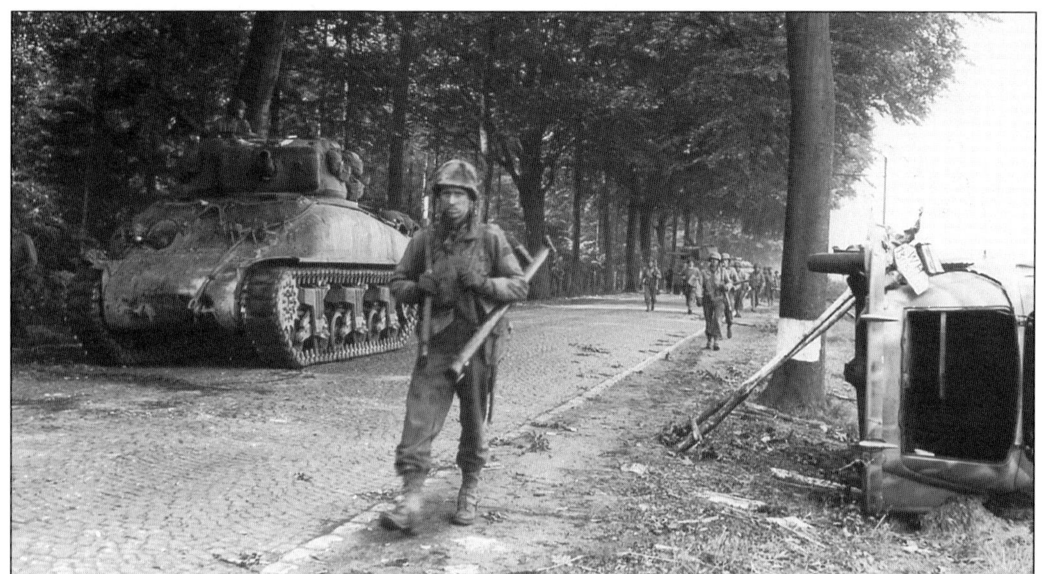

A US bazookaman advances under the watchful eye of a M4A1(76)W of the 66th Arm'd. Regt., 2nd Armored Division on a road near Haaselt in Belgium on 12 September 1944. On the side of the road is an overturned German staff car left behind during the retreat.

In one of the more famous incidents in its distinguished combat career, the 4th Armored Division leapfrogged the Moselle river after the Germans had blown up the main bridges by finding a ford over the National Canal near Bayon. The Germans had thought that the canal was impassible to tanks due to deep mud, but the M4A3(76)W managed to get over the bank and drag out the M4A1 stuck in the mud. This action was instrumental in capturing the key city of Nancy on the way to the German border.

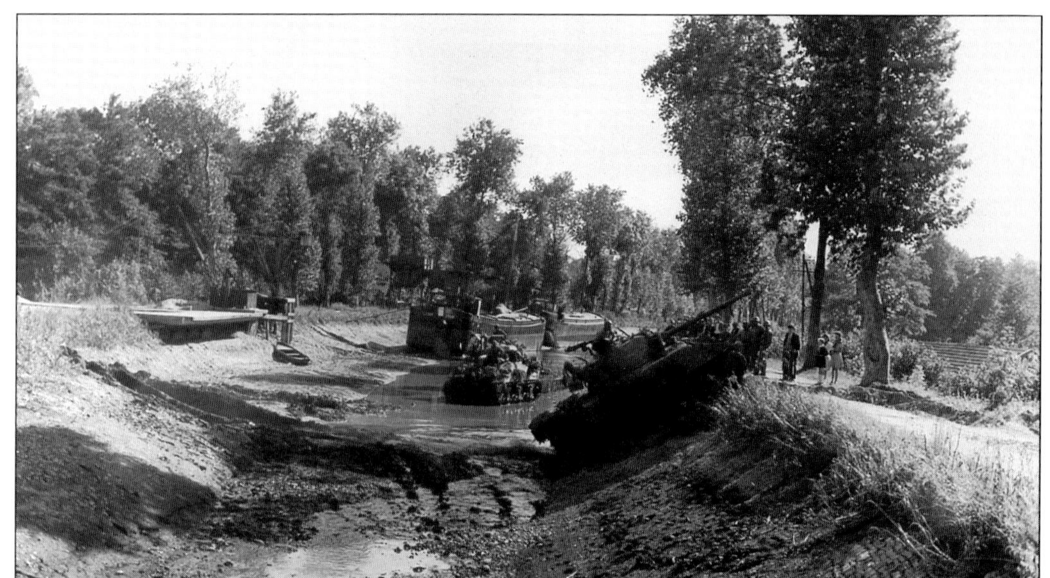

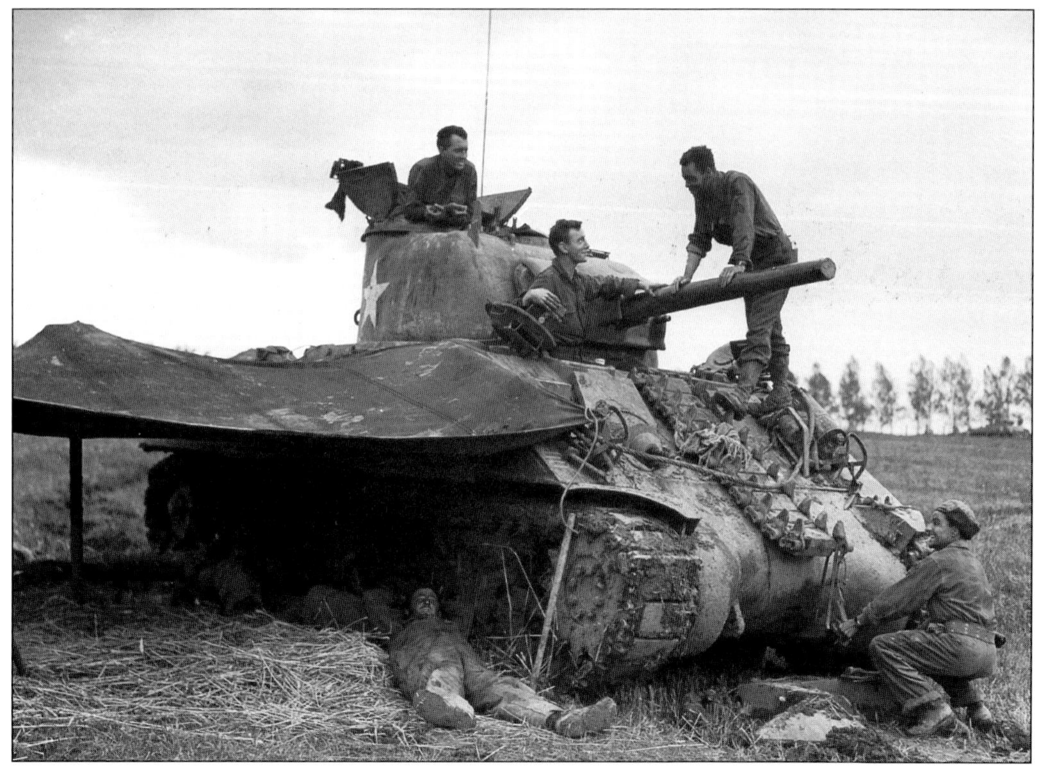

The crew of a M4 of the 37th Tank Battalion, 4th Armored Division bed down for the night after a day of fighting near Chateau Salinas in northwestern France. This battalion was commanded by Maj. Creighton Abrams, after whom today's M1 Abrams tank is named. This gives a good view of the intermediate style of 75mm gun turret, fitted with the wider, improved M34A1 gun mount.

From 19 to 22 September 1944, the 4th Armored Division fought elements of the German 5th Panzer Army near Arracourt in the largest tank-vs.-tank battles since the German army stopped the British 21st Army Group at Caen in Normandy in July. Even though the German force included a substantial number of new Panther tanks, the more experienced 4th Armored Division decisively defeated the German attack, destroying 107 tanks and 30 StuGs for a loss of 14 M4 tanks and 7 M-5A1 light tanks. This rare view of the battlefield after the fighting shows three knocked out Panthers and a M4A3(76)W.

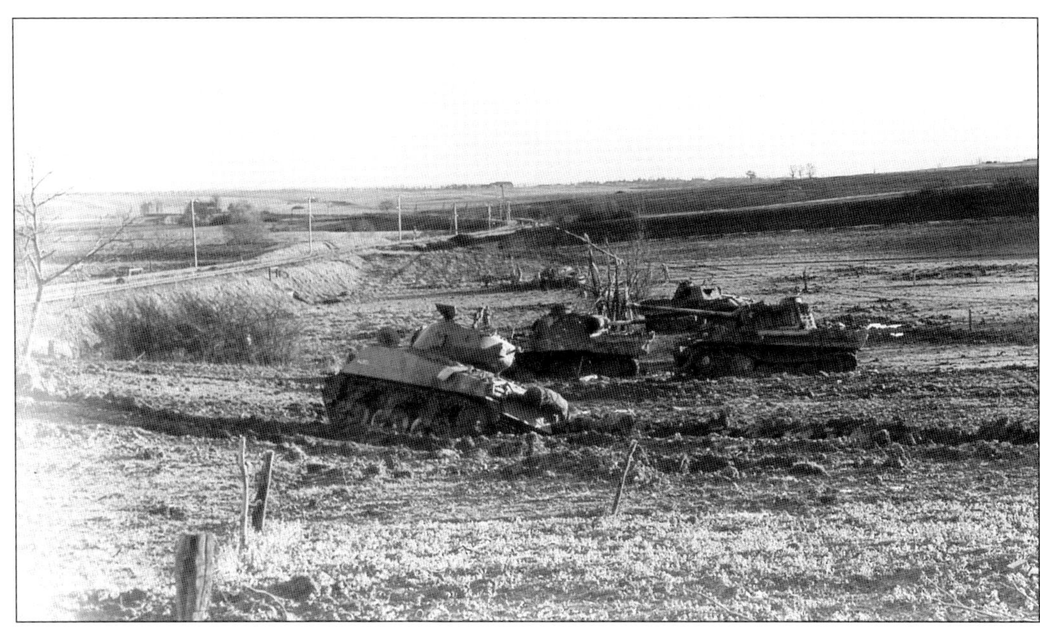

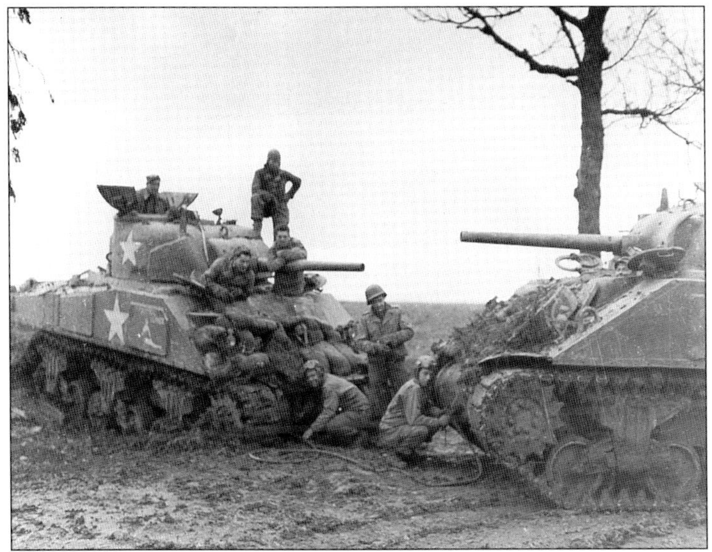

A M4 of the 6th Armored Division tries to help pull another M4 out of the mud. One of the most serious shortcomings of the M4 Sherman was its poor floatation in soft soil, mud and snow. By the late autumn of 1944, many Shermans began to be fitted with extended end-connectors, sometimes called duck-bills, which marginally improved traction in poor conditions.

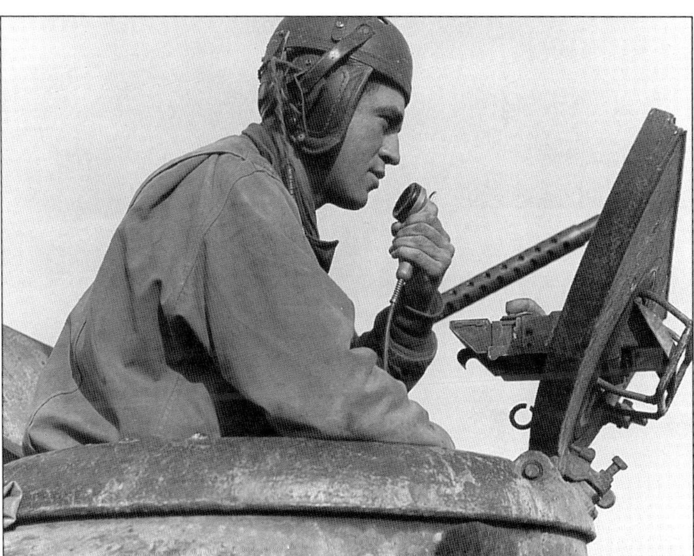

Capt. J. F. Brady, commander of A Company, 35th Tank Bn., 4th Armored Division shortly after the Arracourt tank battle. This gives a good view of the standard US Army tanker's helmet as well as the tank commander's inter-tank microphone. The tanker's helmet was not armored, so in some units, a normal steel helmet was worn instead when riding outside the tank.

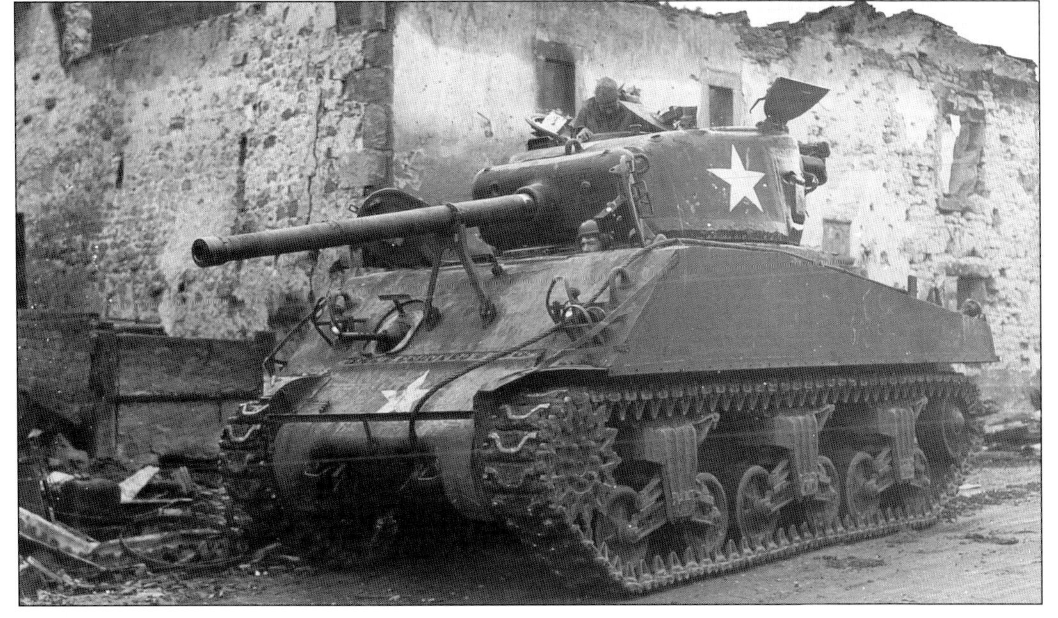

A M4A3(76)W medium tank of the 756th Tank Bn., supporting the 3rd Infantry Division near Brouvelieures, France in October 1944. The crew has begun to weld metal strips to the glacis plate as the first step in applying a layer of sandbags to add further protection to the tank. The M4 was not well protected against typical German anti-tank weapons like the panzerfaust and panzershreck, which led to many improvised armor improvements in the field.

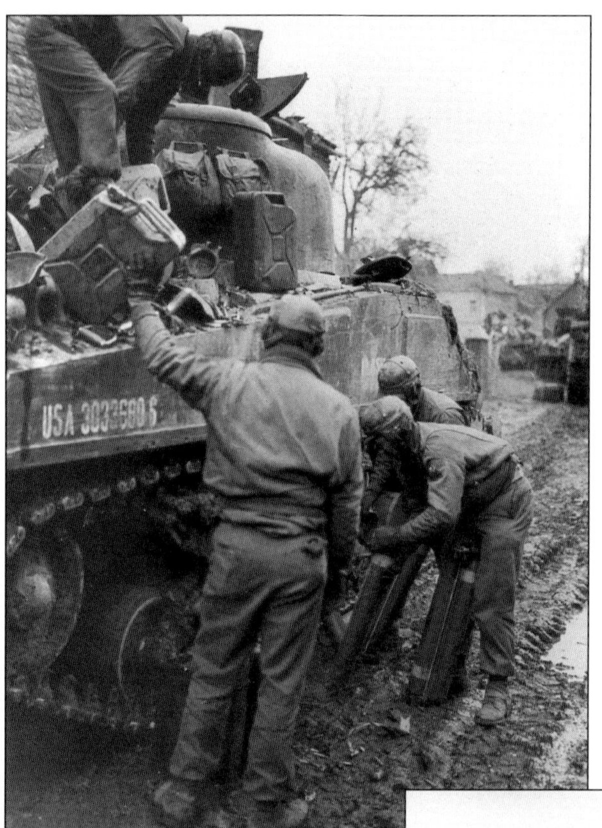

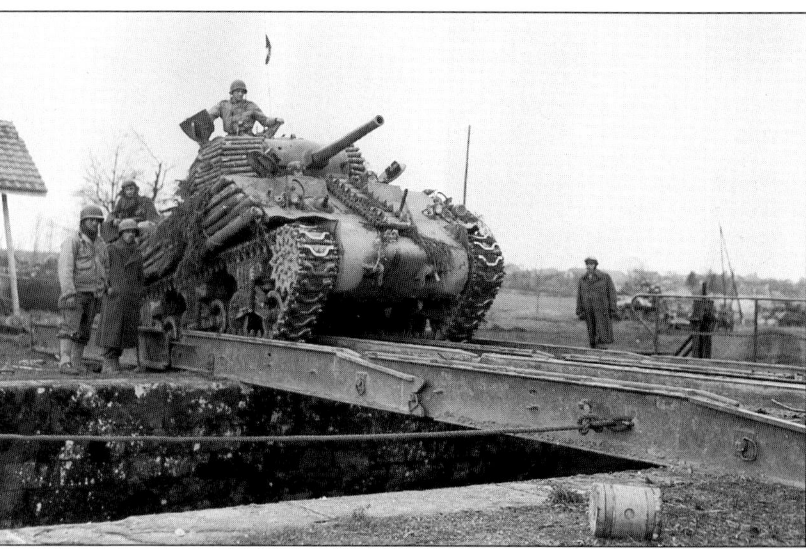

Tankers of the 2nd Armored Division fuel and rearm their M4 tank in Beggendorf, Germany on 17 November 1944. Shortages of fuel in the autumn of 1944 limited the Allied drive on Germany and caused considerable bickering between British and American field commanders as to who should receive priority for fuel and supplies.

A M4A2 tank of the French 5th Armored Division crosses a treadway bridge near Belfort on 20 November 1944 during the siege of that city. The use of logs as improvised protection had greater psychological value than ballistic effect when facing German panzerfaust rocket grenades.

The crew of a M7 105mm HMC of the 276th Armored Field Artillery attached to Patton's 3rd Army repair a damaged track near Brulange, France on 17 November 1944. Like the M4 tank on which it was based, the M7 underwent continual evolutionary improvement through the war, including the M7B1 variant based on the M4A3 chassis.

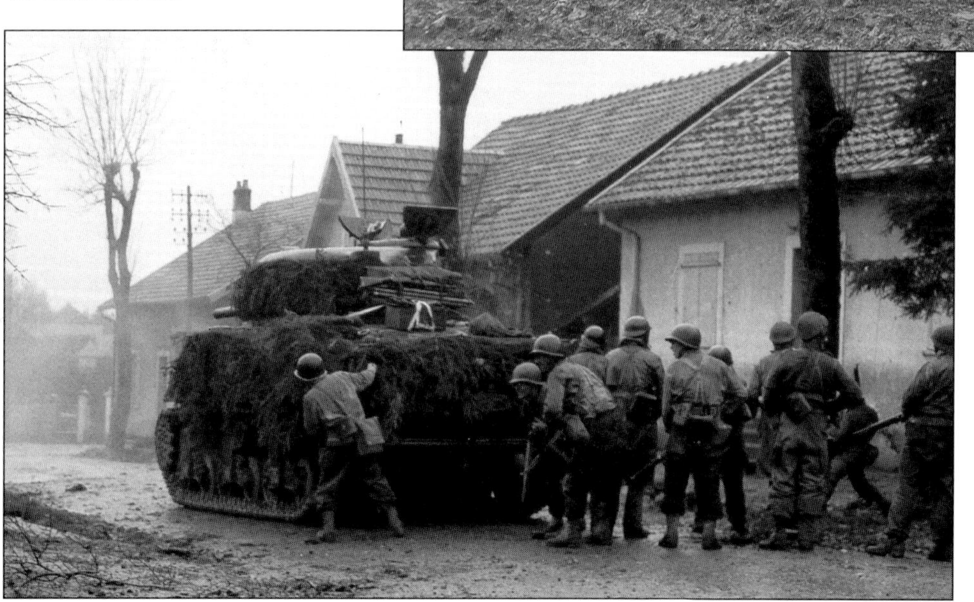

The M4 was frequently used to provide infantry support. Here, a well camouflaged M4A2 of the French 5th Armored Division provides cover for a French infantry platoon during the fighting in the outskirts of Belfort on 20 November 1944. Although the Free French Army was equipped mainly with US equipment and uniforms, some French armored units managed to locate pre-war French crew helmets as can be seen on several of the troopers behind the tank.

A M4A3(76)W of the 6th Armored Division disabled by a German mine near Hellimer on 25 November 1944. Engineers have marked the vehicle with tape to prevent the curious from stumbling into the minefield. The tank is so deeply bogged in the mud that an armored recovery vehicle would be needed to repair it.

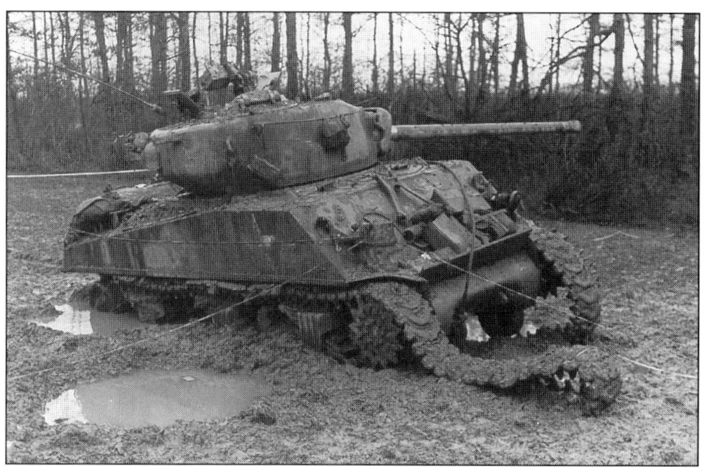

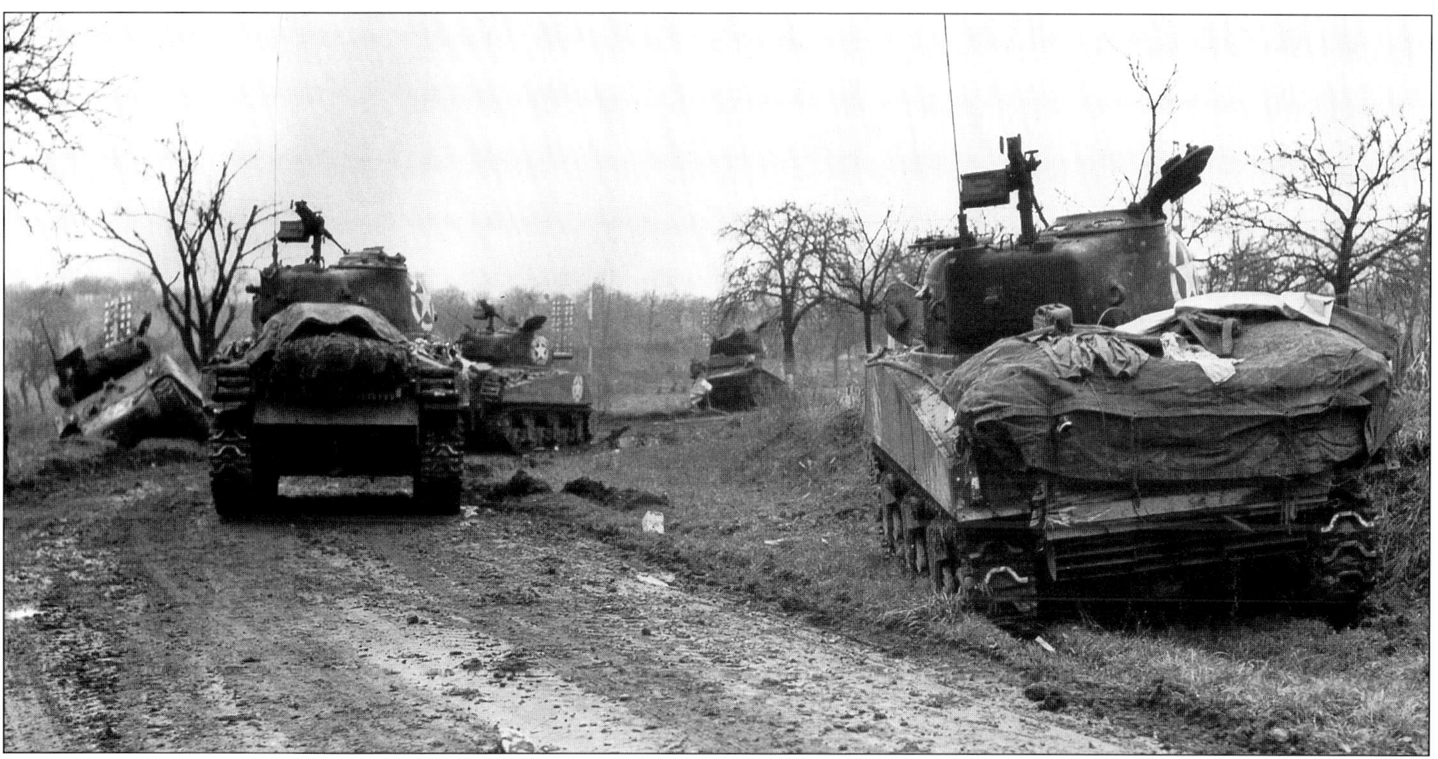

A column of M4A3(75)W of the 14th Armored Division pass by three other Shermans knocked out by German mines near Barr, France on 29 November 1944. These are very late production M4A3(75)W tanks, evident from the late style 75mm gun turret with its improved commander's vision cupola, and the raised rear bustle casting.

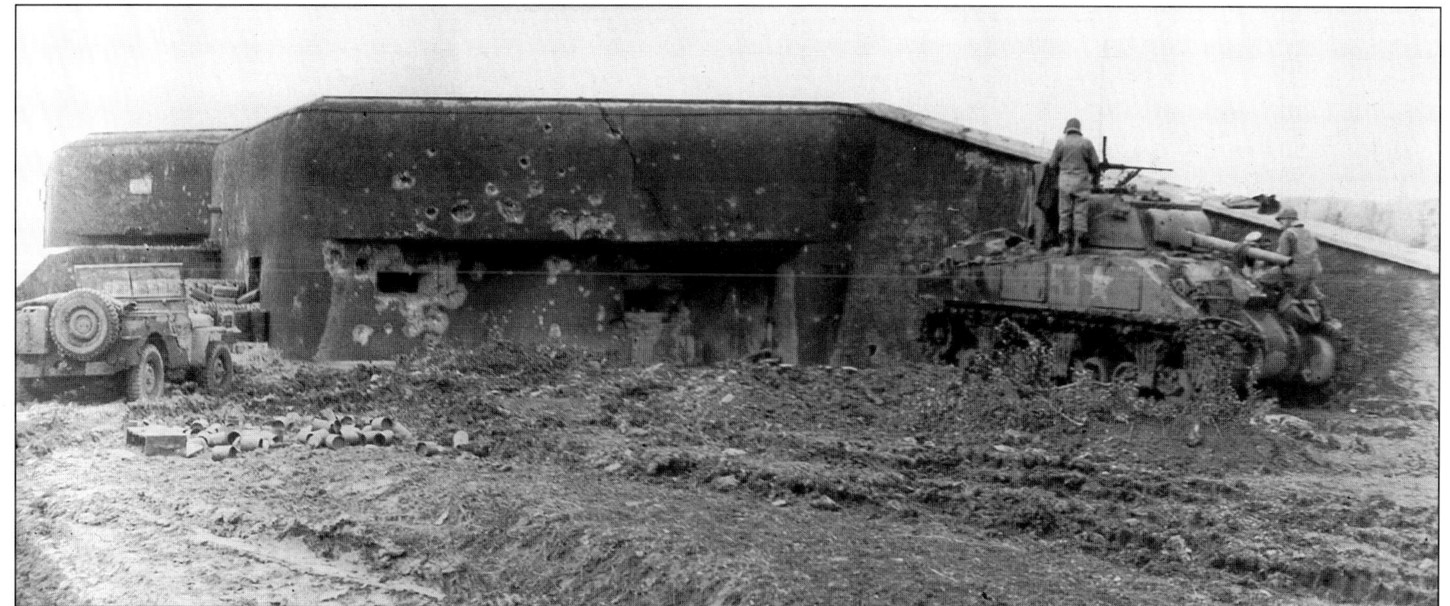

A M4 of the 6th Armored Division takes a break near a pock-marked pillbox of the German Siegfried line near Kappel, Germany on 1 December 1944.

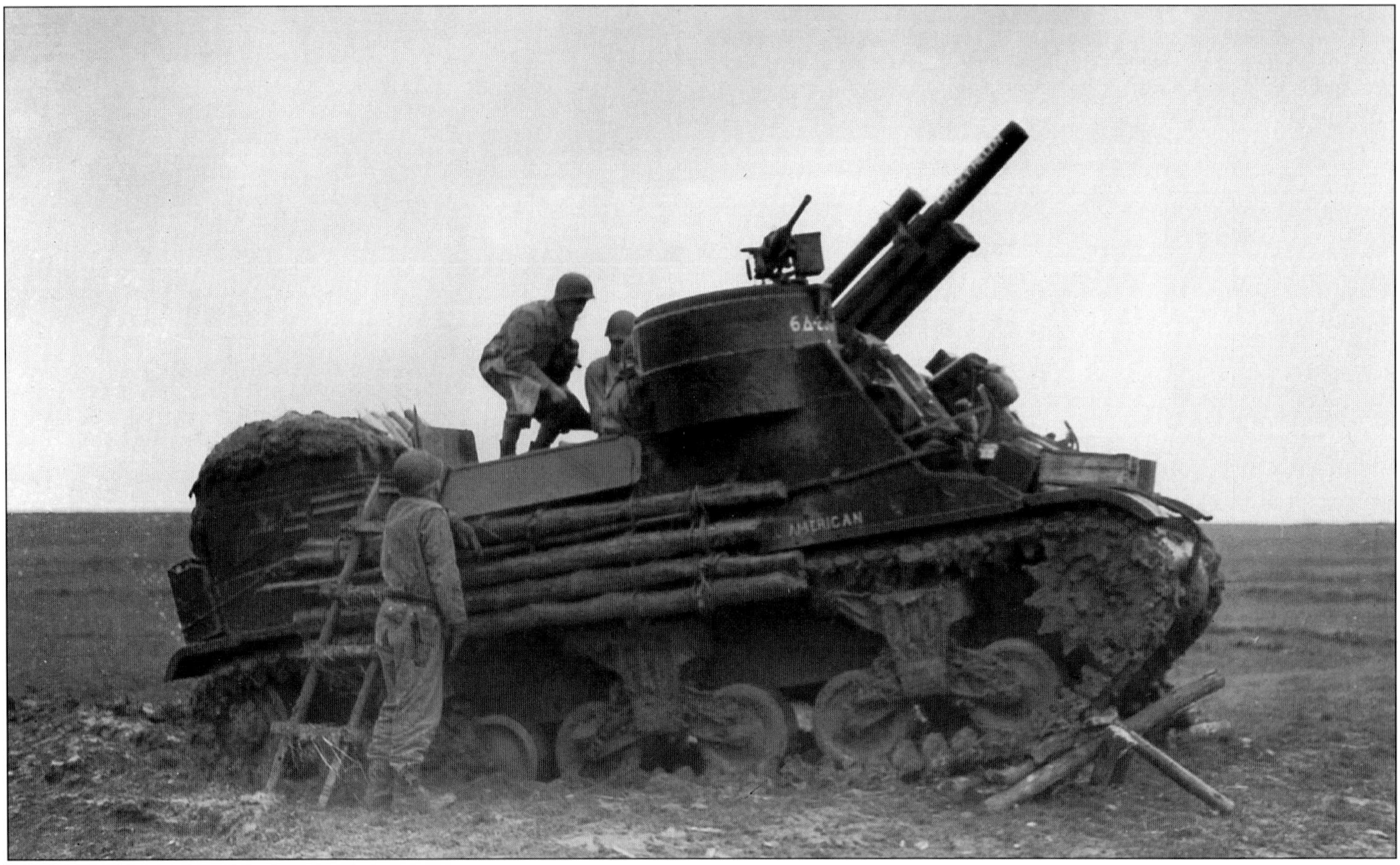

A M7 105mm HMC of the 231st Armored Field Artillery Bn., 6th Armored Division is propped up an improvised ramp to give a higher elevation for long range shelling of German positions near Kleinblitterdorf, Germany on 7 December 1944. The vehicle has the name "All-American" on the hull side, probably indicating a vehicle of A Battery, while the name "Crazy Helen" is painted on the howitzer tube.

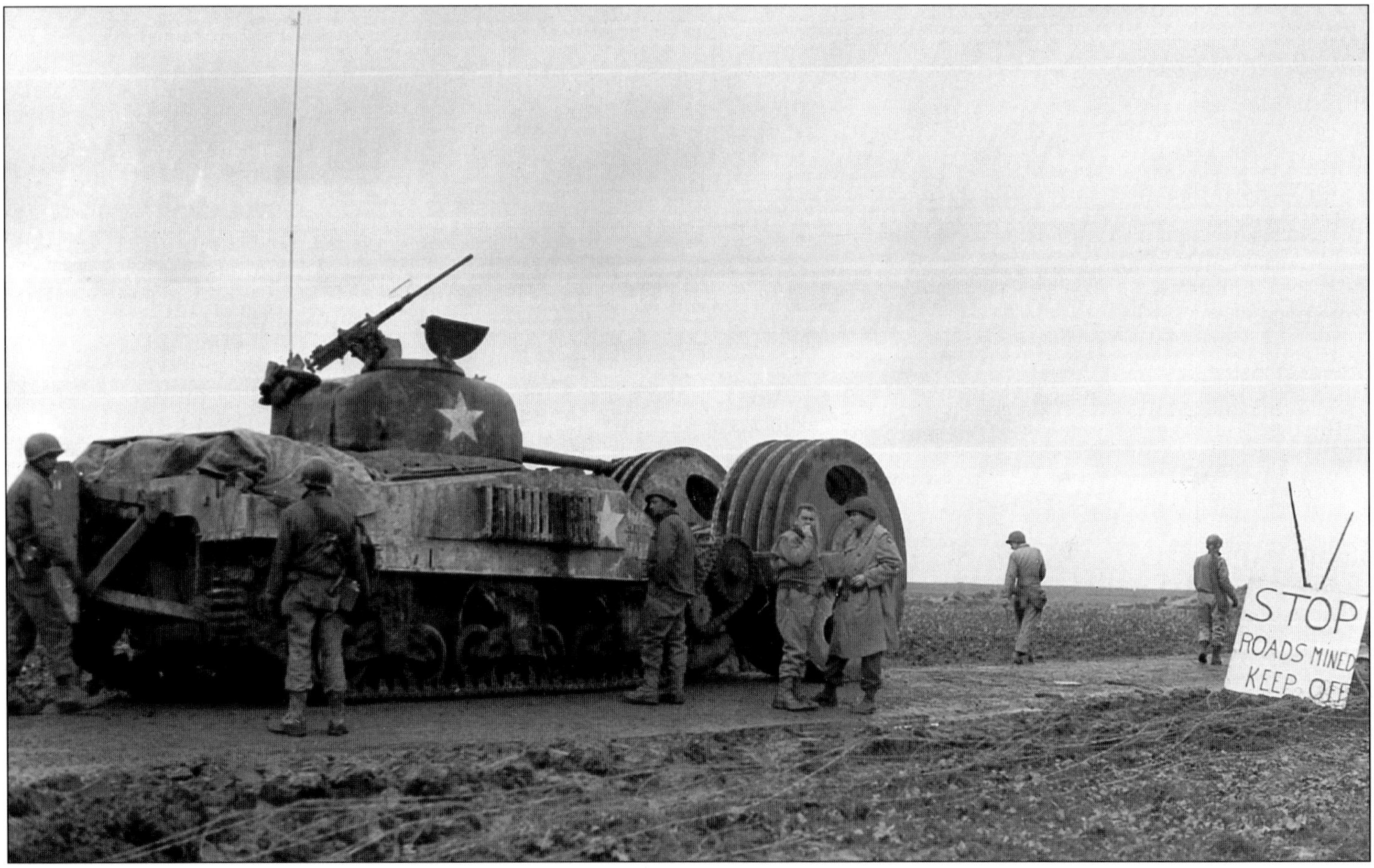

One of the more outlandish anti-mine devices was the T1E3 "Aunt Jemima" named after the character in the advertisements for a popular pancake batter. This example is being put to the test by the US 9th Army near Beggendorf, Germany on 11 December 1944. The large rollers could withstand a limited number of mine detonations, and then the large discs would have to be replaced.

Battle of the Bulge

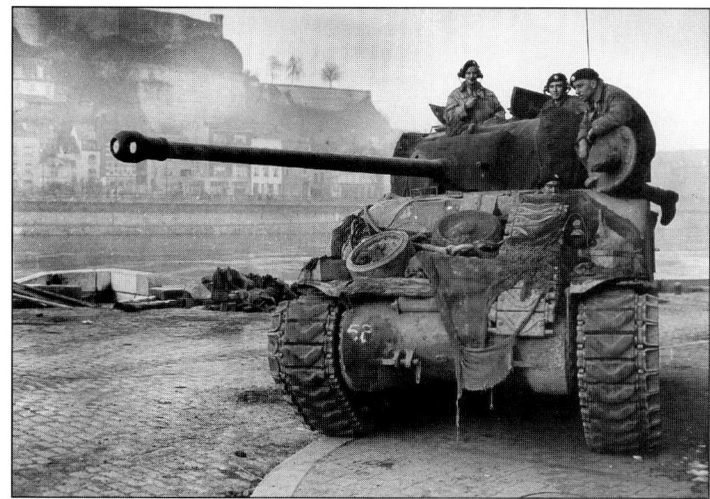

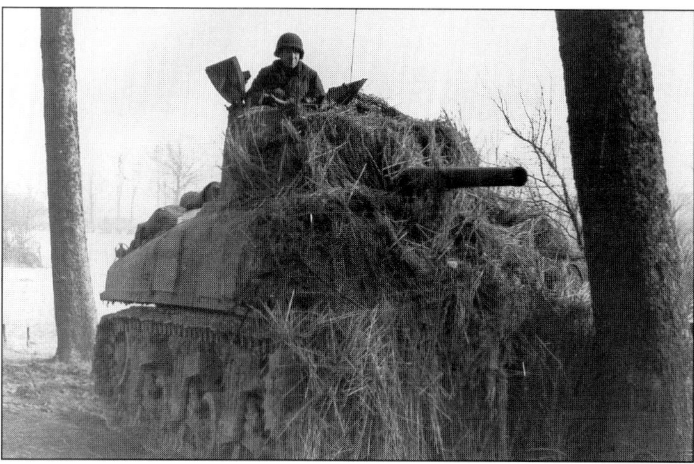

A M4A1 tank of the 3rd Armored Division stands watch over a road near Manhay, Belgium during the attempts to stem the tide of the German offensive in the Ardennes on 23 December 1944. The crew has covered the front of the tank with straw to provide camouflage.

During the Ardennes fighting, several British armor units provided support for the US Army efforts especially along the northern edge of the battle-zone. This Sherman Firefly of the 29 Armoured Brigade was assigned to guard duty at an intersection in Namur, Belgium to prevent German paratrooper forces from capturing key sites. The Firefly used the 17-pounder, the most effective anti-tank armament fitted on the Sherman tank. One US tank battalion was equipped with Fireflies in Italy, but received them too late to see combat action.

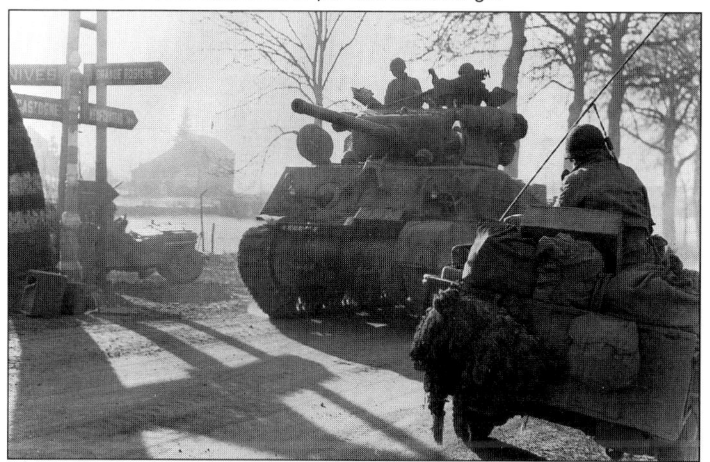

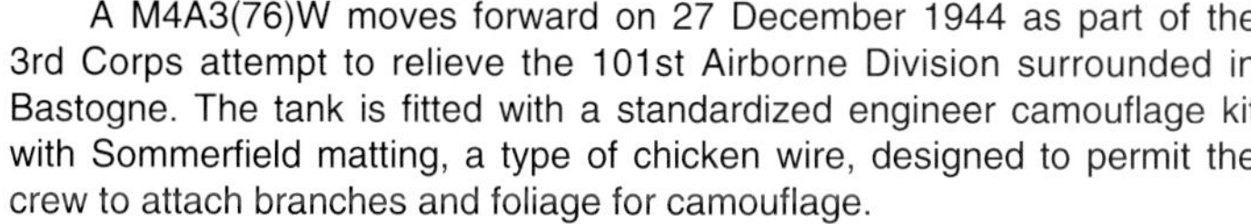

A M4A3(76)W moves forward on 27 December 1944 as part of the 3rd Corps attempt to relieve the 101st Airborne Division surrounded in Bastogne. The tank is fitted with a standardized engineer camouflage kit with Sommerfield matting, a type of chicken wire, designed to permit the crew to attach branches and foliage for camouflage.

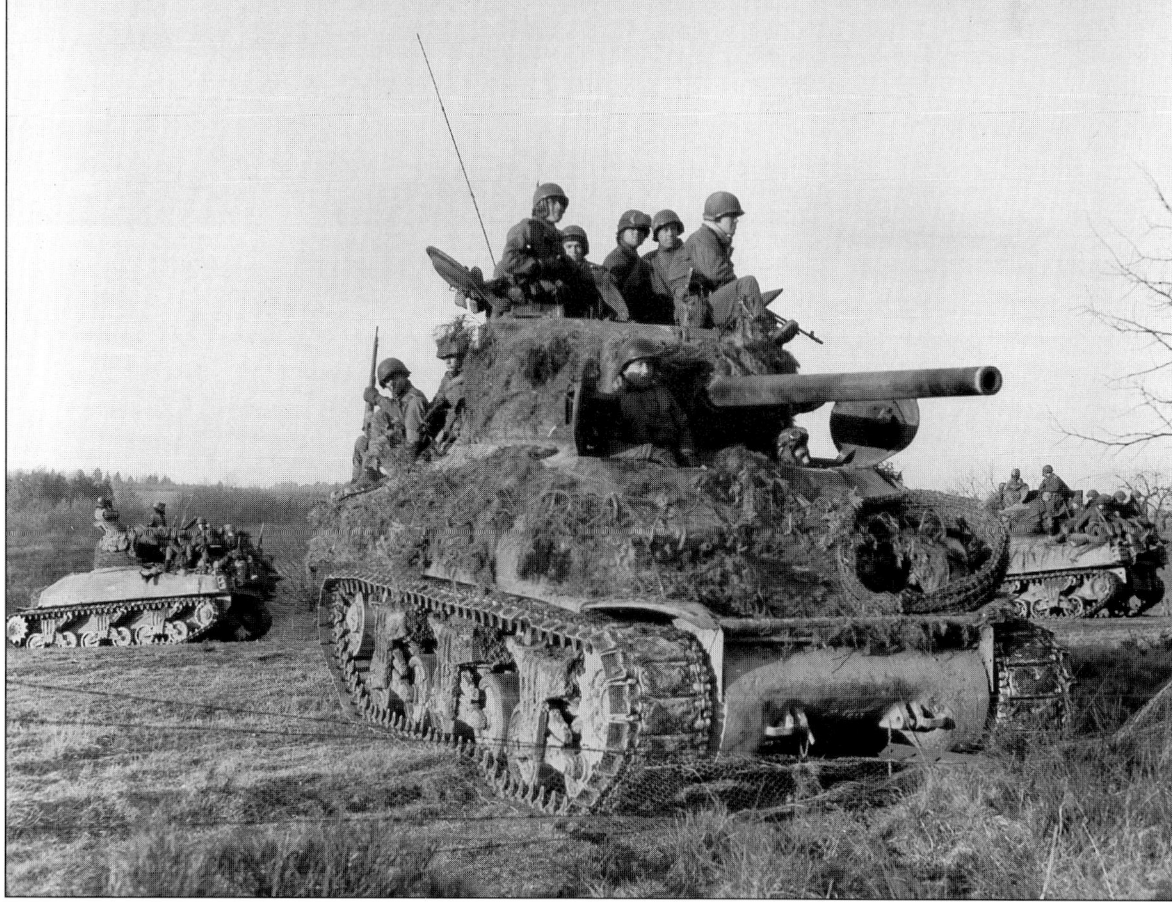

A well camouflaged M4A1(76)W of the 2nd Armored Division carrying troops of the 291st Rgt., 75th Infantry Division during attacks on the German positions in Frandeux, Belgium during the Battle of the Bulge. It is usually forgotten that the first few weeks of the battle were not snowy as is so often thought.

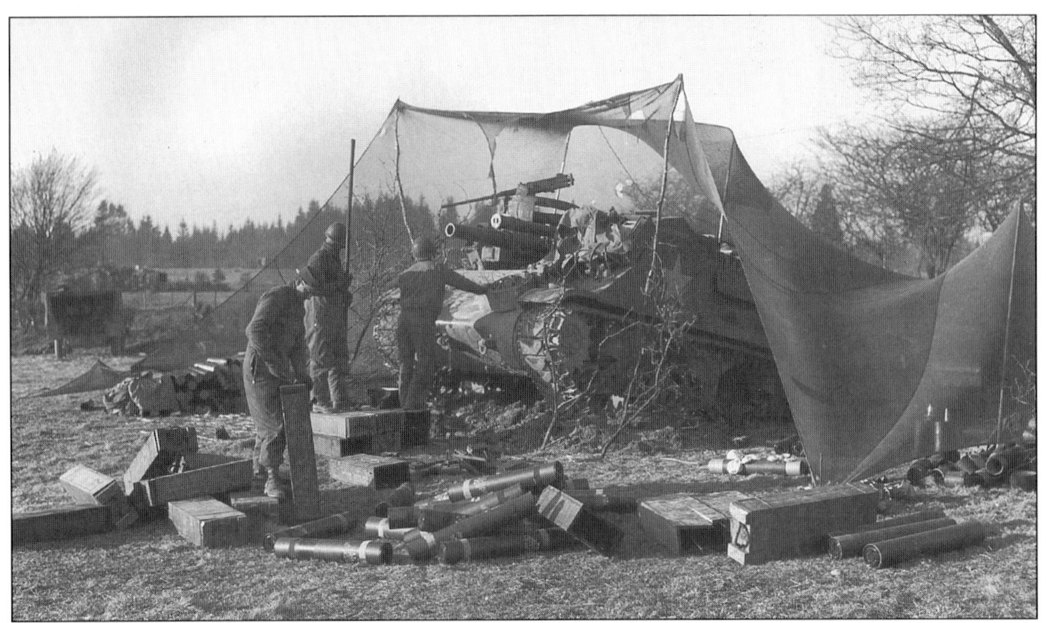

A M7 105mm HMC crew prepares ammunition for another fire mission in support of the 7th Armored Division's heroic defense of St. Vith on 27 December 1944. The 7th Armored Division's defense of St. Vith along with several US infantry division held the northern thrust of the German offensive, but at a heavy cost in men and equipment. St. Vith was captured by Grenadier-Regiment 294 on 21 December 1944 after intense fighting.

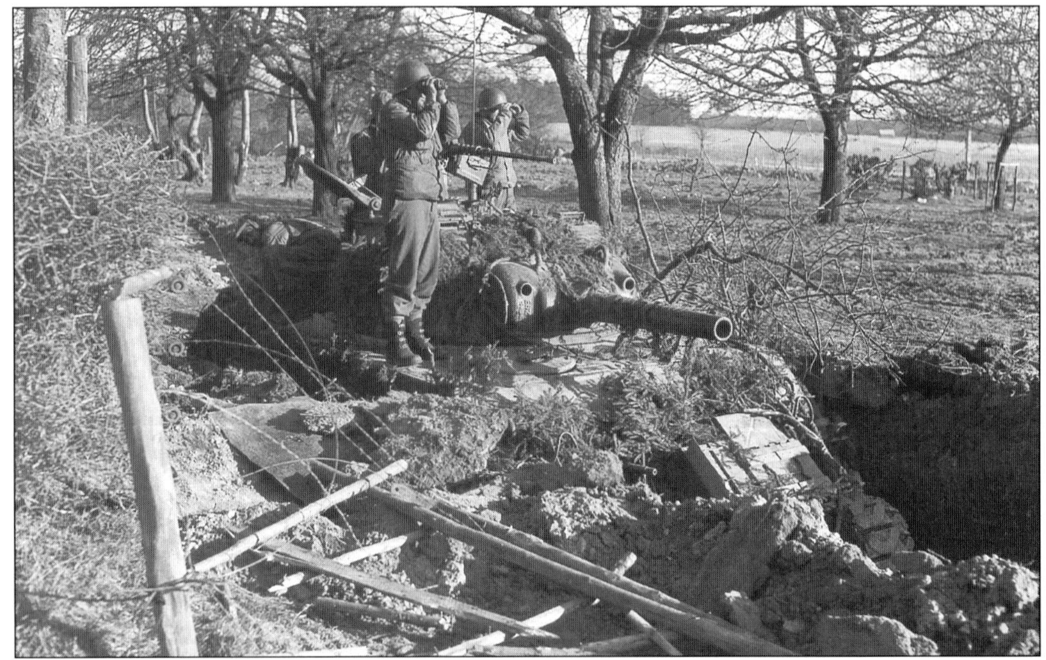

A well entrenched M4A3(105) howitzer tank of the 7th Armored Division is set up in an ambush position to cover a key road in the Manhay sector of the front, 27 December 1944.

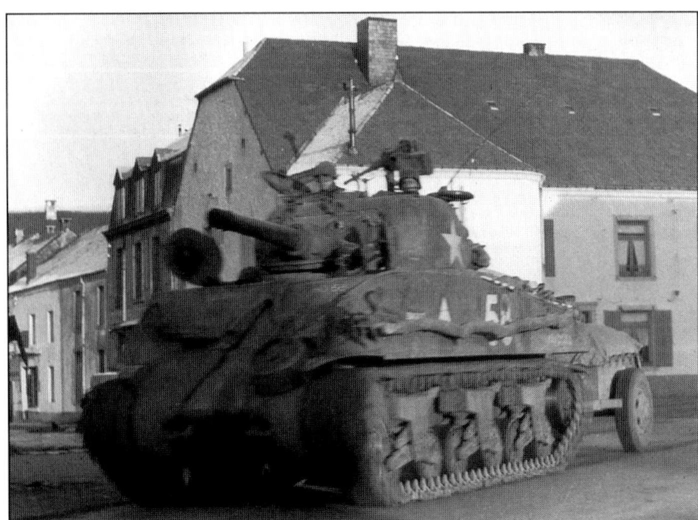

A M4A3(105) howitzer tank of the 6th Armored Division passes through Habay-la-Neuve on its way to Bastogne on 29 December 1944. The howitzer tank version of the Sherman usually towed a single axle trailer to carry additional ammunition.

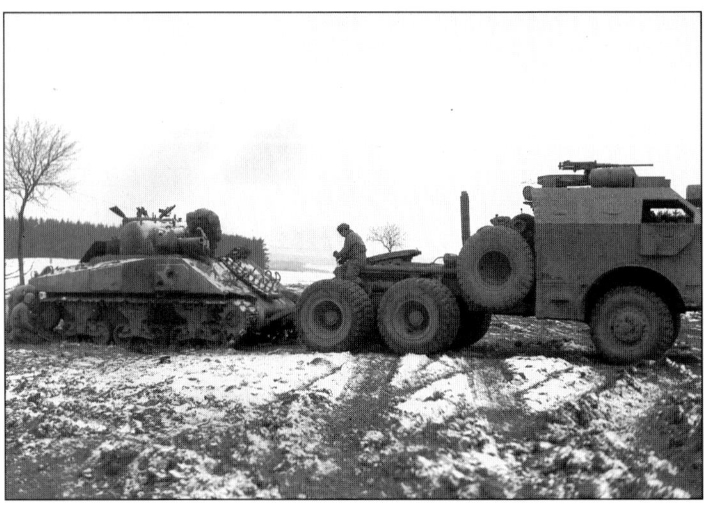

The first armor unit to break into Bastogne from Patton's 3rd Army was Abram's 37th Tank Battalion. This remarkable assault came at a price as is evident in this recovery of a 4th Armored Division M4 knocked out in the outskirts of Bastogne. A close examination of the hull side shows why many crews painted out the white US stars on the hull side.

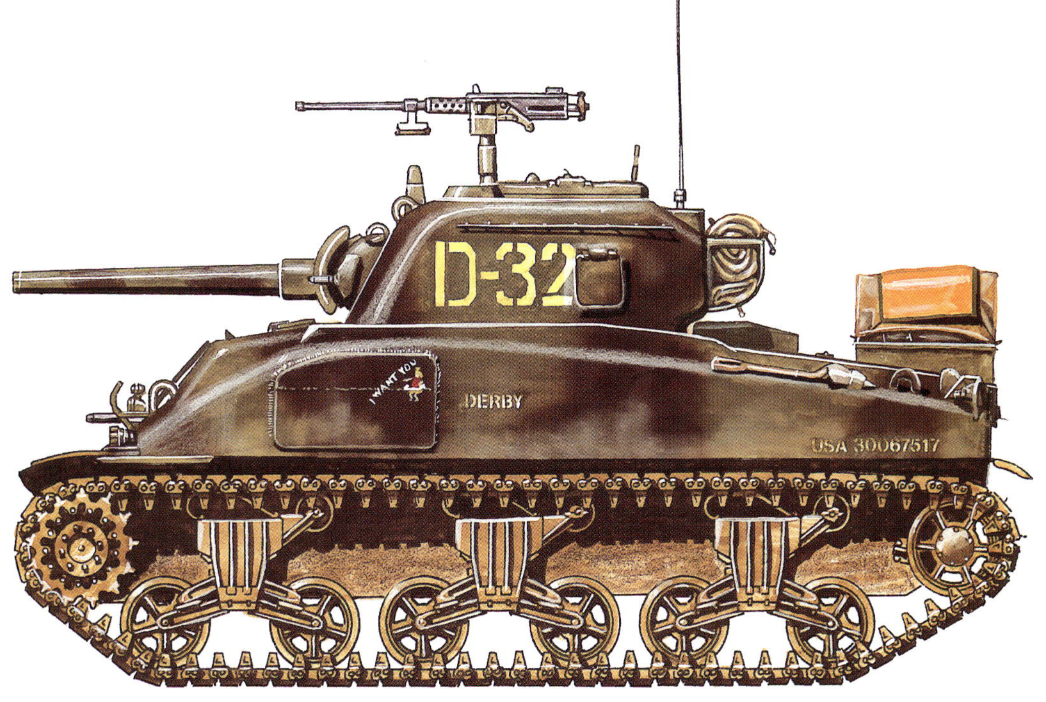

M4A1, 66th or 67th Arm'd Regt., 2nd Armored Division, Normandy, July 1944. The 2nd Armored Division camouflage painted their tanks prior to their introduction into combat during the Normandy break-out operations. A sprayed-on pattern of Earth Brown was applied over the usual olive drab. Vehicle numbers were applied in yellow, beginning with the company letter, a dash, the platoon number, and the tank number. In some cases, this number was repeated on the turret rear; this vehicle had a sheet metal basket welded to the rear with the number painted on it. A vehicle name was painted on the hull side in white. This vehicle had a small cartoon of a doll in a high-chair painted on the side with the caption "I Want You". The crew attached a platform at the rear of the engine deck for attaching personal gear and tarps. On top of the gear is an AL 140 flourescent red identification panel. These were designated AP-50-A and came in a set consisting of an AL 140 neon red and AL 141 neon yellow panel (both with white reverse backing). During combat, units would be instructed which colors or combinations of colors would be used. These panels served to identify Allied equipment since it was found in Italy that the roof stars painted on vehicles soon became covered in dust and were not sufficiently visible to Allied fighter bombers.

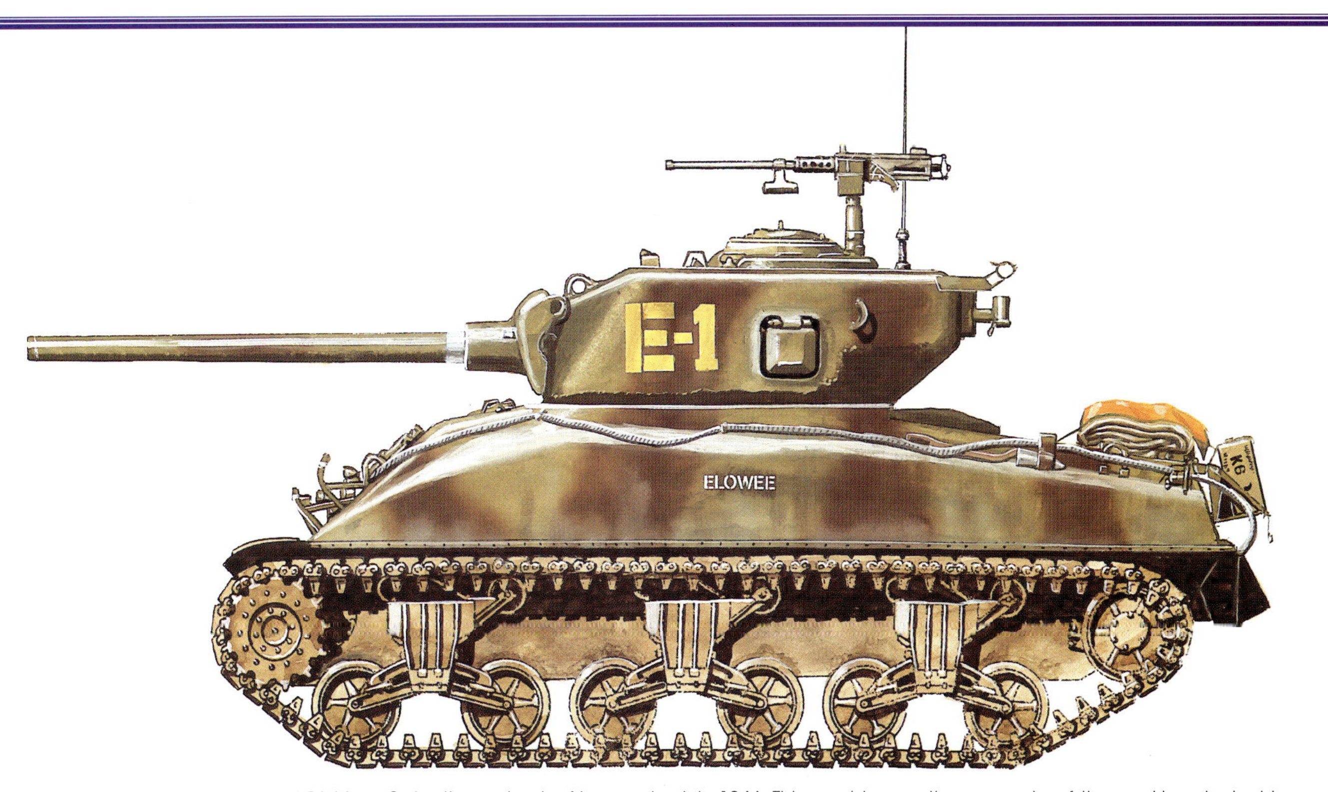

M4A1(76)W, 2nd Armored Division, Cotentin peninsula, Normandy, July 1944. This provides another example of the markings typical in Normandy with the 2nd and 3rd Armored Divisions. The vehicle is finished in a spray-painted pattern of Earth Brown and olive drab. The vehicle name is Elowee and the individual number is E-1 indicating the company commander. The turret insignia on this particular tank was painted out before it entered combat at the time of the St. Lo break-out operation in July.

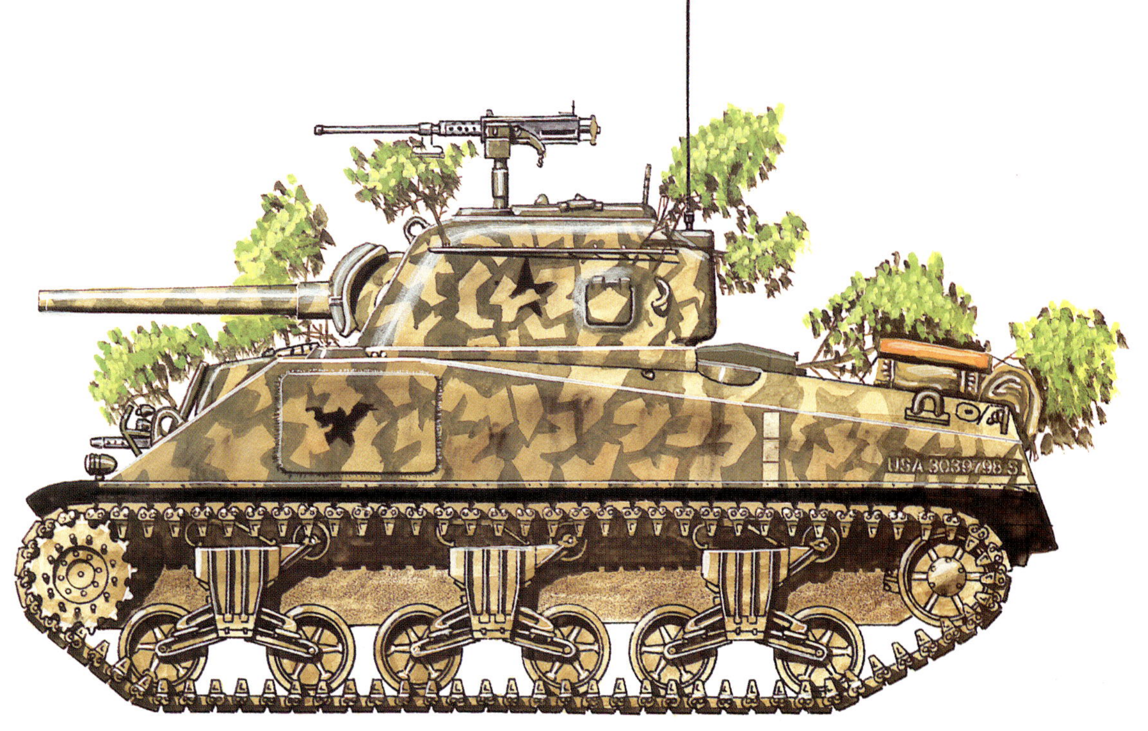

M4, 3rd Platoon, 8th Tank Bn., 4th Armored Division, Britanny, July 1944. Among the three tank battalions of the 4th Armored Division, the 8th Tank Bn. took the greatest care with camouflage. Before the attack on Coutances, the battalion applied an improvised camouflage using a concoction of mud. In addition, wire was strung along the tank to attach foliage. On this illustration, the foliage has been omitted from the left side to better show the camouflage pattern. Notice also that the white stars have been painted out. The battalion also used a white band, 18 inches high on the hull side and on the center of the engine access door on the rear of the hull to indicate platoon. One long bar was 1st, a bar broken in two parts was 2nd, and broken in three was 3rd Platoon as seen here.

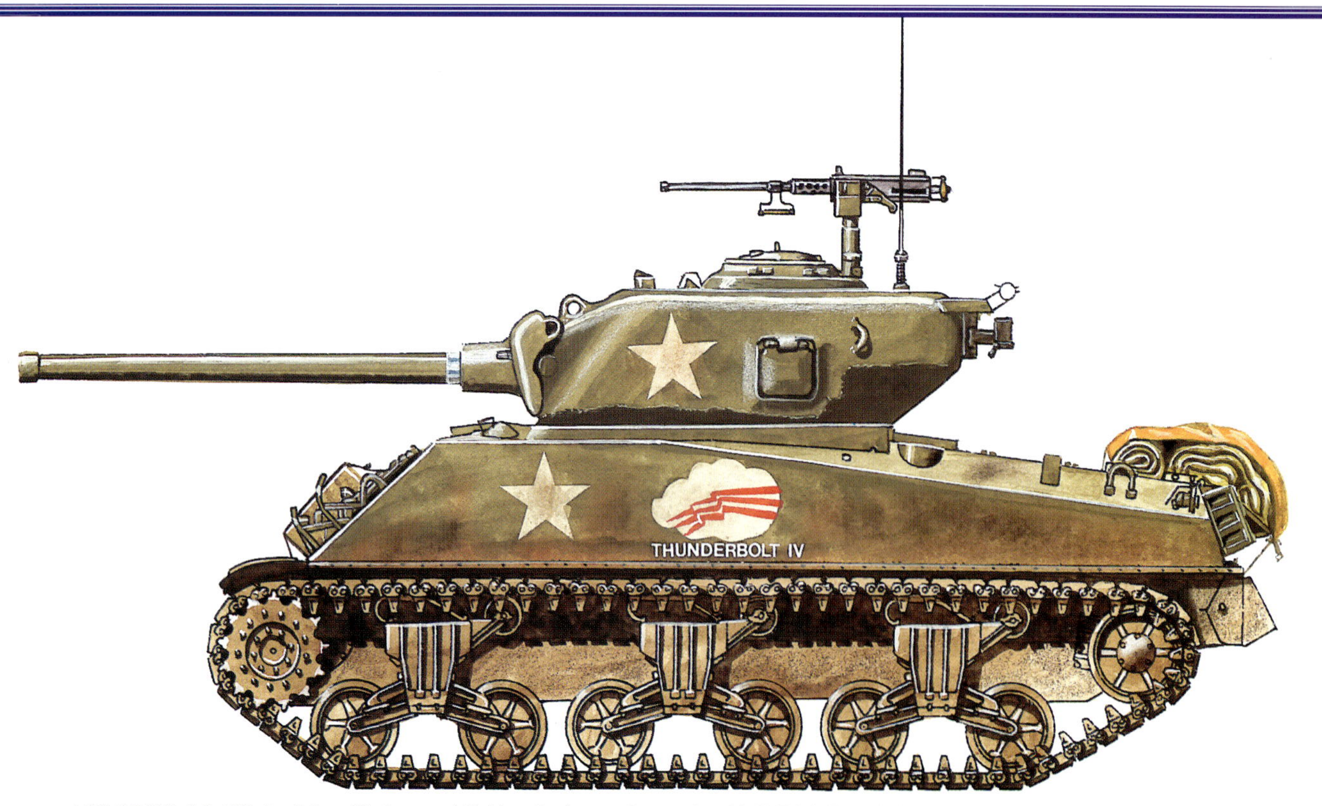

M4A3(76)W, HQ, 37th Tank Bn., 4th Armored Division, Bastogne, December 1944. This is Thunderbolt IV, the command tank of Maj. Creighton Abrams at the time of the Battle of the Bulge. Abrams had three previous Sherman tanks that were either knocked out or worn out prior to receiving his first 76mm Sherman in November 1944 while fighting in the Lorraine. All had the white and red Thunderbolt marking. For whatever reason, Abrams kept the white turret and hull insignia even though many other tanks in the division painted it out. Besides being a superb unit commander, Abrams was probably one of the highest scoring American tankers during the war, as his battalion saw more tank-vs.-tank combat than nearly any other and Abrams' was the highest scoring crew in the battalion.

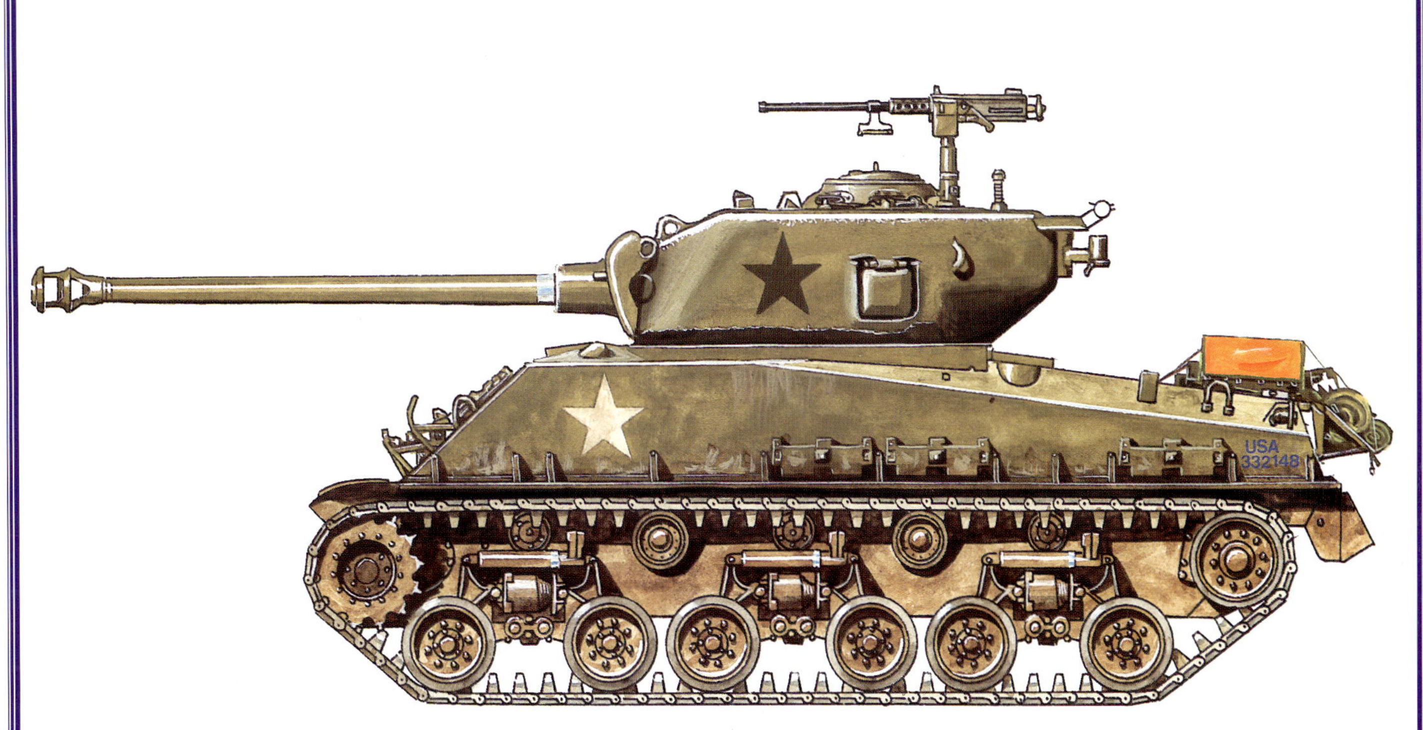

M4A3(76)W HVSS, 4th Armored Division, Bastogne, January 1945. The 4th Armored Division received a small number of HVSS Shermans in December 1944 as reinforcements to make up for their losses during the drive to relieve Bastogne. This is a fairly typical example, showing the roof star painted out, but the hull star still left.

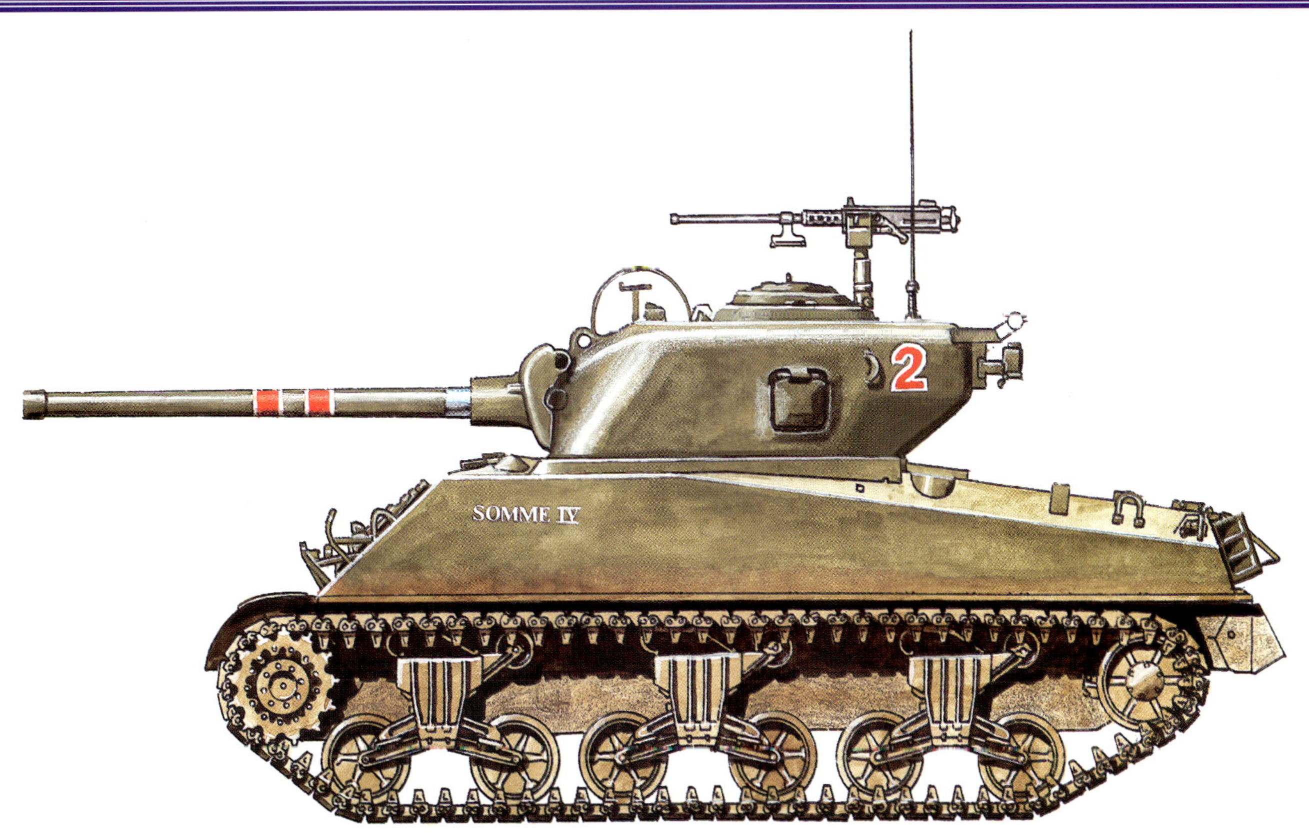

M4A3(76)W, 4th Tank Battalion, 1st Armored Division, St. Lucia, Italy, October 1944. The 1st Armored Division began receiving 76mm Shermans in August 1944 to replace losses suffered during the drive on Rome. Most were left in overall olive drab. After the division was reorganized from heavy to light configuration, the markings pattern changed. The platoon bands were kept for the barrel, but edge in white for better visibility. But the new markings used a number instead of bars on the turret rear for ease of identification. Under the new configuration, each battalion had four companies, and the color pattern was red, white, yellow, blue. The crew has added a set of circular steel rod hoops over an improvised artillery sight mounted in front of the gunner's station on the right turret roof. The vehicle name, Somme IV, does not follow the usual practice of beginning the name with the company letter, which in this case would be "A".

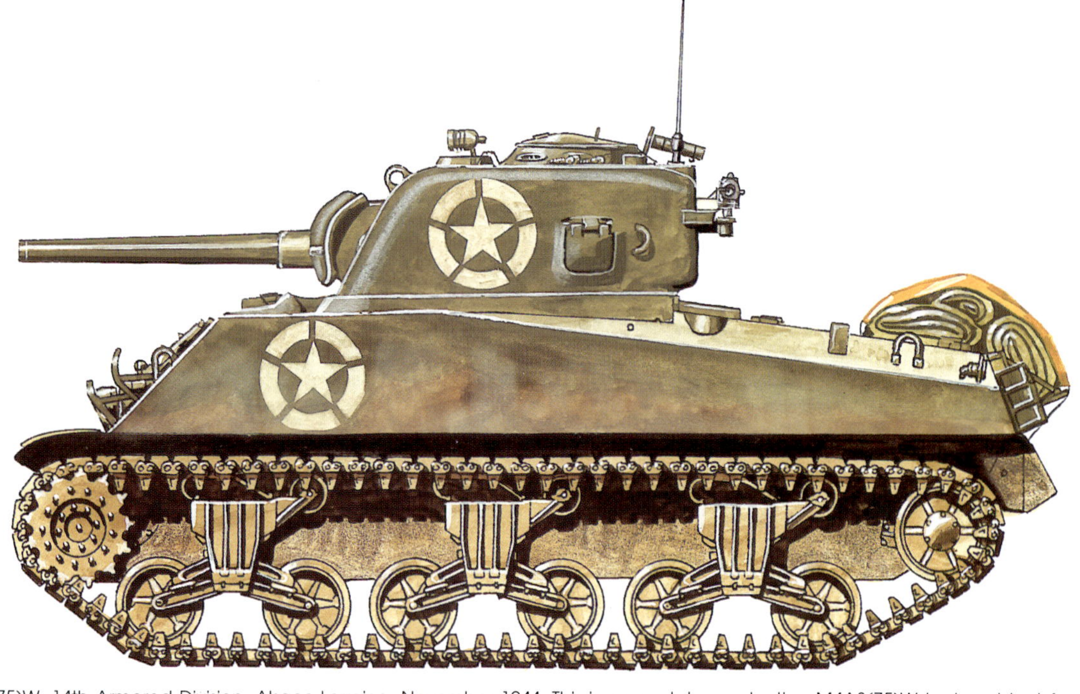

M4A3(75)W, 14th Armored Division, Alsace-Lorraine, November 1944. This is a very late production M4A3(75)W tank, evident from the late style 75mm gun turret with its improved commander's vision cupola, and the raised rear bustle casting. Surprisingly, the tank retains the standard Normandy invasion stars with circular surrounds. These were usually applied by depots prior to issuing replacement tanks. In all probability, the division did not have enough time (or paint) to paint the stars out before using them in combat.

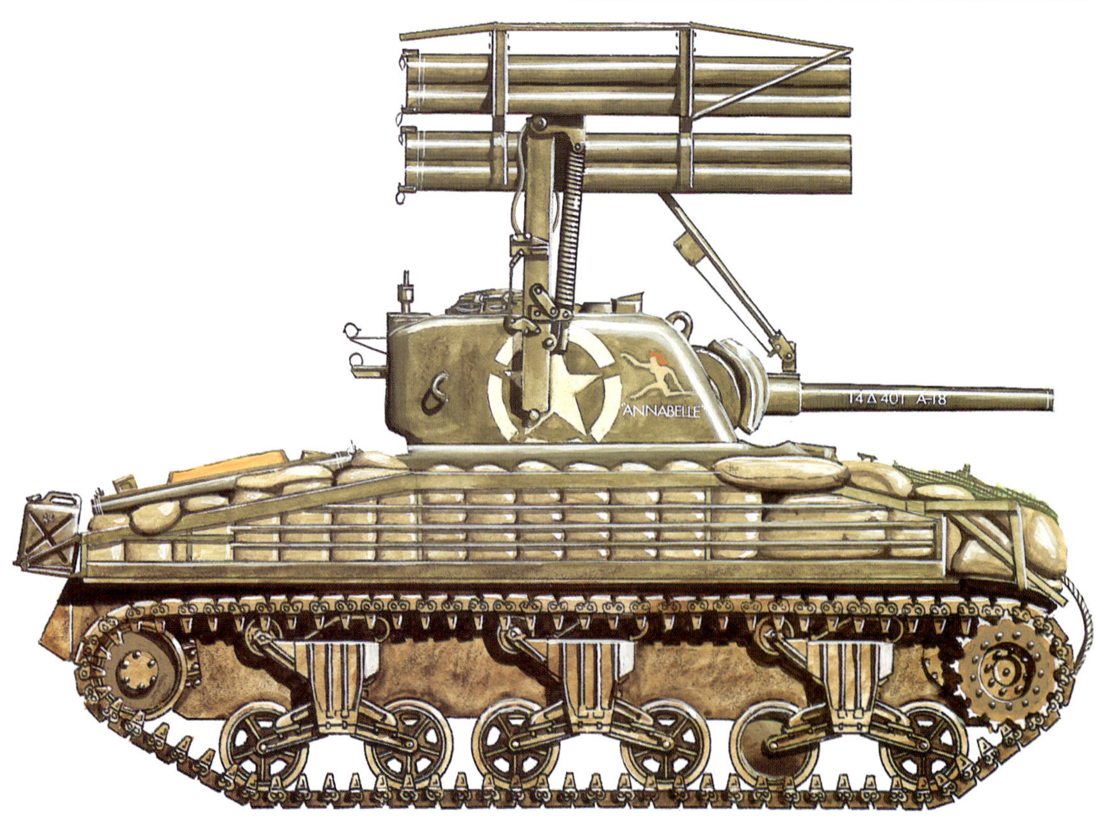

M4A1 with T-34 Calliope MRL, A Co., 40th Tank Bn., 14th Armored Division, Obermodern, Germany, 3 March 1945. Like so many other 14th Armored Division vehicles, this M4A1 has been thoroughly sand-bagged. However, the turret had been kept free of the usual sand-bag armor, so revealing the old vehicle markings. These include a very prominent white star, obscured after the T-34 Calliope was welded over it. In addition, there is a small pin-up painted in front of it with the name Annabelle below. On the gun barrel is the vehicle ID code, 14Δ40T A-18.

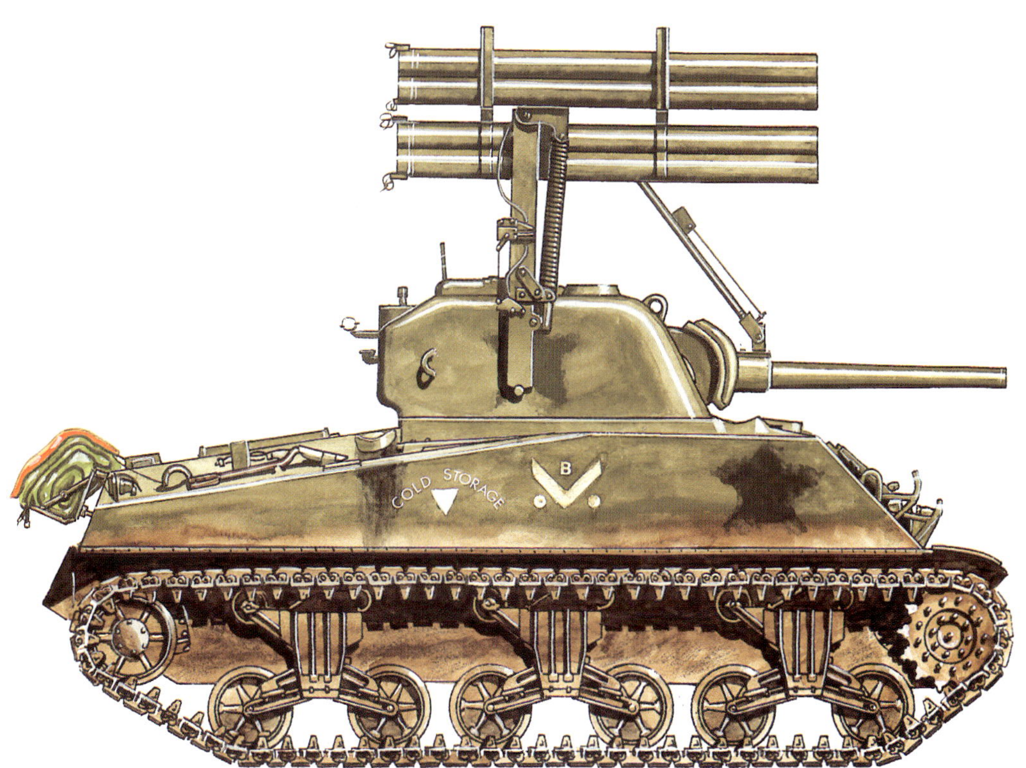

M4A3(75)W, 2nd Platoon, B Co., 714th Tank Bn., 12th Armored Division, Fletrange, France, 1945. The 12th Armored Division had a complex set of markings to identify its components. The 23rd Tank Bn. was identified by an upward-pointing chevron, the 43rd Tank Bn. by a horizontal bar and the 714th Tank Bn. (as seen here) with a downward- pointing chevron. The Company letter was placed centrally above this tactical sign, in this case, B. Below the sign were small circles indicating the platoon, in this case, 2nd Platoon. This tank also had its one name, Cold Storage, marked over a triangle insignia on the hull side.

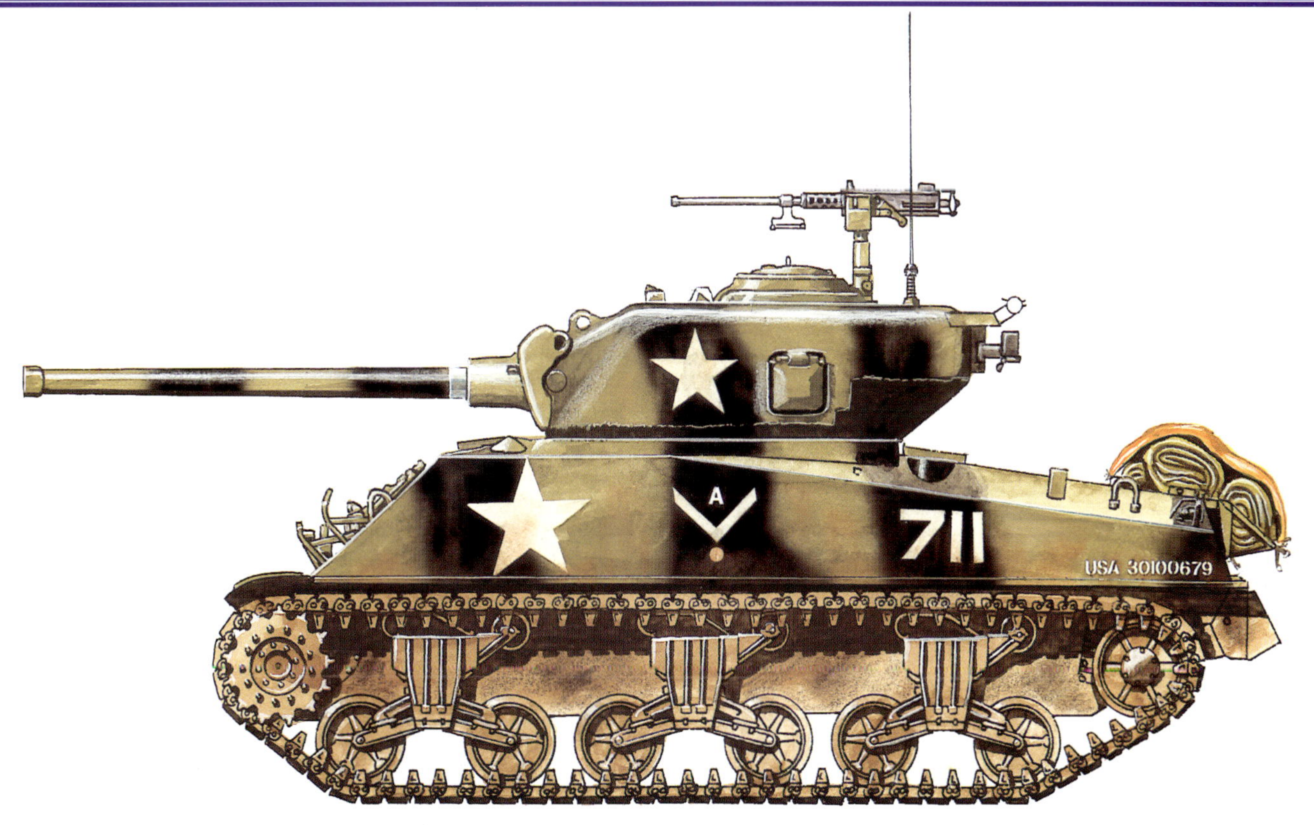

M4A3(76)W, 1st Platoon, A Co., 714th Tank Battalion, 12th Armored Division, Germany, 1945. This tank provides another example of the 12th Armored Division insignia. The tank is camoulfage painted in black over olive drab, the most common color combination in late 1944 and early 1945. Besides the unit tactical insignia, the vehicle also carries a tactical number on the hull rear. In all probability the first digit indicated the battalion, the second the company or platoon and the third, the vehicle. Standard US stars are carried in the official positions.

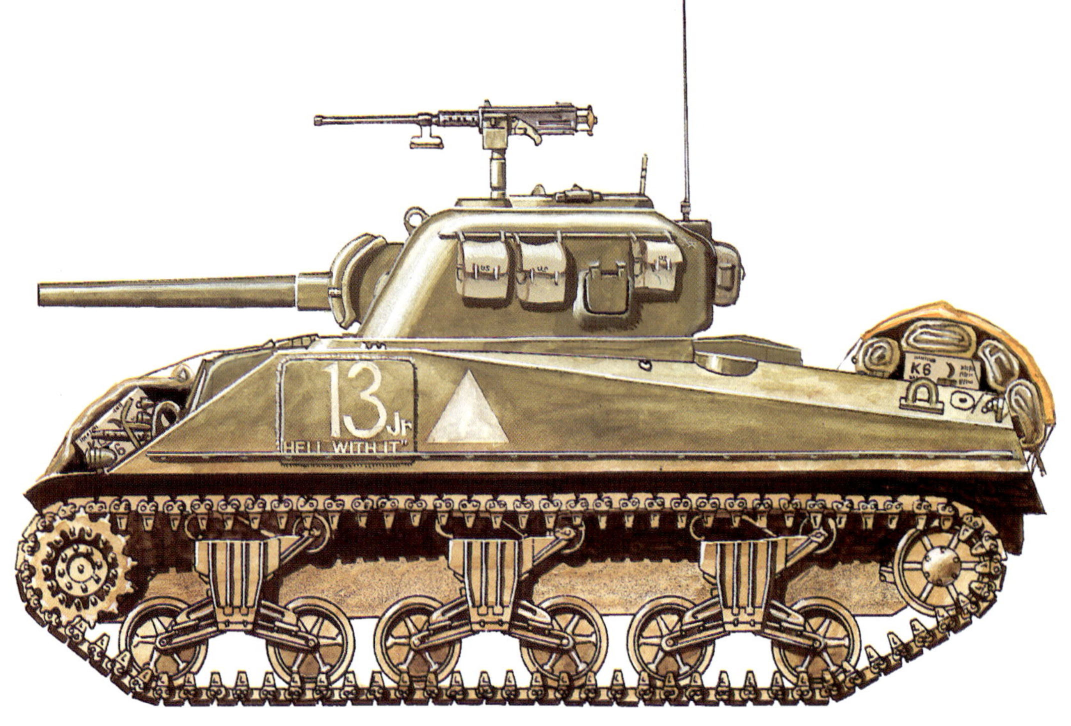

M4, 15th Tank Bn, 6th Armored Division, Lanensalz airbase, Germany, April 1945. The 6th Armored Division did not regularly use any complicated markings. Many of its tanks sported a white triangle insignia, but it is not clear if this served as a battalion or divisional insignia. This tank is numbered, oddly enough, as 13 Jr., which suggests it replace an earlier number 13. Below this marking is the slogan "Hell With It". This tank had a four inch strip of sheet metal welded about five inches above the lower hull sponson sides. This was apparently intended as a type of fender when the vehicle was fitted with extended end-connectors. The new fender partly covered the markings as seen here. This tank also had a fairly standard steel rod frame welded to the upper turret side for storage.

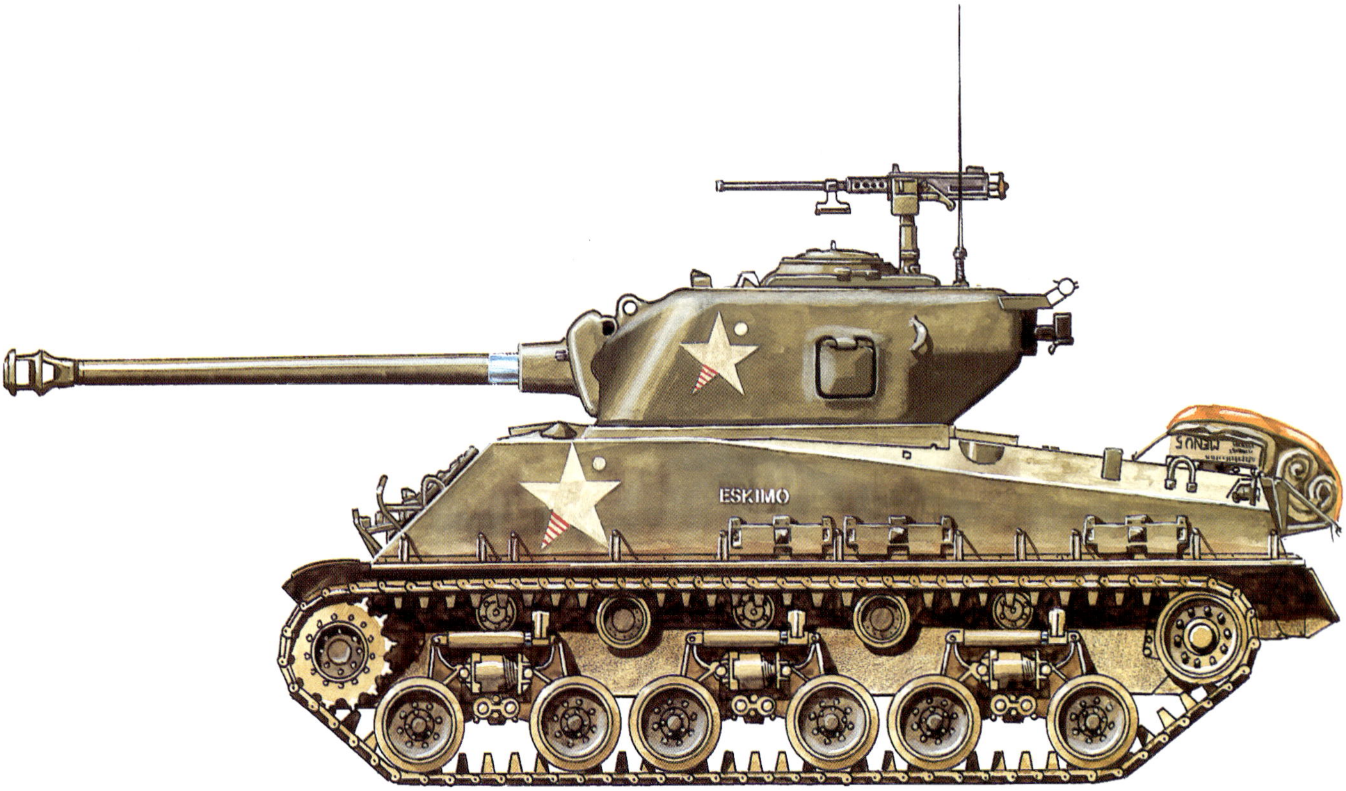

M4A3(76)W HVSS, 41st Tank Battalion, 11th Armored Division, Rhine river, Germany, March 1945. The 11th Armored Division used a unique method to identify its tank battalions. Small red bands were painted on the arms of the turret and hull star: 22nd Tank Bn. (12 o'clock arm); 41st Tank Bn. (7 o'clock arm); 42nd (9 o'clock arm). The company was indicated by the number of red bands, 5 bands for E company as seen here. In addition, the platoon was indicated by a small circle.

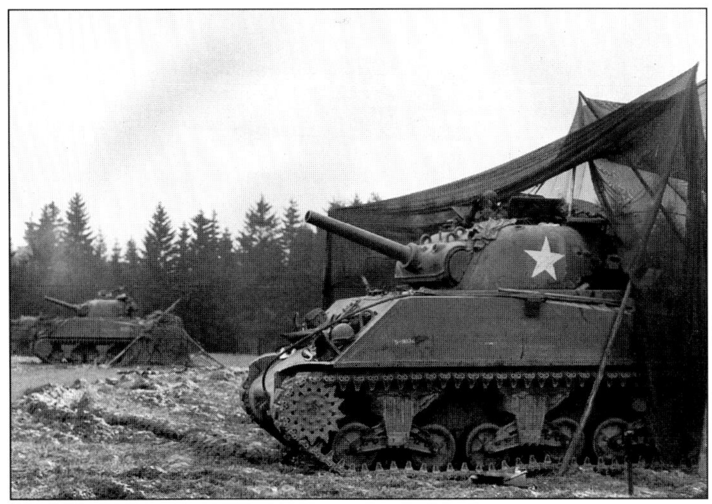

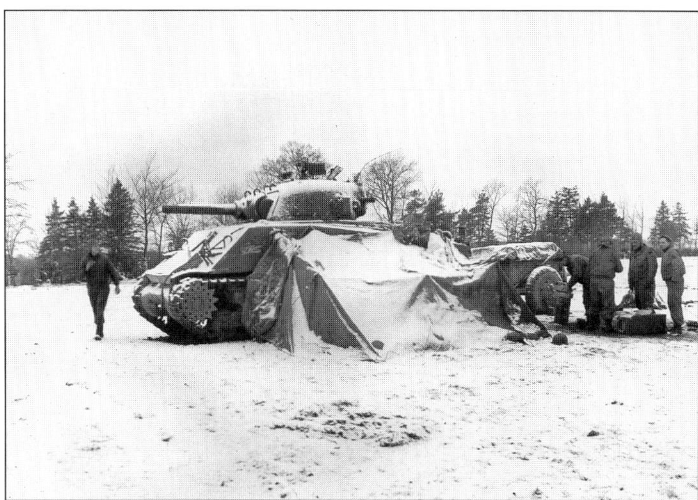

M4A3(105) howitzer tanks from the 750th Tank Bn. fire on German positions from a field near Manhay, Belgium. Like most artillery vehicles, they have been provided with camouflage netting.

Snow began to fall heavily at the end of December, as tankers of the 5th Arm'd. Regt. gather around a fire to warm behind their M4A3(105) howitzer tank near Eupen, Belgium.

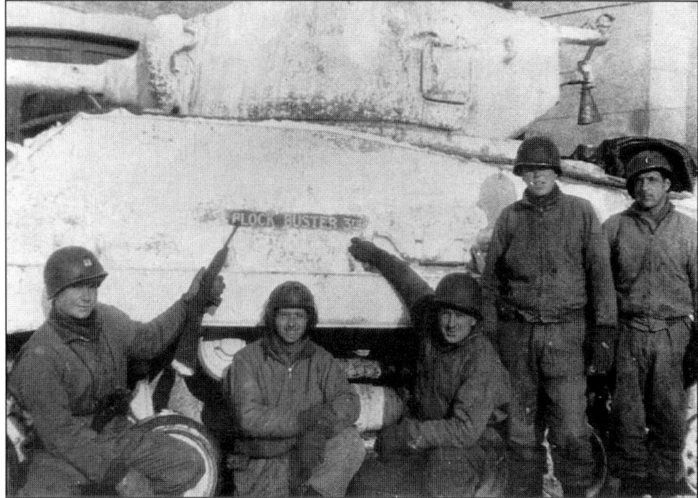

One of the first units into Bastogne was B Co., 37th Tank Bn, 4th Armored Division led by Capt. James Leach. This photo was taken inside Bastogne, and Capt. Leach is seen pointing to the nickname of his tank-Block Buster 3rd. The 37th Tank Battalion began receiving the new M4A3(76)W HVSS tanks around the time of the Bastogne operation, one of the earliest combat uses of this new Sherman version. This version is popularly called the M4A3E8 or "Easy Eight" though this was not its official name. (Col. James Leach)

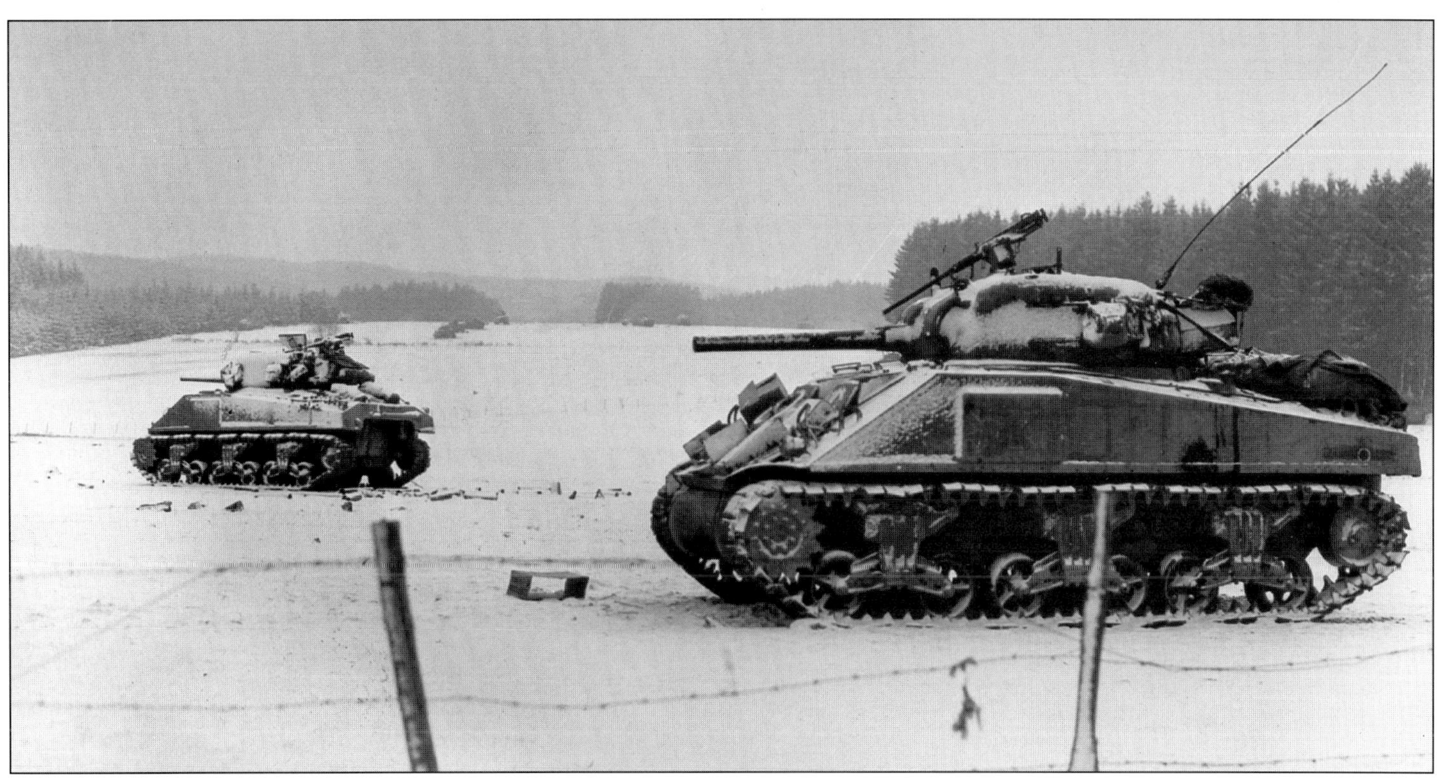

Wind-whipped snow covers M4 tanks of the 4th Armored Division deployed in a clearing near Sainlex, Belgium on the road to Bastogne. It was a credit to the durability of the Sherman that many of these original M4 tanks made it all the way from the Normandy fighting in July 1944 to Bastogne in December 1944.

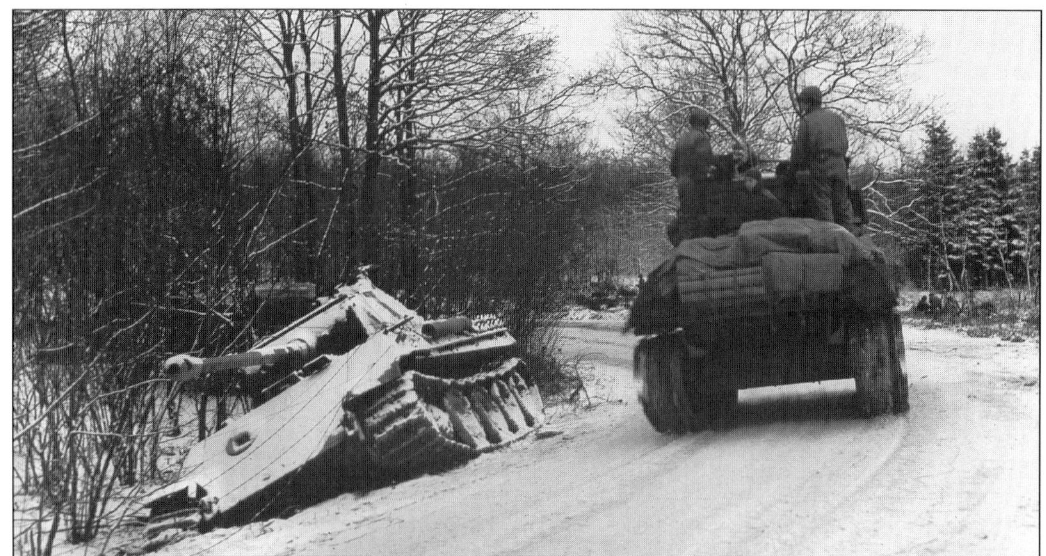

A M4A3(76)W of the 2nd Armored Division passes a disabled German Panther Ausf. G of the 2. SS-Panzer Division along the Erezee road outside Grandmenil, Belgium on 2 January 1945. The Panther was one of the Sherman's most difficult opponents, and was encountered far more frequently than the rare Tiger I.

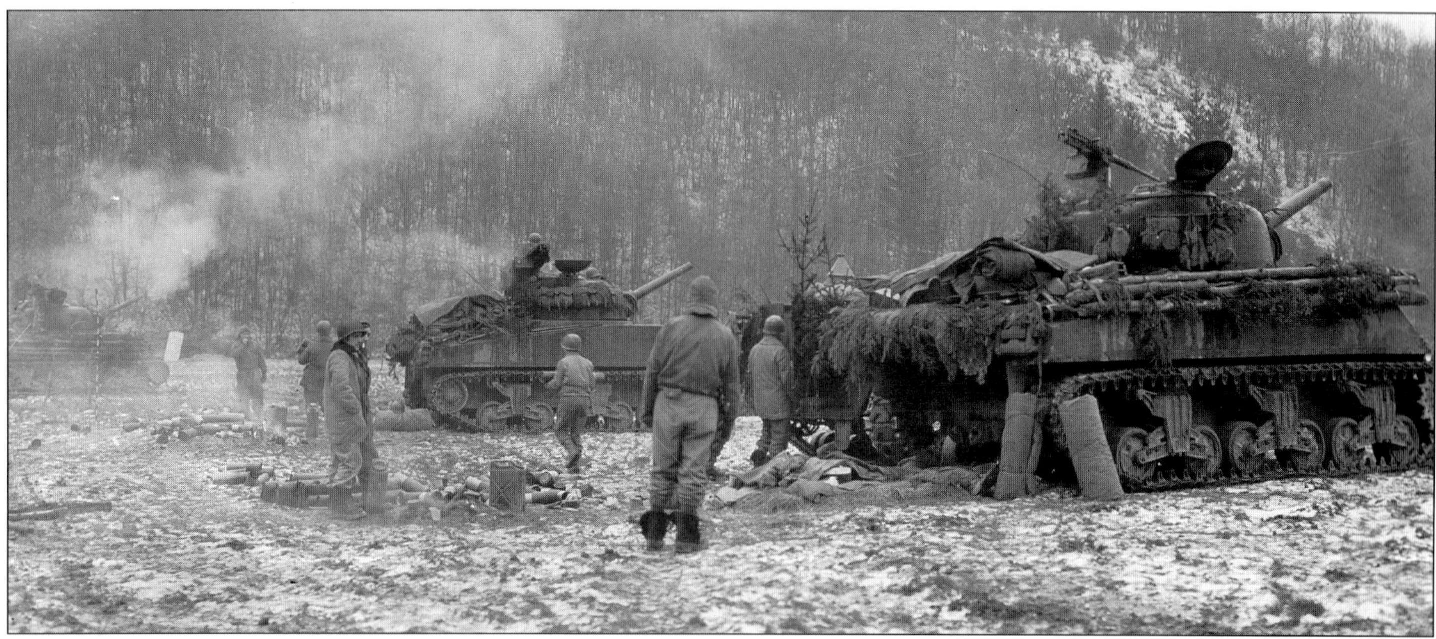

M4(105) howitzer tanks provide fire support for the 32nd Arm'd. Regt., 3rd Armored Division during the fighting near Trou-de-Bra, Belgium on 3 January 1945.

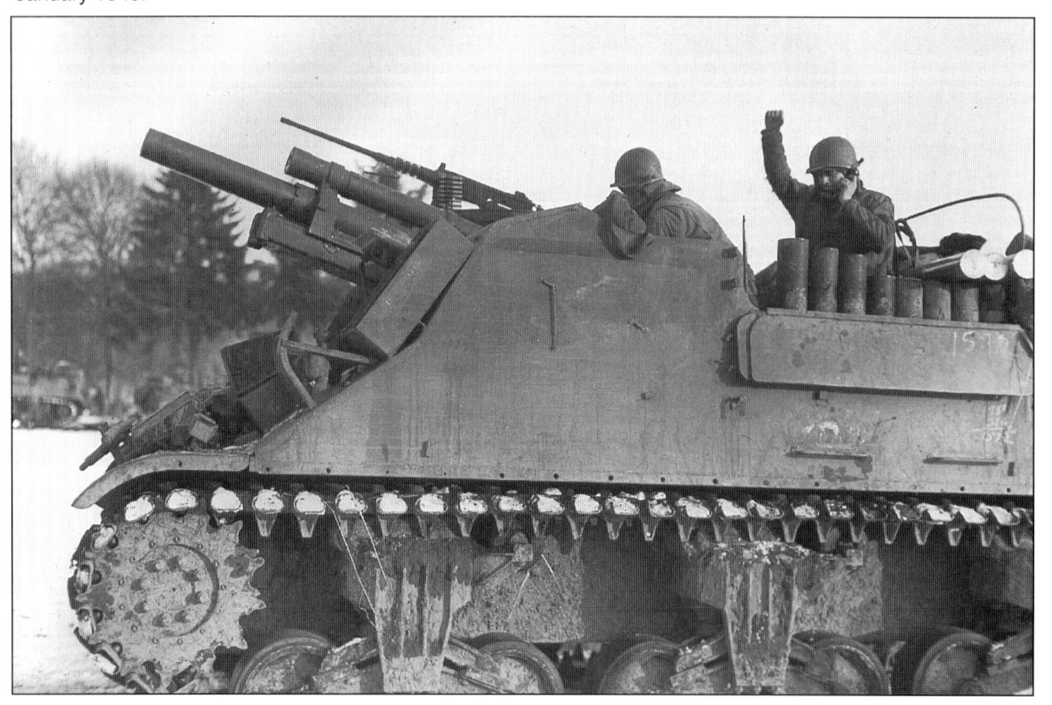

The crew of a M7 105mm HMC of C Battery, 274th Armored Field Artillery await the order to fire on German positions outside Bastogne during the counteroffensive to end the German siege. This self-propelled artillery unit was one of several transferred from France during Patton's Third Army drive to relieve Bastogne.

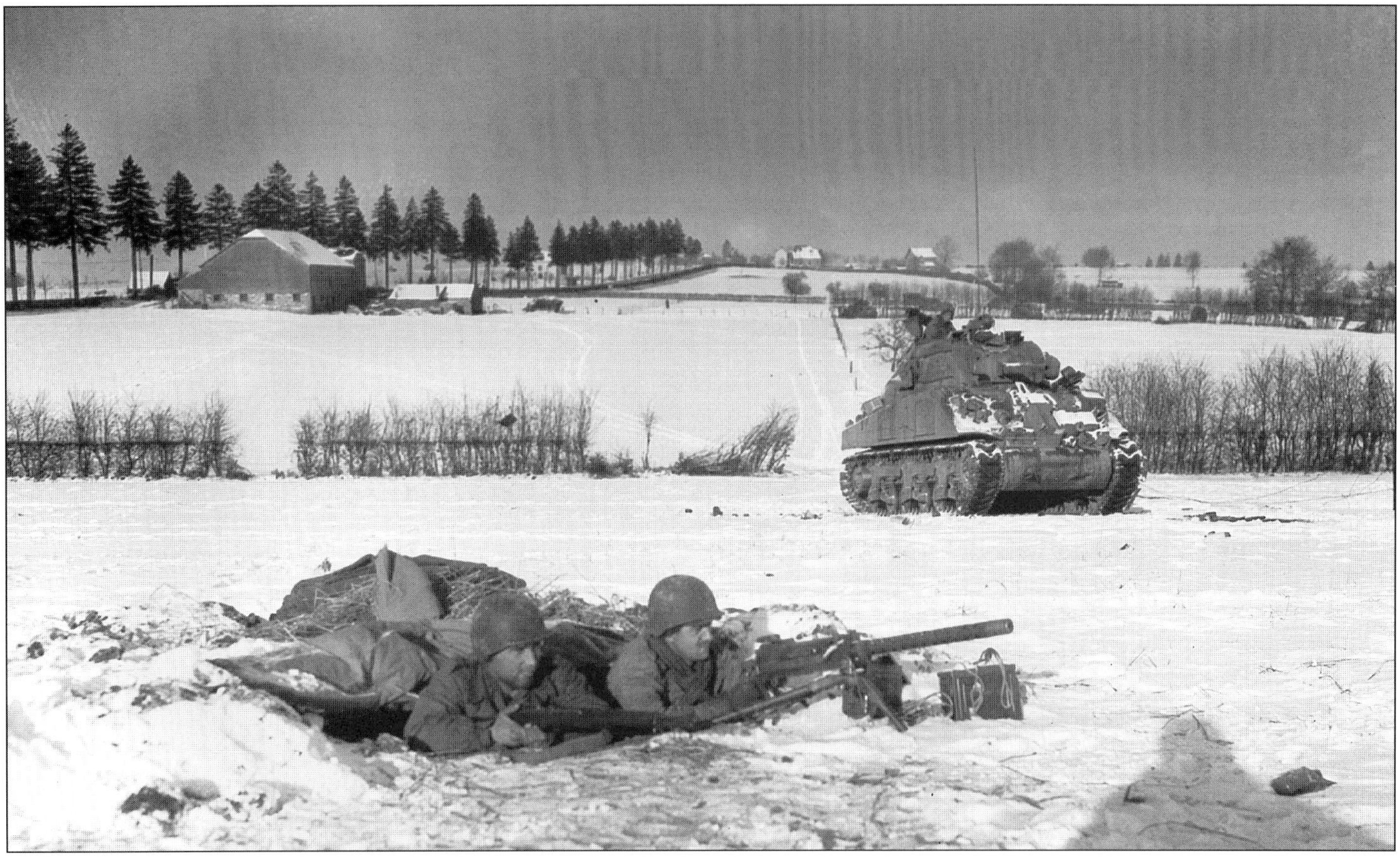

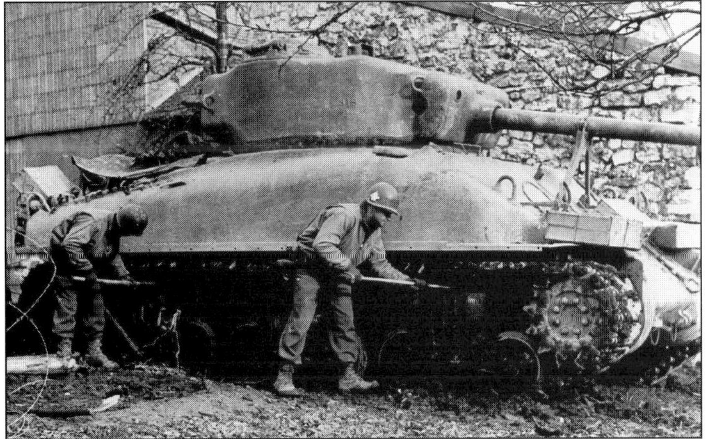

In a scene evocative of the fighting in the Ardennes, a M4 tank of the 4th Armored Division moves past an entrenched .30 cal machine gun team of the 104th Infantry in the fighting to keep the Bastogne corridor open on 3 January 1945.

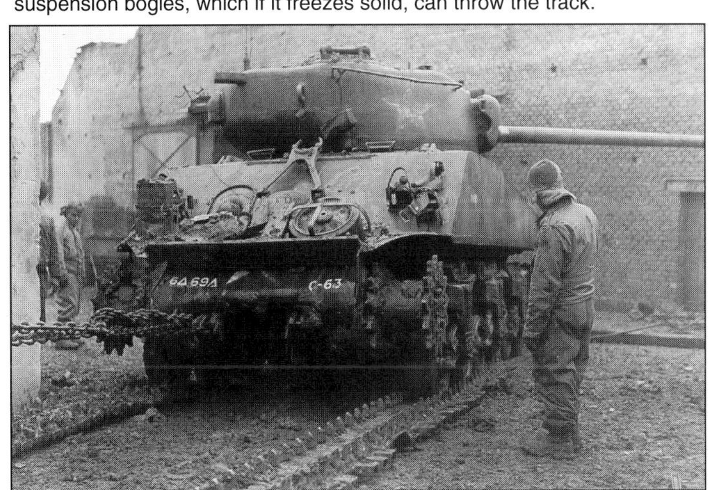

The crew of a M4A1(76)W of the 2/32 Arm'd. Regt., 3rd Armored Division does routine track repair during a lull in the fighting around Trou-de-Bra, Belgium on 3 January 1945. They are cleaning out mud from the suspension bogies, which if it freezes solid, can throw the track.

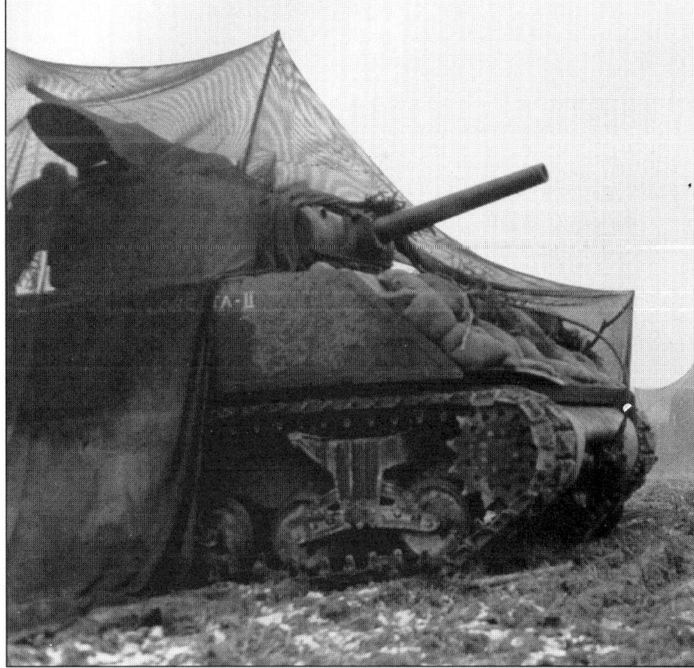

Loretta II and other M4(105) howitzer tanks fire on German positions in support of the 66th Arm'd. Regt. of the 2nd Armored Division during fighting near Amonines, Belgium on 4 January 1945. This tank is sporting a layer of sand-bags for protection against German panzerfausts.

A tank crew uses a truck to help put the track back on a M4A3(76)W of the 69th Tank Bn., 6th Armored Division. This track is fitted with extended end connectors for better floatation in muddy conditions.

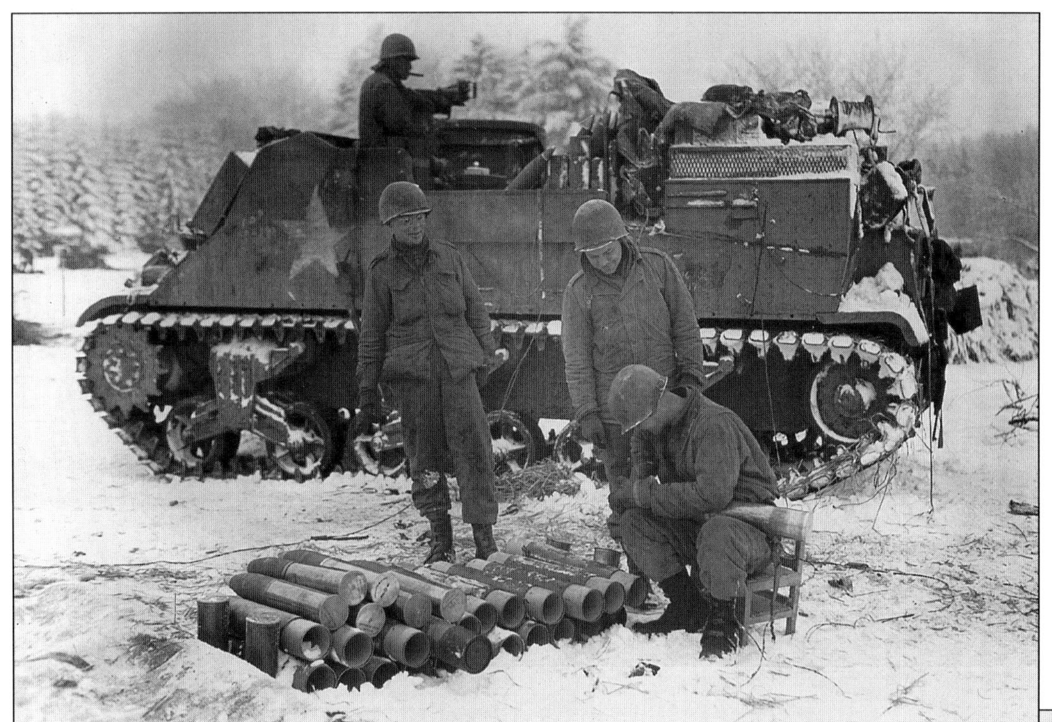

A gunner from Battery C, 274th Armored Field Artillery Regiment sets a fuze on a 105mm howitzer round during fire support operations in Bastogne on 5 January 1945. The ammunition came packed in cardboard tubes as seen stacked under the ammunition in the foreground. The M7 105mm HMC in the background is fitted with duck-bill extenders on the track for better performance in the snow and mud.

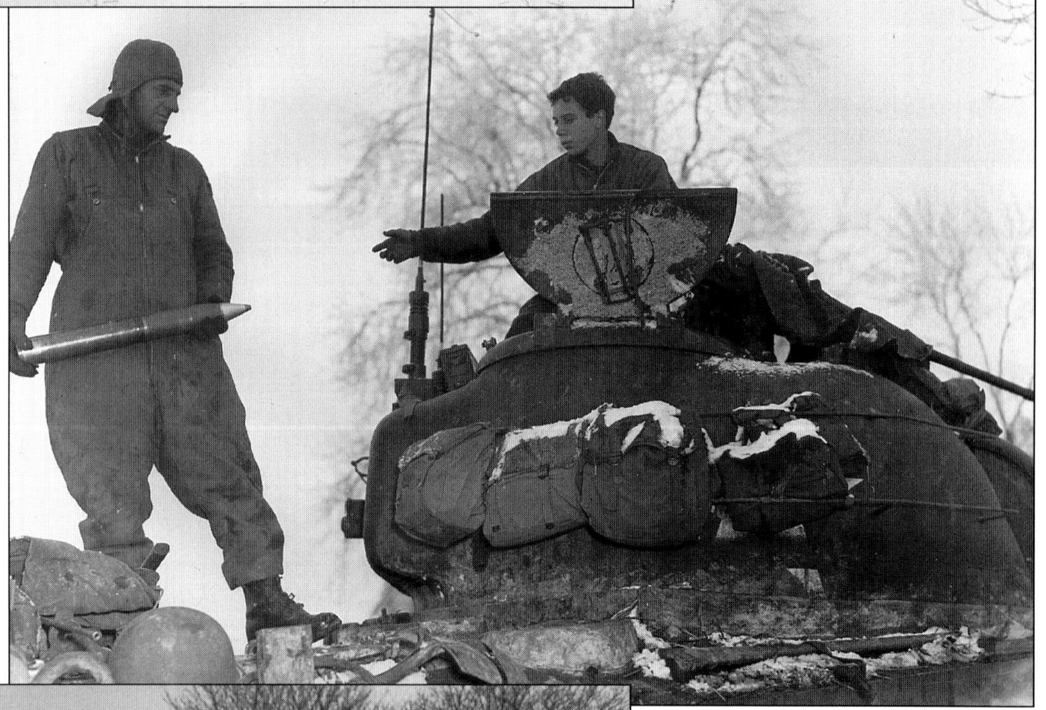

The crew of a M4A3 load 75mm high-explosive ammunition into their tank during a lull in the fighting near Jodenville, Belgium on 5 January 1945. Many crews had additional racks welded to the turret sides to attach their knapsacks and other kit.

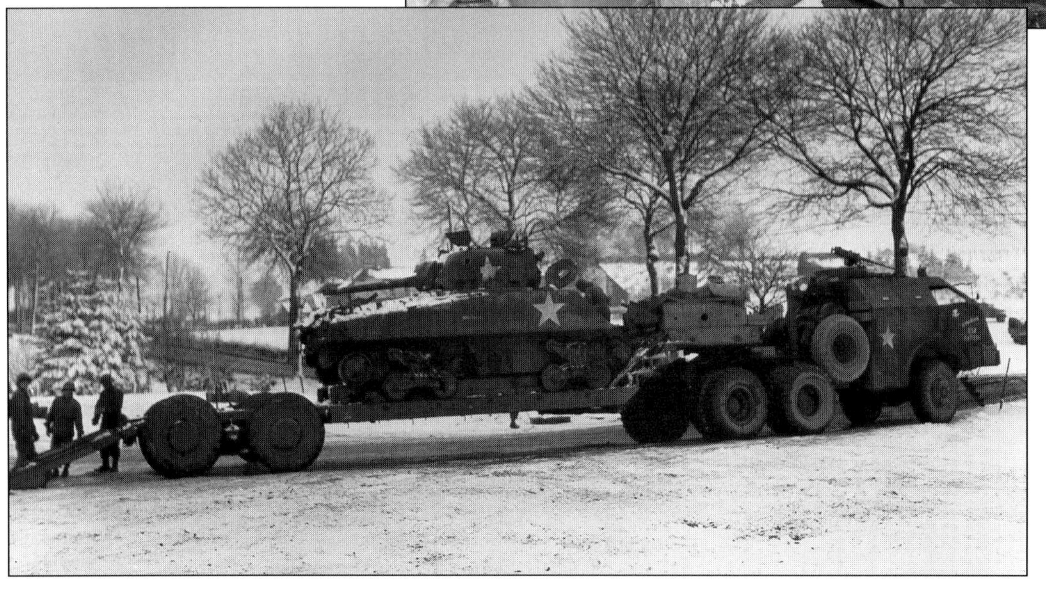

A M-25 Dragon Wagon 40-ton tank transporter is used to recover a knocked out M4A3 from Patton's Third Army outside Bastogne after the fighting near the city on 6 January 1945. Two large penetrations can be seen on the turret, evidently from tank or anti-tank guns.

A M7 105mm HMC of the 212th Arm. Field Arty. Bn., 6th Armored Division fires from beneath a snow-camouflaged net during fighting around the city on 8 January 1945. This battalion set a record 1,000 rounds per day during the fighting, about double the normal performance. In the foreground is a neat stack of empty ammunition tubes.

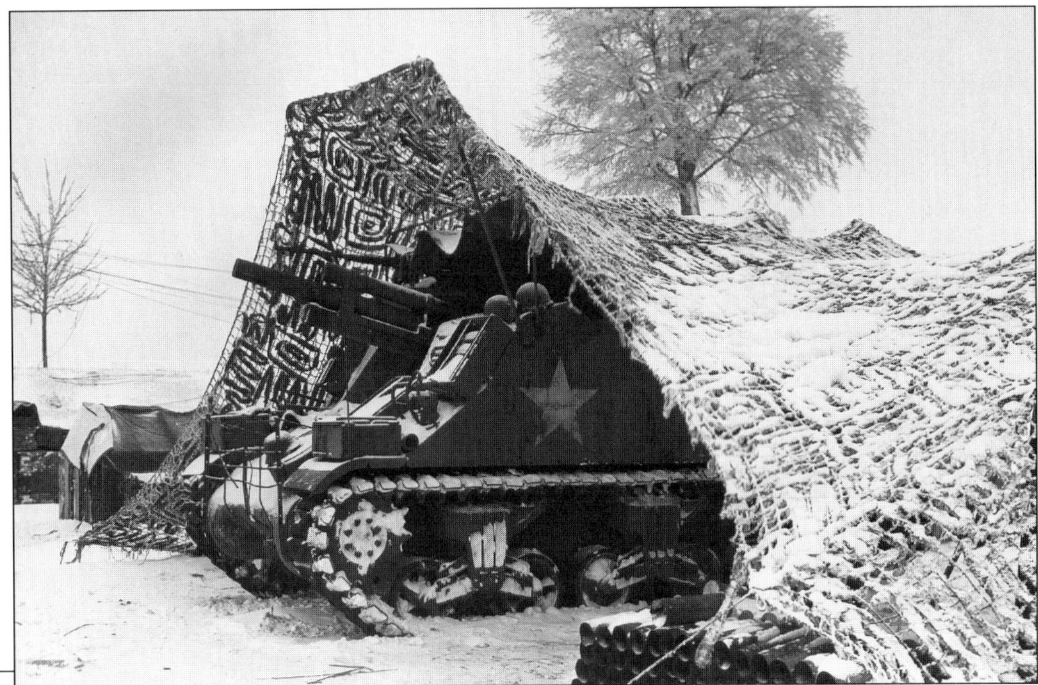

A new M4A3(76)W HVSS of the 4th Armored Division covering the H-4 highway outside Bastogne on 8 January 1945. The Battle of the Bulge was the first time that this new version of the M4 appeared in combat. The new HVSS suspension on this version had a wider track for better performance in snow or mud. Notice that the turret star has already been painted out.

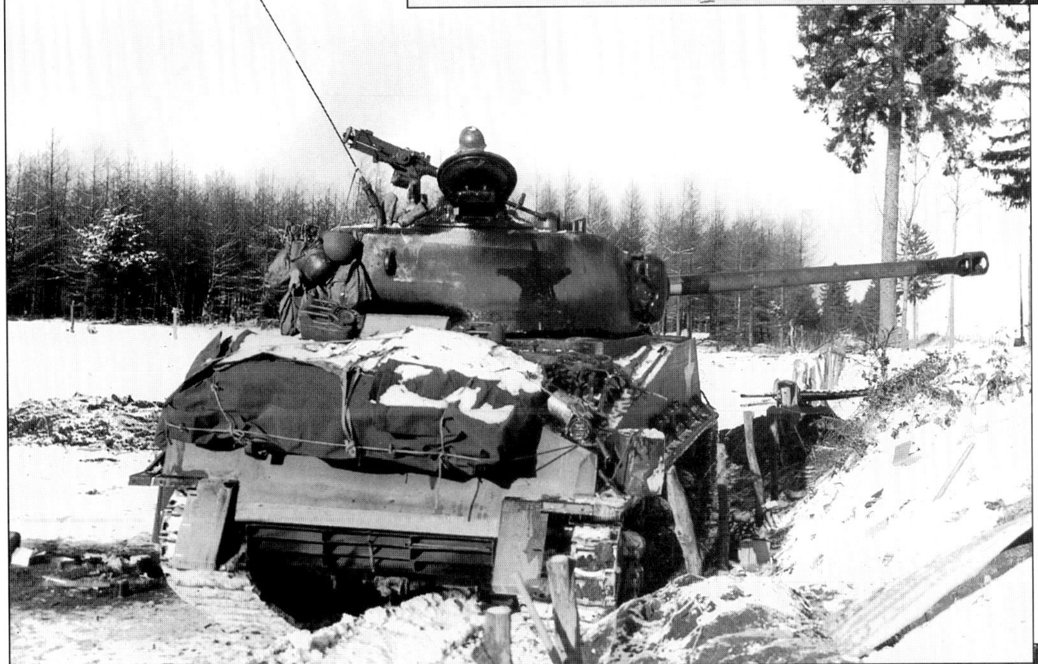

A M4A3(75)W leads a column of infantry from the 75th Division as they move into Basse, Belgium, to relieve the 82nd Airborne Division. This tank has the duck-bill extenders on its track and appears to have sand-bag armor on the glacis plate as well.

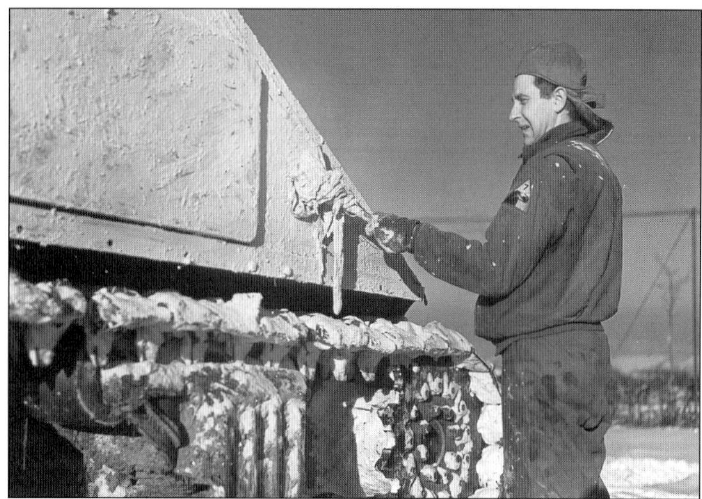

During the later phases of the Battle of the Bulge, many tanks were camouflage painted with lime whitewash. This was not a particularly delicate procedure as is evident from the scene of a 7th Armored Division tanker painting his M4 near Xhorie, Belgium on 11 January 1945.

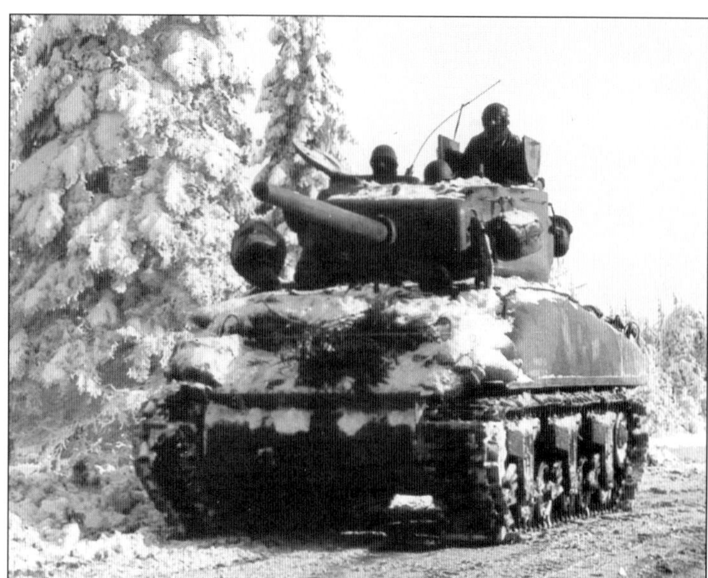

A M4A1(76)W moves along a snow-covered road near Odeigne, Belgium on 11 January 1945. It has extended end-connectors fitted to the track for better floation in snow.

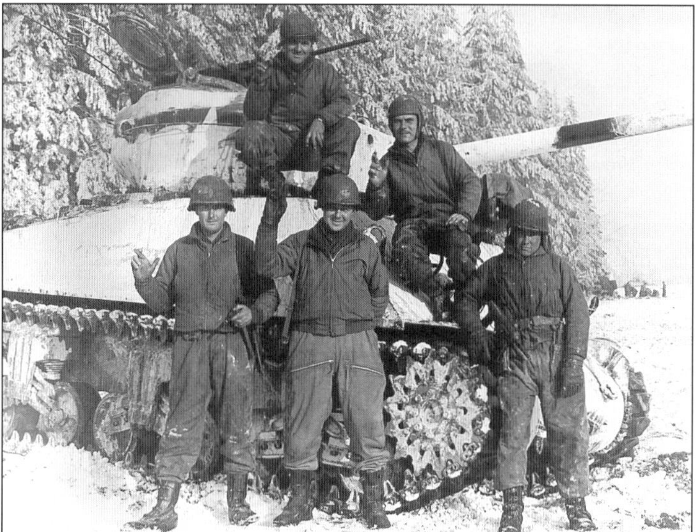

The crew of an M4A3(76)W command tank of Capt. John Megglesin of the 42nd Tank Bn., 11th Armd. Div., cross their fingers for luck. This new tank was the third they had been issued in two weeks of fighting. The two previous tanks had been knocked out, fortunately without the loss of a single crewman. It was a grim statistic that one crewman was killed on average every time a Sherman tank was knocked out.

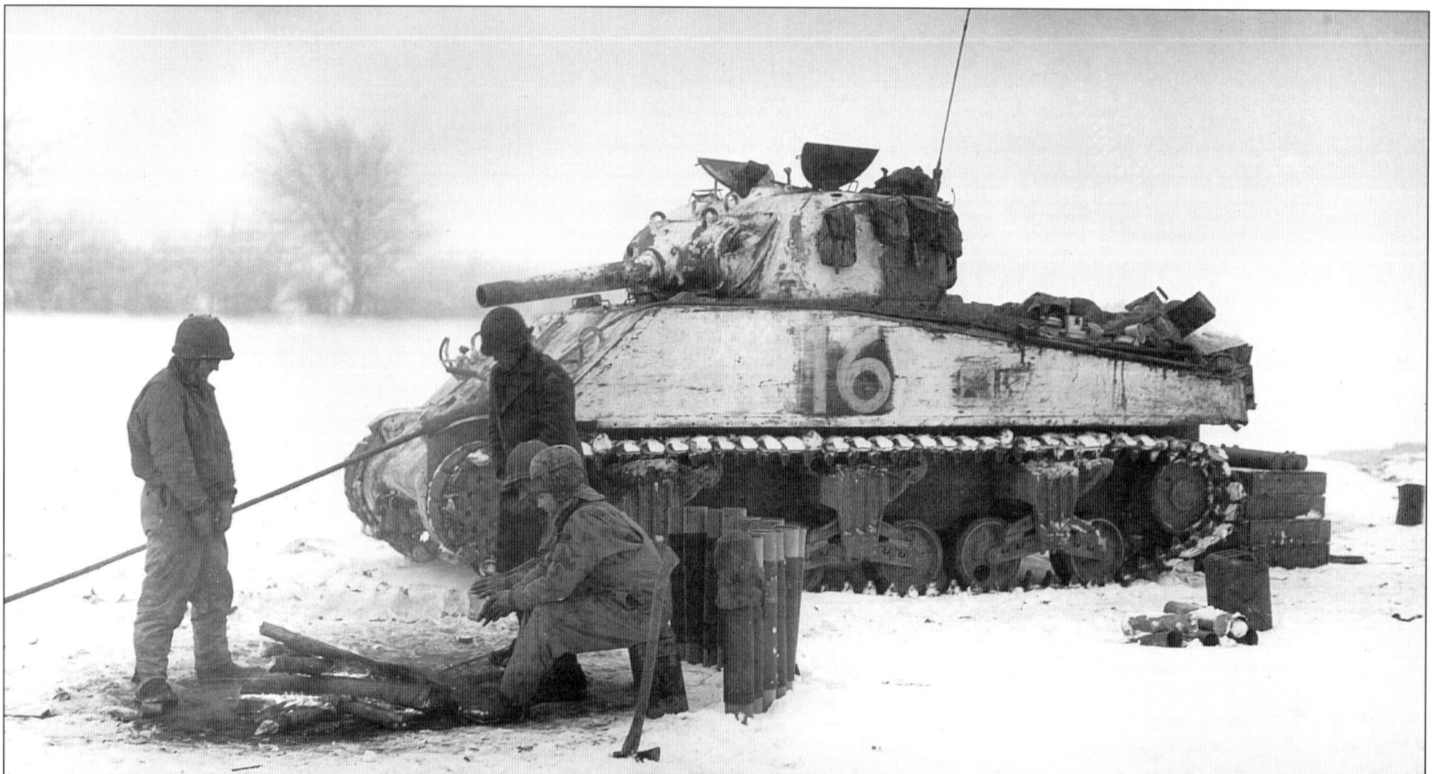

The crew of a M4(105) howitzer tank warm themselves over a fire after having cleaning the bore of their tank's howitzer. The tank has been given a quick coat of whitewash camouflage, leaving the individual vehicle number exposed.

The sign at the edge of the road says it all: Vers Bastogne (Towards Bastogne) as a M4A3(75)W leads a column to Longchamps on 13 January 1945. By mid January, the German offensive in Belgium had been decisively defeated and US forces began attacking towards Germany again.

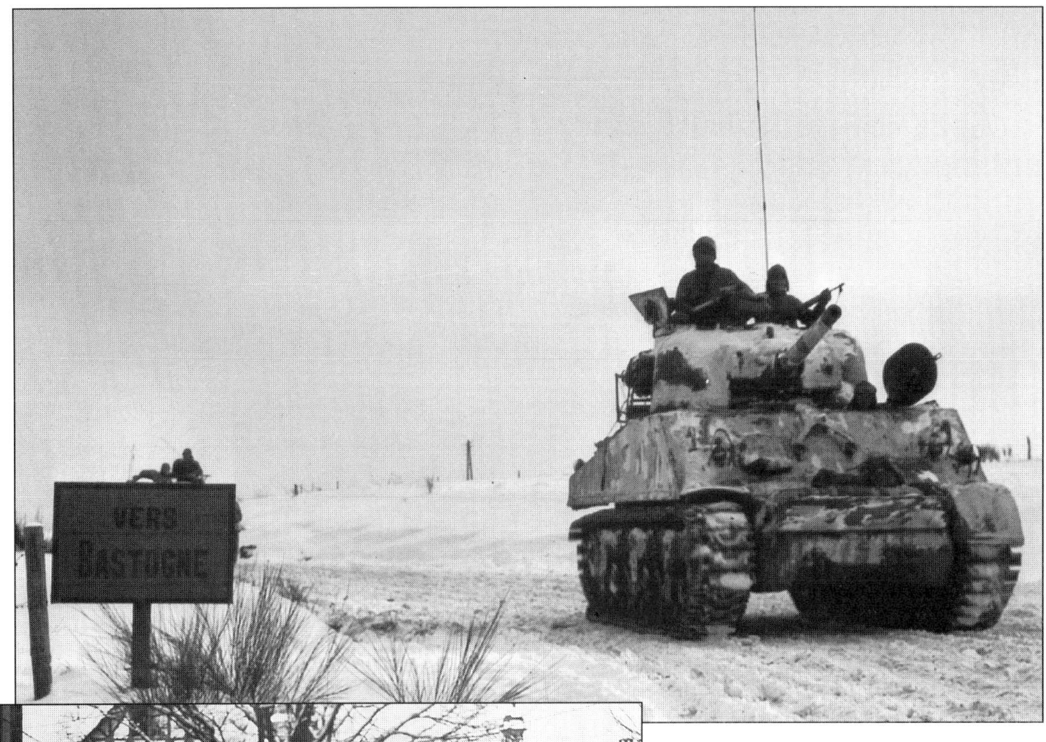

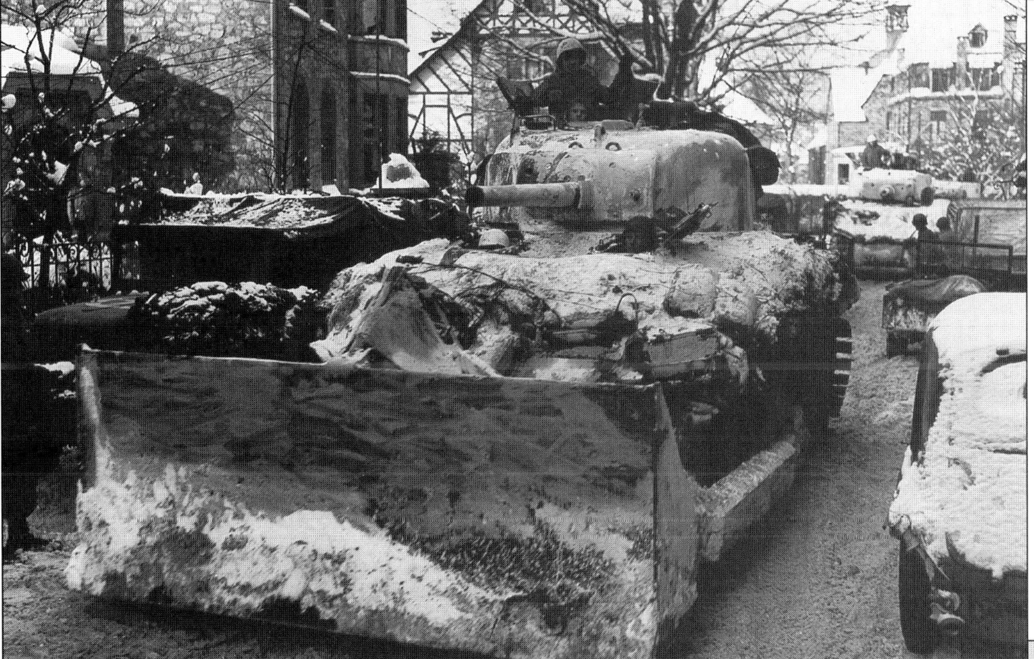

A snow covered M4A1 fitted with an M-1 tank mounted bulldozer passes through Malmedy on 13 January 1945 as the 743rd Tank Bn. moves up to support the 38th Infantry Division. During the Ardennes fighting, the bulldozer tanks were often used to clear roads instead of their traditional chore of digging emplacements.

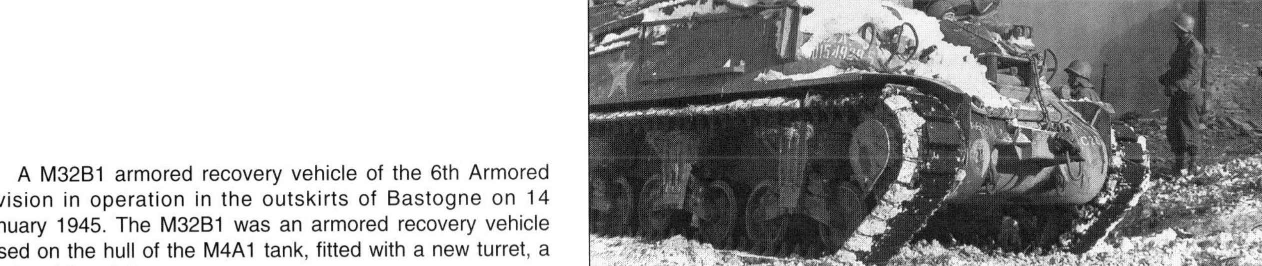

A M32B1 armored recovery vehicle of the 6th Armored Division in operation in the outskirts of Bastogne on 14 January 1945. The M32B1 was an armored recovery vehicle based on the hull of the M4A1 tank, fitted with a new turret, a winch, and an A-frame crane.

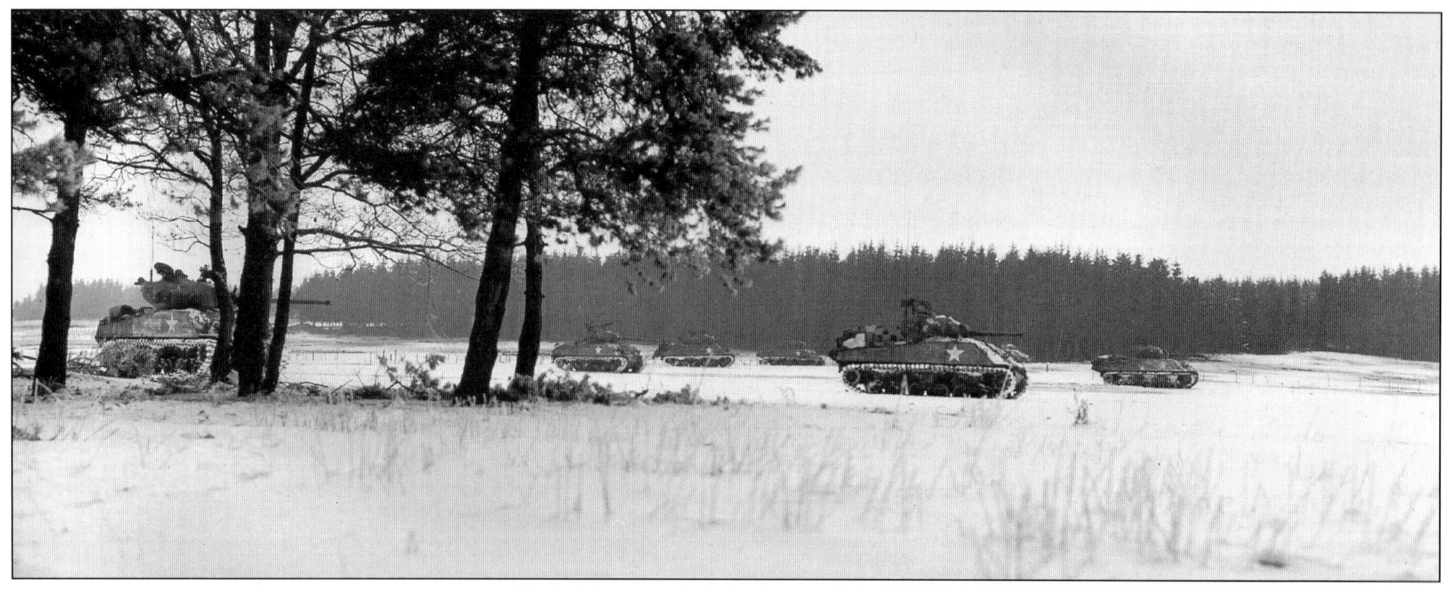

A rare view of a Sherman unit deployed for combat. A company of tanks from the 11th Armored Division await orders to attack German positions in the town of Compogne, Belgium on 15 January 1945.

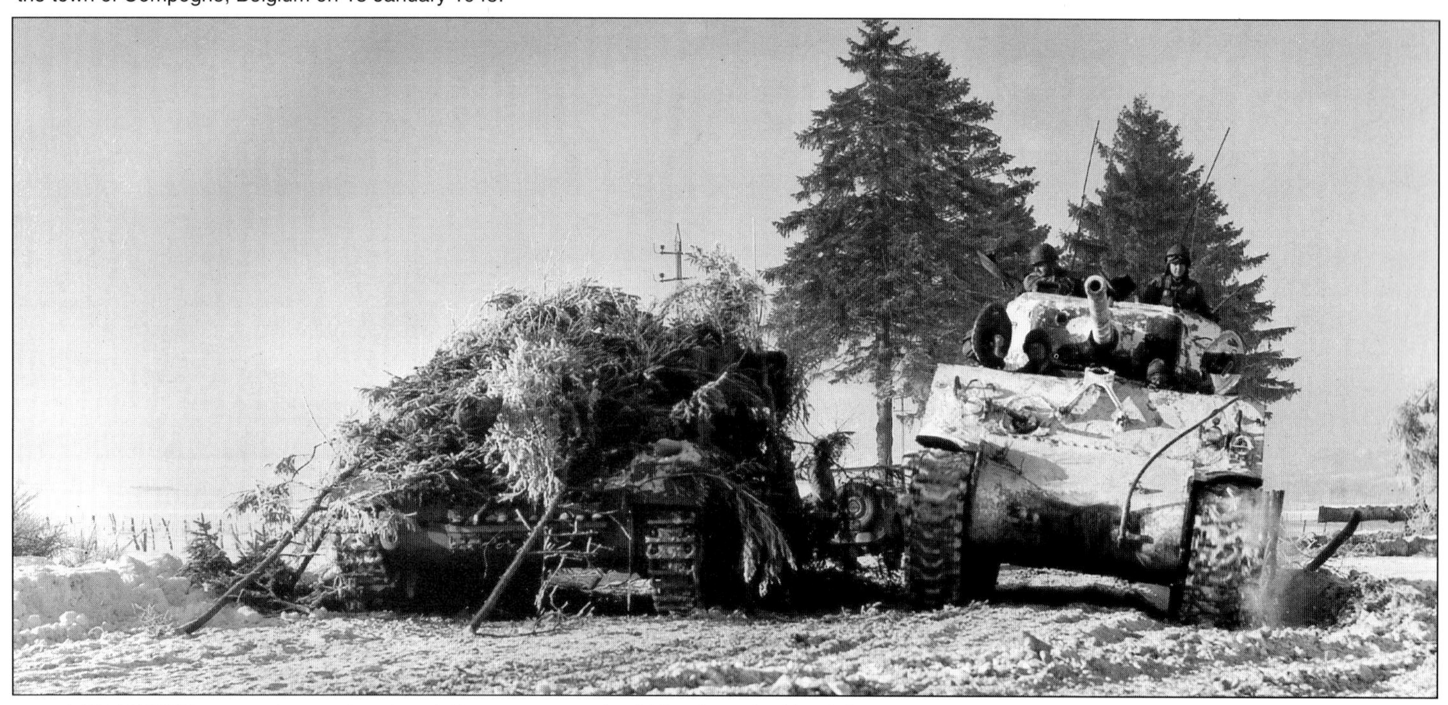

A M4A3(76)W passes by an abandoned German armored vehicle along the Houffalize road outside Bastogne on 15 January 1945. The German vehicle appears to be a Pz.Kpfw IV tank, but is so well camouflaged that it is difficult to tell!

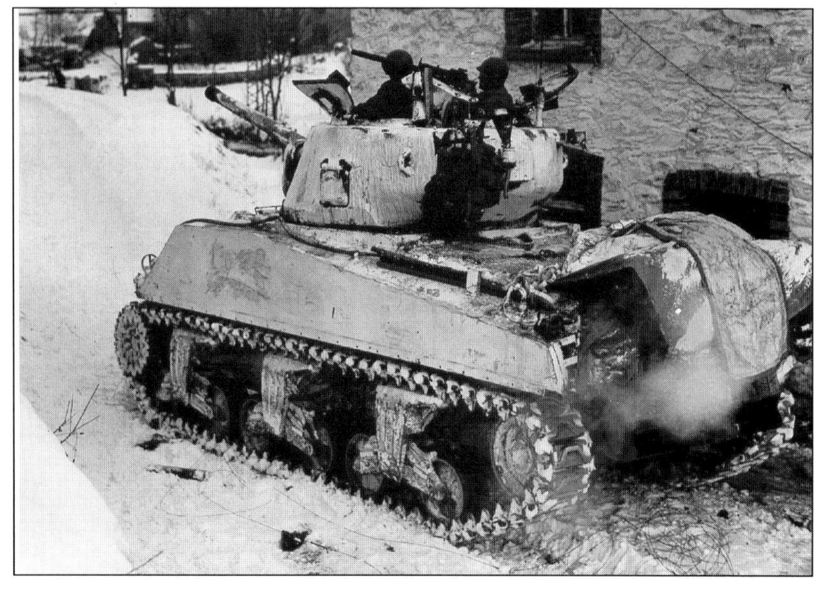

A M4A3(76)W of the 750th Tank Bn. moves into Salmchateu, Belgium while supporting an attack by the 75th Division on 16 January 1945. The usual .50 cal. M2 Browning HB heavy machine on the turret has been replaced by a .30 cal. machine gun.

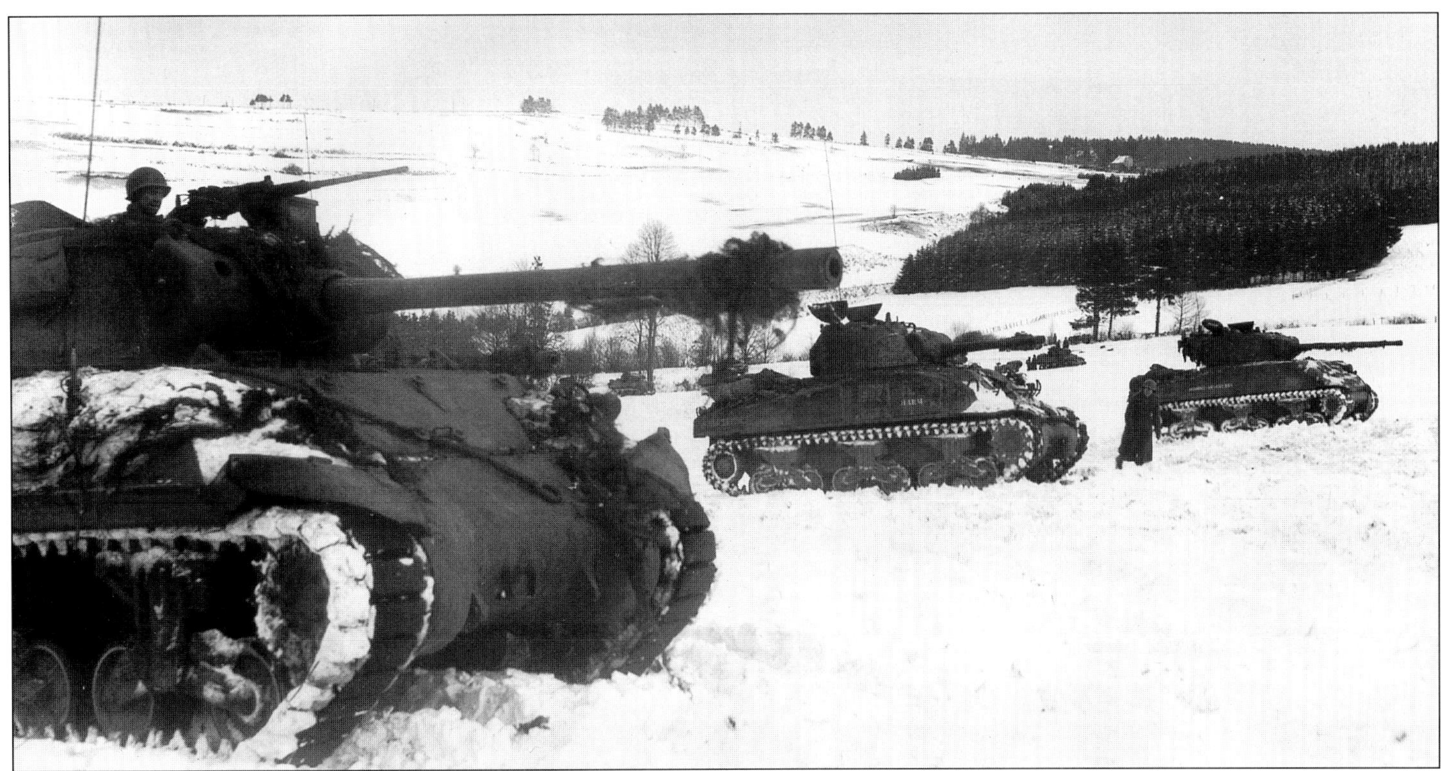

A task force composed of M36s from the 702nd Tank Destroyer Bn. (on the left) and M4 Shermans of the 66th Arm'd. Regt. of the 2nd Armored Div. prepare for an attack on Houfallize, Belgium on 16 January 1945. During the Ardennes fighting, it was common to attach a few M36 tank destroyers to tank battalions since their 90mm gun was the only sure way to deal with German heavy tanks.

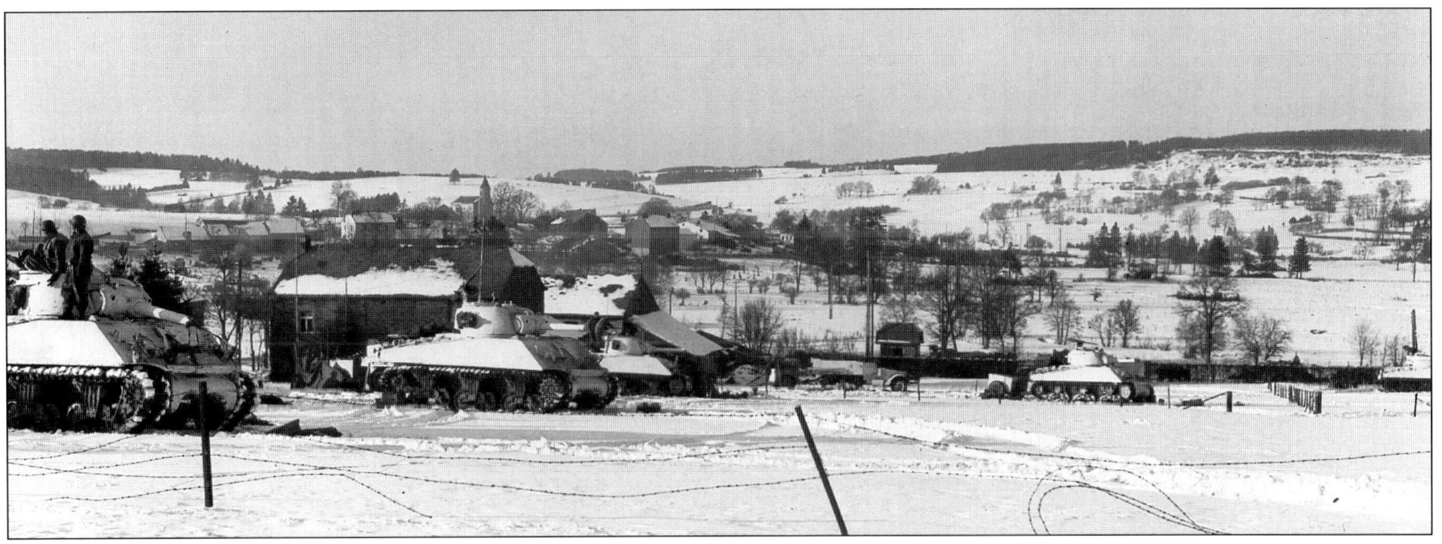

M4(105) howitzer tanks of the HQ Co. of the 774th Tank Bn. provide fire support for the 3rd Armored Division and 75th Infantry Division on 16 January 1945. In the distant background is a M3 half-track being used to bring up additional ammunition for the howitzer tanks.

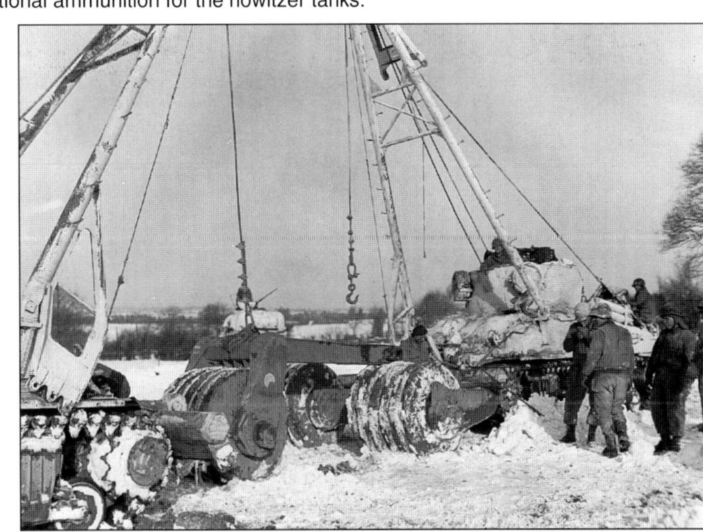

A pair of M32B1 armored recovery vehicle use their A-frame cranes to attach a T-1E1 Aunt Jemima mine roller. The T-1E1 is a different configuration than the T-1E3 shown earlier, with three sets of smaller rollers instead of two sets of large rollers.

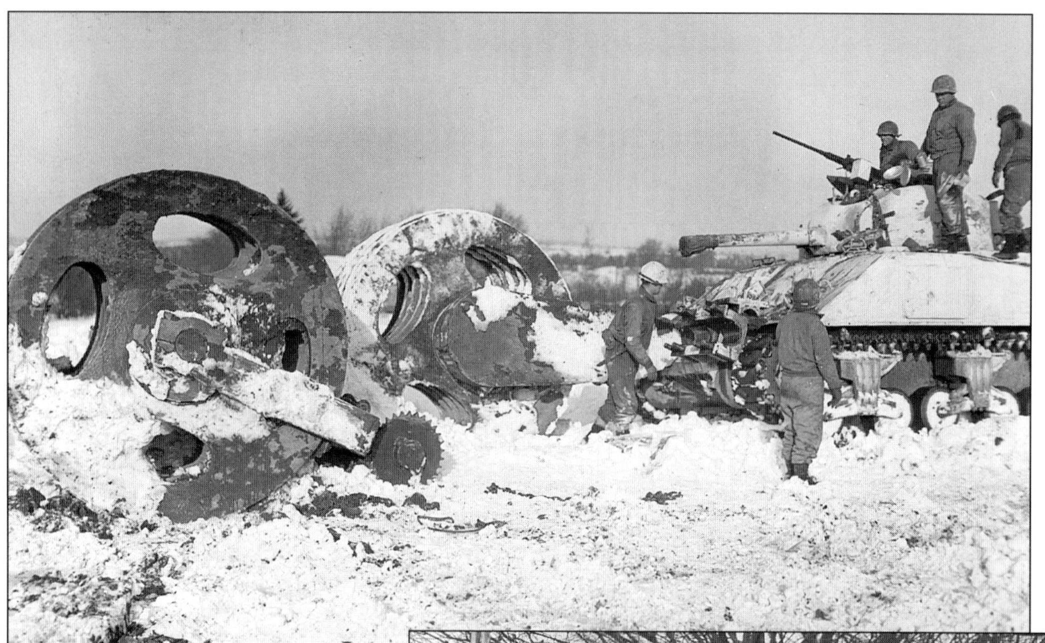

Engineer crews assist in mounting a T-1E3 mineroller on the front of a M4A3 tank near Wiesme, Belgium on 16 January 1945. This was the first time that mine rollers were employed during the Battle of the Bulge, as the Germans began mining roads during their retreat.

A M32B1 armored recovery vehicle of the 2nd Armored Division pushes a T-1E1 mineroller assembly during the fighting near Houfalize, Belgium on 16 January 1945.

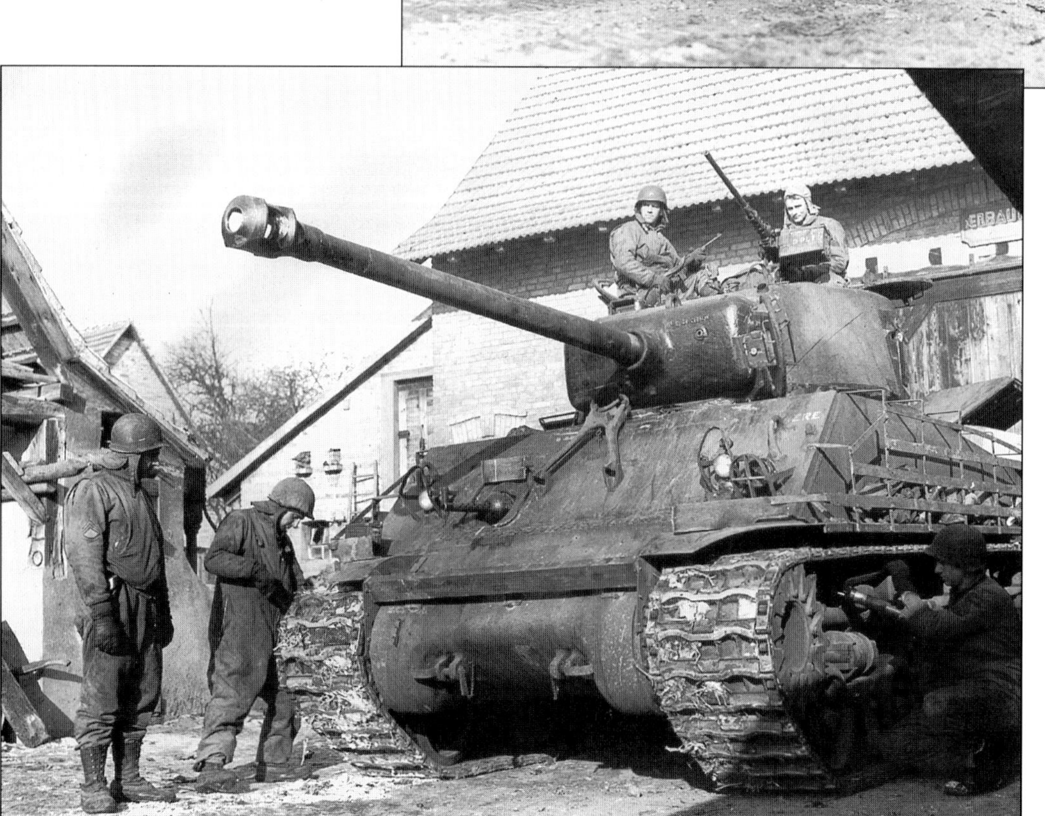

A new M4A3(76)W HVSS tank is prepared by the 48th Tank Bn, 14th Armored Division before being committed to the fighting in Belgium. The crewman on the right is making certain that the new HVSS suspension is well lubricated. The tank has already been fitted with a mounting cage on the side for sand-bag panzerfaust protection.

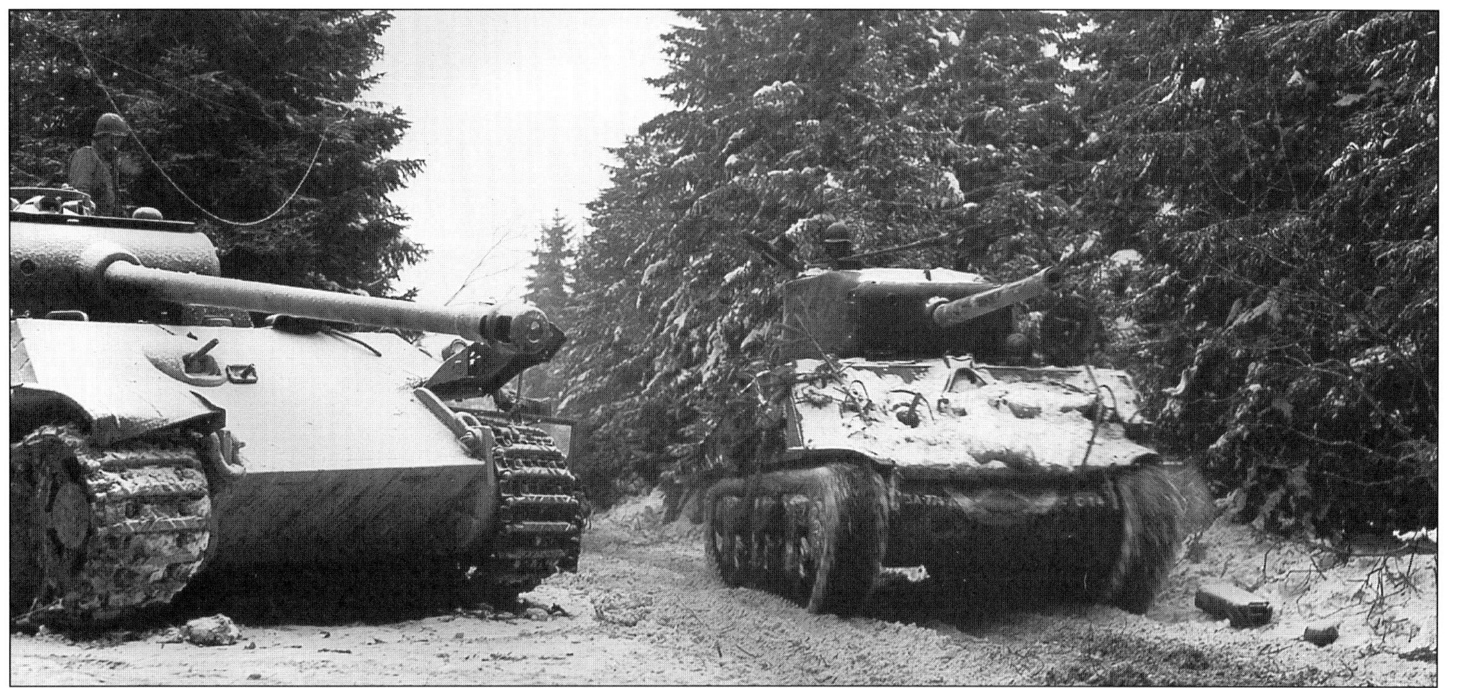

A M4A3(76)W passes by a German Panther Ausf. G knocked out along the road near Bovigny, Belgium during the 3rd Armroed Division's pursuit of the retreating German forces on 17 January 1945.

A tank crew from A Company, 774th Tank Bn. give their M4A3(76)W a snow camouflage paint job. This photo gives a good view of the extended end connectors (duckbills) and shows how easily damaged they became under intense use.

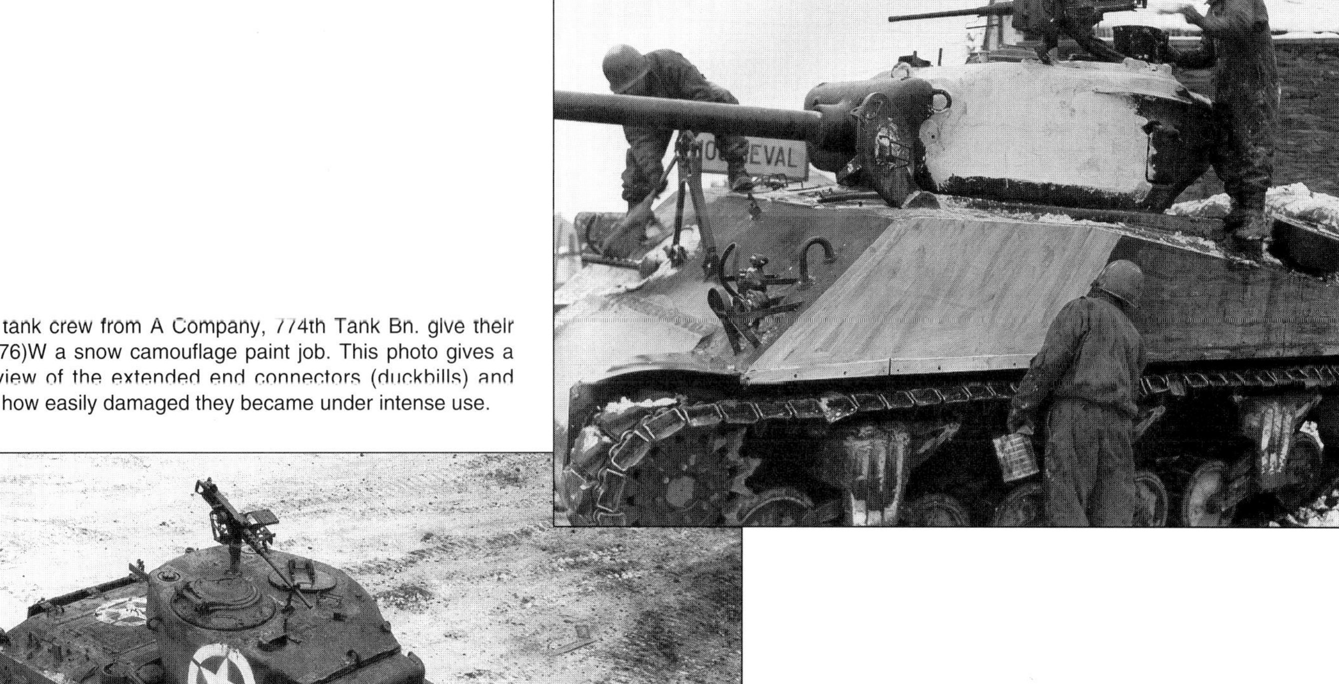

A depot-fresh M4A3(76)W HVSS (aka M4A3E8) prior to be shipped to US tank units in Belgium. The ordnance depots often painted the tanks with official markings, but when issued to the troops, the conspicuous white stars would usually be painted over with olive drab or black paint. The only star usually left intact was the one on the engine deck.

A M4A3(75)W knocked out by panzerfaust from German troops in the neighboring church. The Germans' SdKfz 251 half-track is configured as an ambulance with Red Cross insignia painted on the side.

A M4 of the 738th Tank Battalion fitted with a T-1E3 mine roller passes by a cemetery in Recht, Belgium while supporting the US 1st Army. The device at the rear of the tank is a pusher plate which enabled a second tank to give the mine-roller tank a helpful nudge if it got stuck. The rollers often got stuck in soft soil, so it was often necessary to operate as a team with a second tank behind.

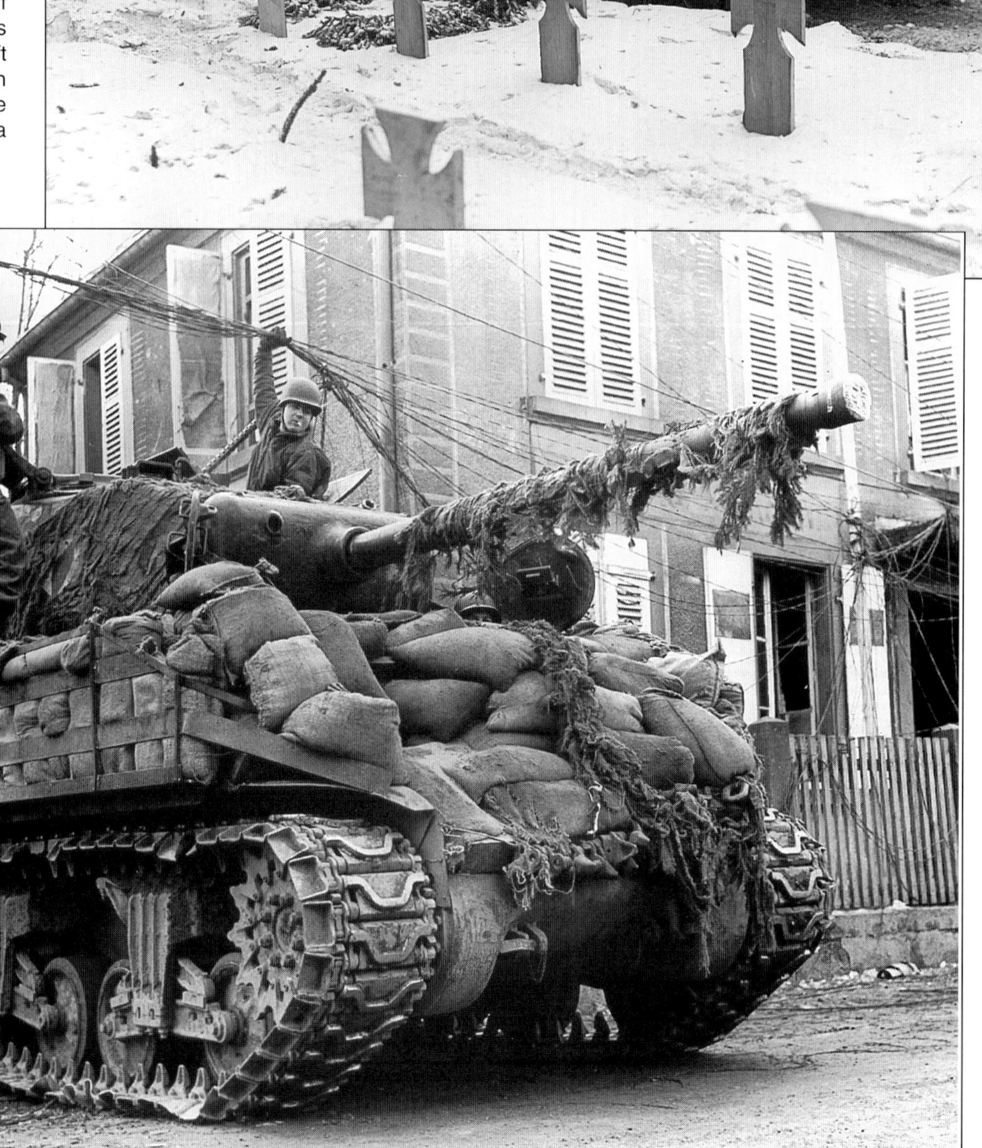

A new M4A3(76)W is transferred to the 14th Armored Division in Niederbetsdorf in Alsace-Lorraine. By this stage of the war, sand-bag armor protection was becoming increasingly common. The 14th Armored Division was one of the units that systematically equipped its tanks with this type of protection.

A crewman of a M4A3(75)W load ammunition into his tank near Hatten on 20 January 1945. This vehicle is attached to the 48th Tank Bn, US 7th Army and is marked with unusually prominent stars for this stage of the war.

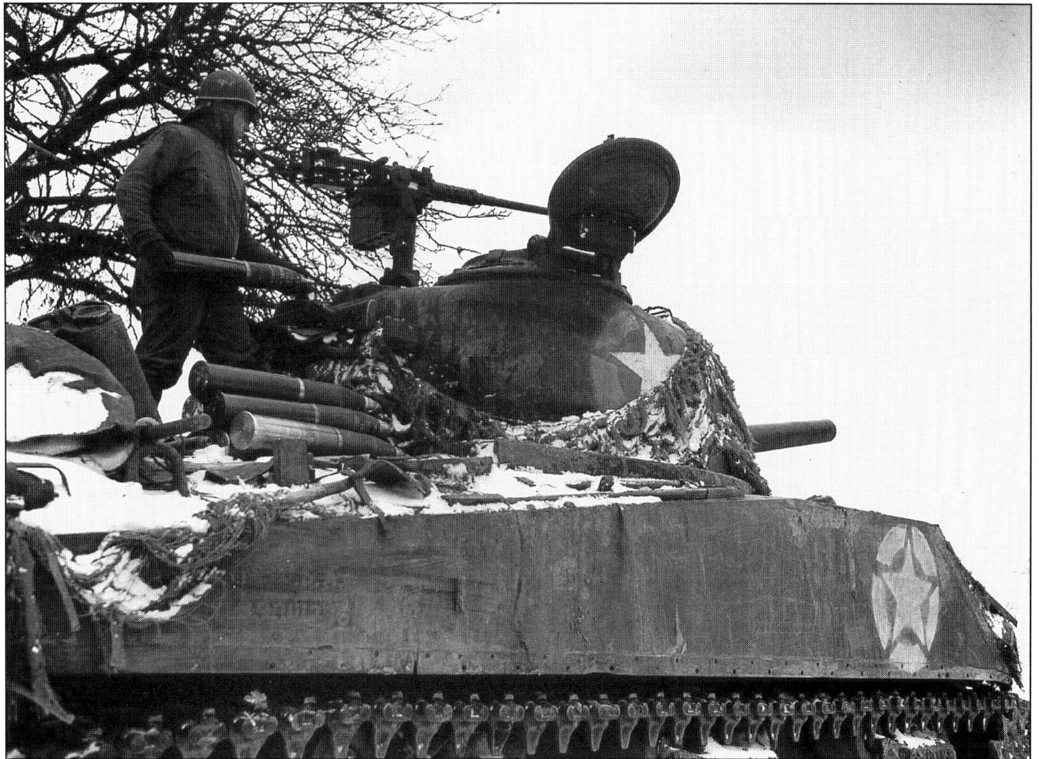

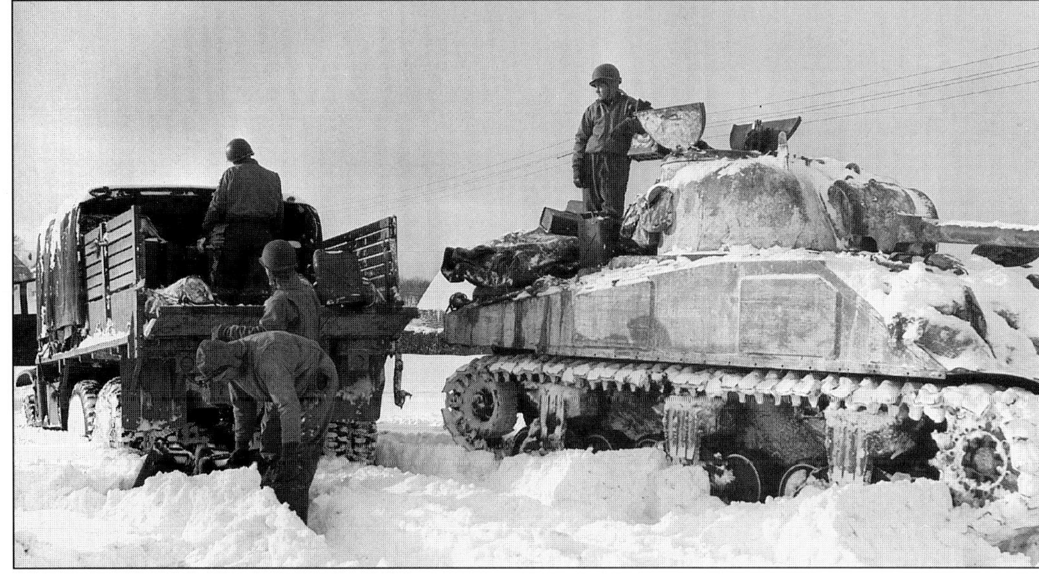

Refueling in the field was usually done using jerricans, not specialized refueling trucks. Here, a M4 tank of the 7th Armored Division near Weims, Belgium is refueled from a 2 1/2 ton truck on 20 January 1945.

Company I, 16th Infantry, 1st Infantry Division ride into combat on the back of a M4A3 tank during their attack in the snow-covered town of Schopen, Belgium in the final phase of the Battle of the Bulge.

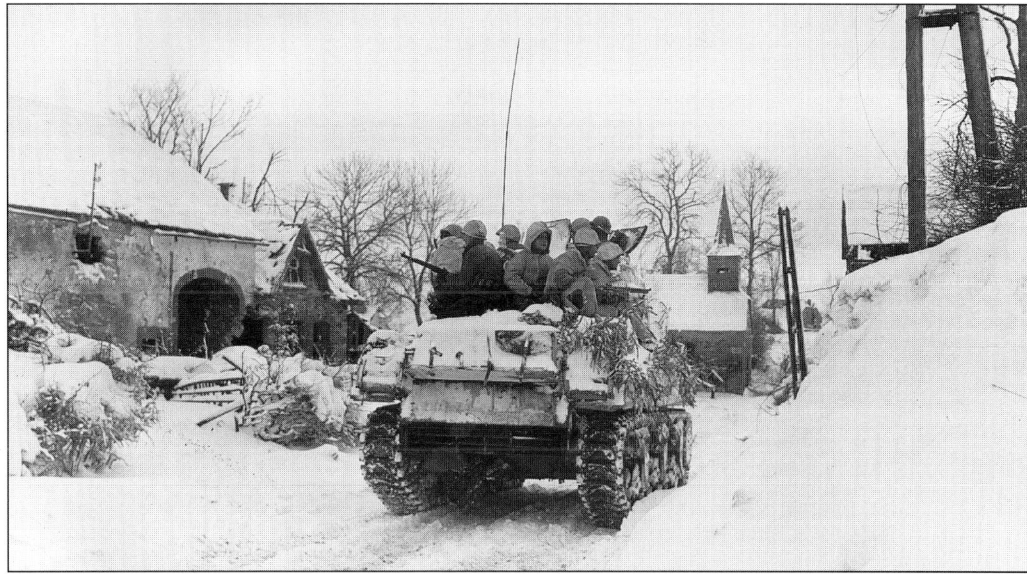

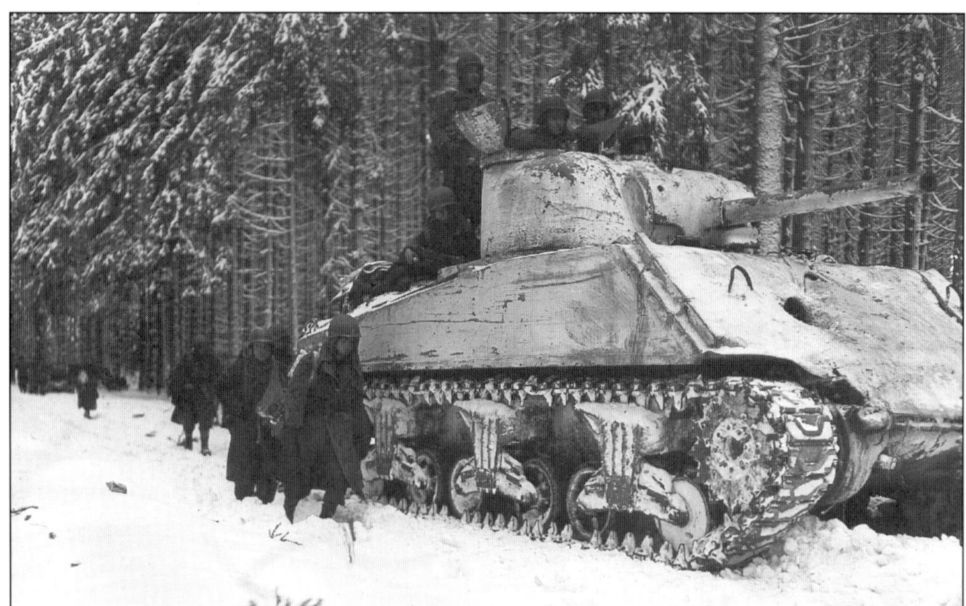

A snow camouflaged M4A3(75)W of the 750th Tank Bn. provides support to an advance by the 75th Infantry Division near St. Vith on 23 January 1945. This tank appears to have a layer of cement armor covering the glacis plate instead of the more common sand-bag armor.

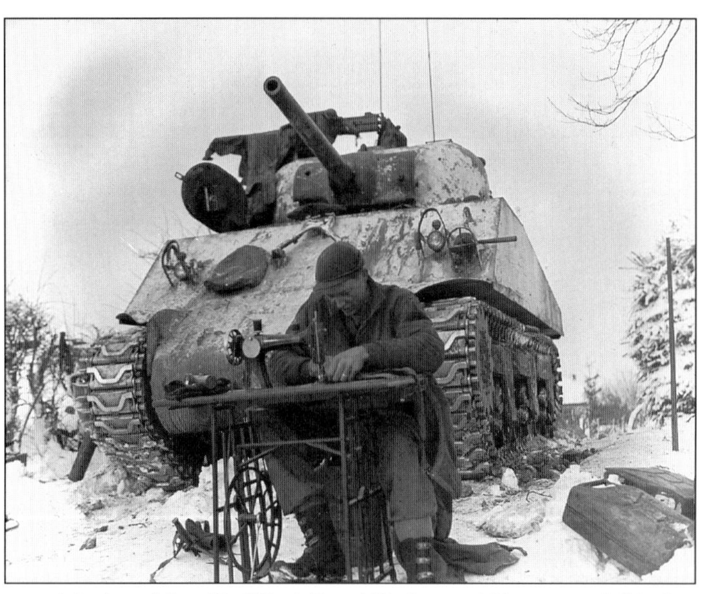

A tanker of the 42nd Tank Bn., 11th Armored Div. uses a lull in the fighting near Steinbach, Belgium to mend his clothes on a sewing machine in front of his M4(75)W tank.

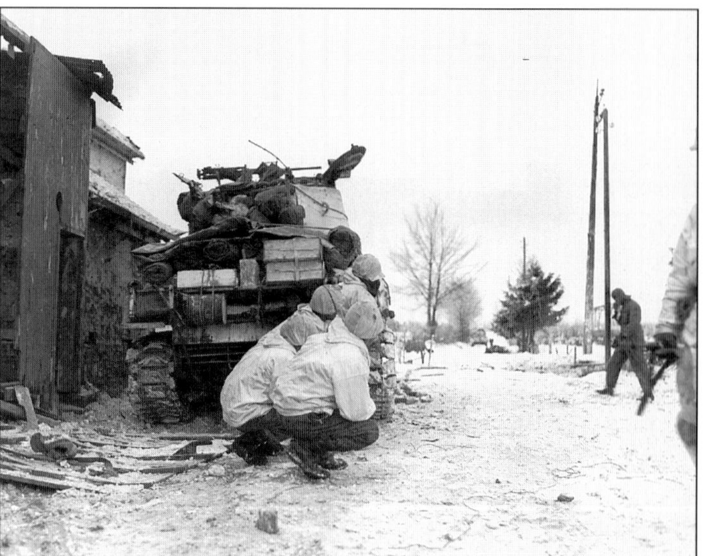

Soldiers of the 23rd Infantry take cover behind a M4A3(76)W of the 7th Armored Division as they move to capture Hunnange on the road to St. Vith on 23 January 1945.

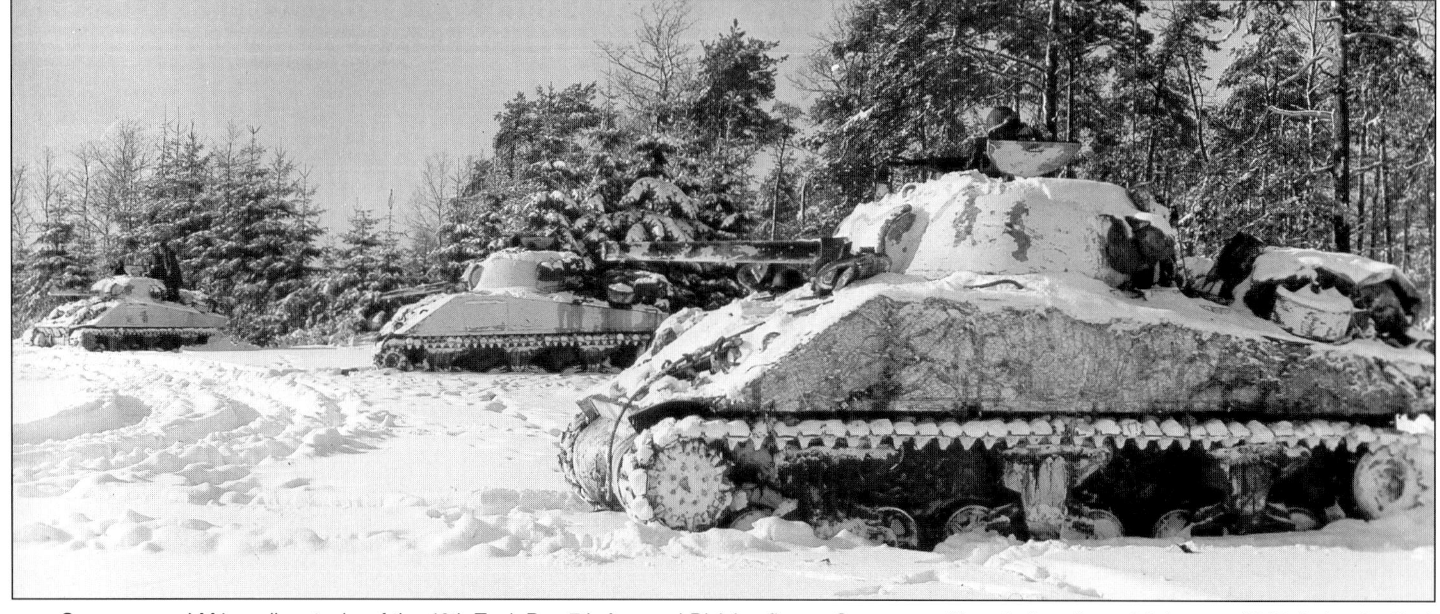

Snow covered M4 medium tanks of the 40th Tank Bn., 7th Armored Division fire on German positions in the city on 24 January 1945 during the final drive to recapture St. Vith from the Germans. The tank in the foreground has its hull side covered in a camouflage net.

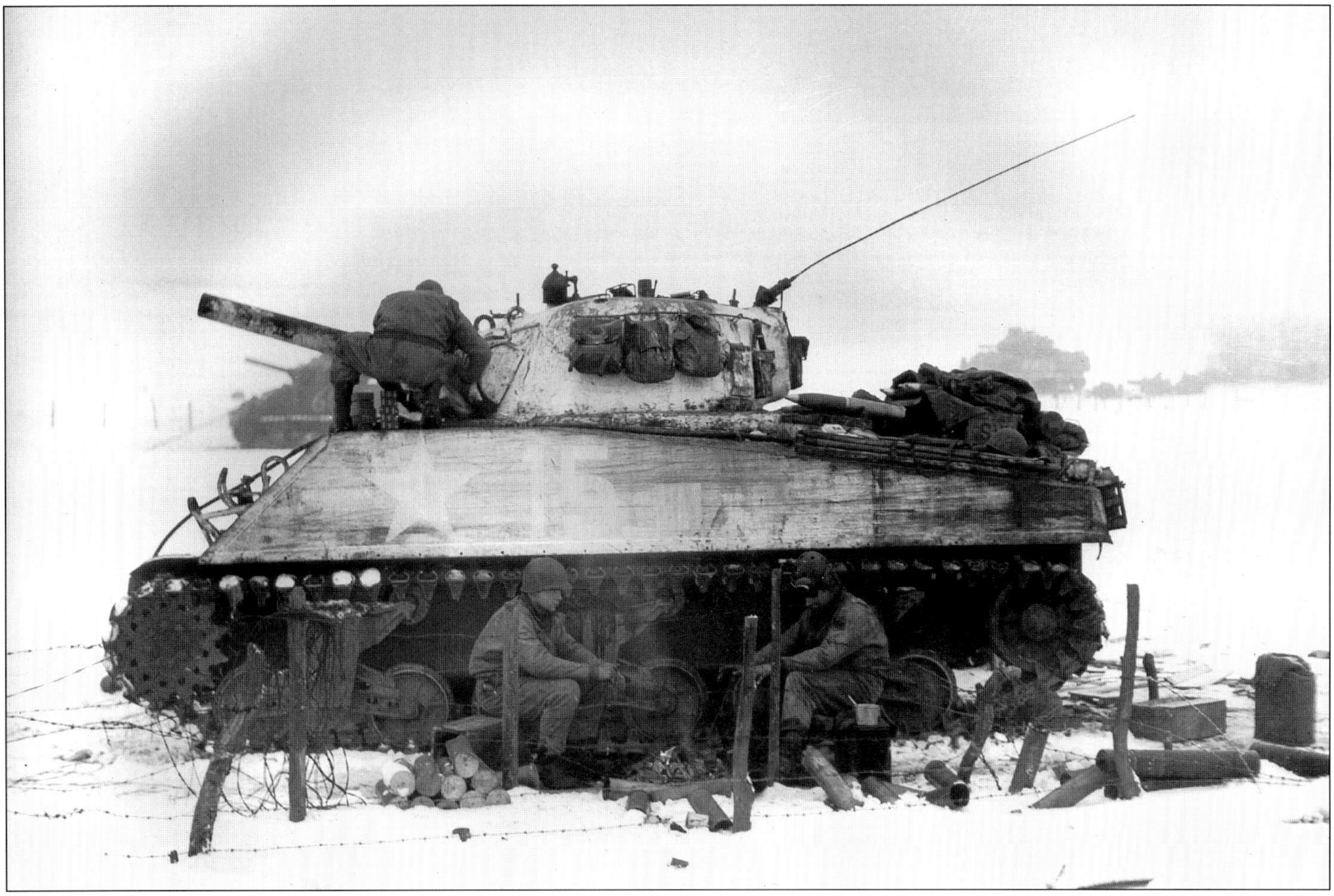

The crew of a M4(105) howitzer tank warm their hands over a fire while awaiting a fire mission while fighting near Trois Vierge, Luxembourg on 24 January 1945. The typical large tactical markings on the hull side, characteristic of the 6th Armored Division, are obscured by the winter whitewash camouflage.

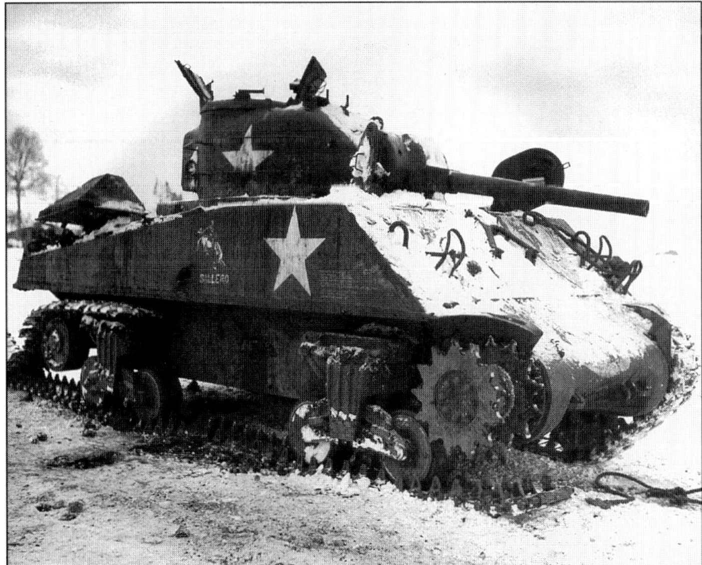

"Ballero", a M4A3(75)W of the 6th Armored Division, knocked out by a German anti-tank gun near Longvilly, Belgium on 25 January 1945.

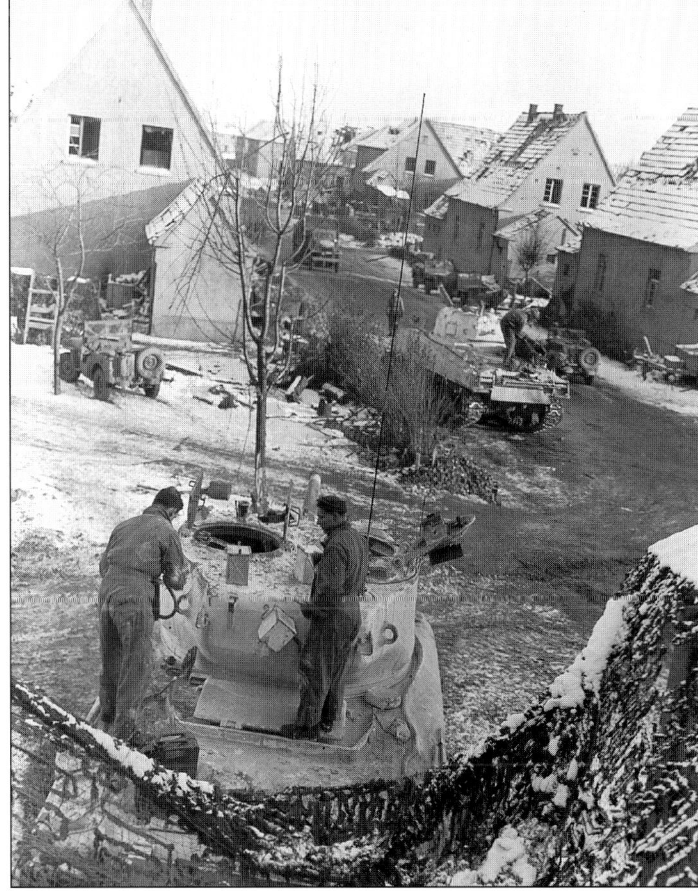

A M4A1(76)W of the 701st Tank Bn. is serviced in a small town in Belgium before moving out in support of the 102nd Infantry Division's advance on 25 January 1945.

The Battle for Germany

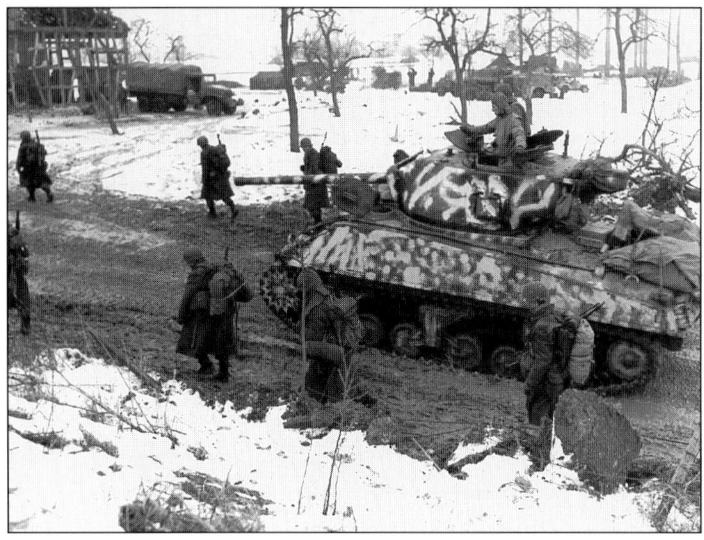

A dapple camouflage M4A3(76)W moves forward alongside soldiers of the 75th Infantry Division during fighting in Riedwihr in the Colmar area of France on 31 January 1945.

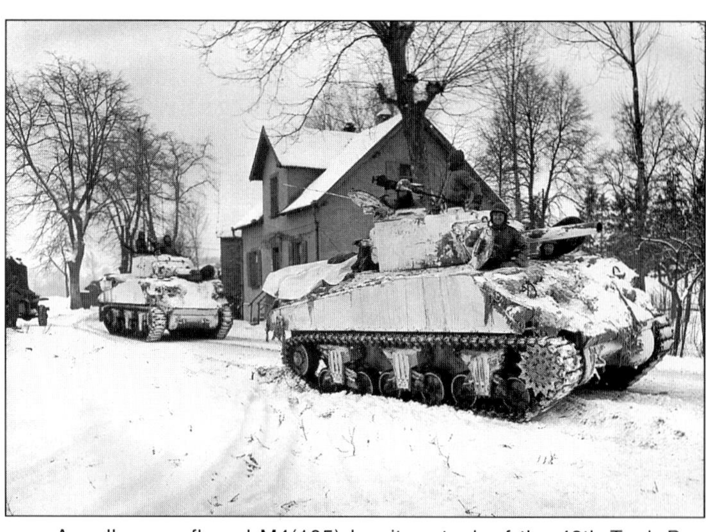

A well camouflaged M4(105) howitzer tank of the 48th Tank Bn. moves forward to positions near Hochdelden in Alsace-Lorraine as the 7th Army prepares to resume its assault towards Germany. The lead tank has sand-bag armor on the glacis plate, obscured by snow and a camouflage net.

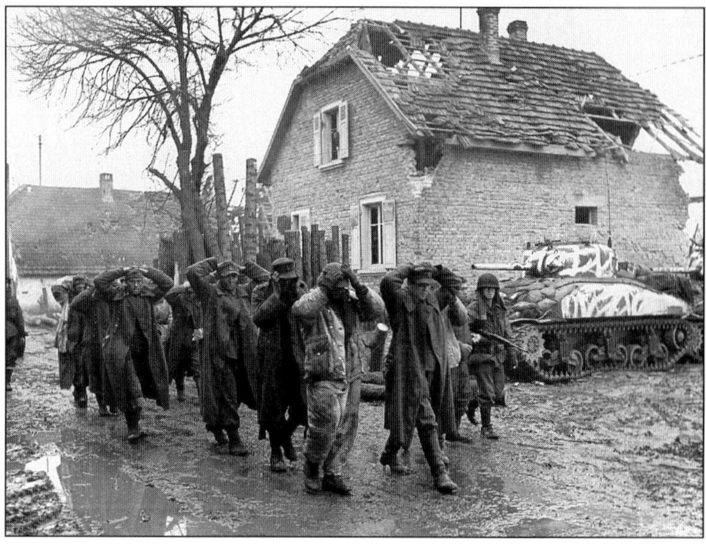

German prisoners are sent to the rear during fighting in Bischwihr, in the Colmar region of France on 1 February 1945. In the background is a remarkably early production M4A1 medium tank, complete with the collarless early gun mantlet and M3 style suspension.

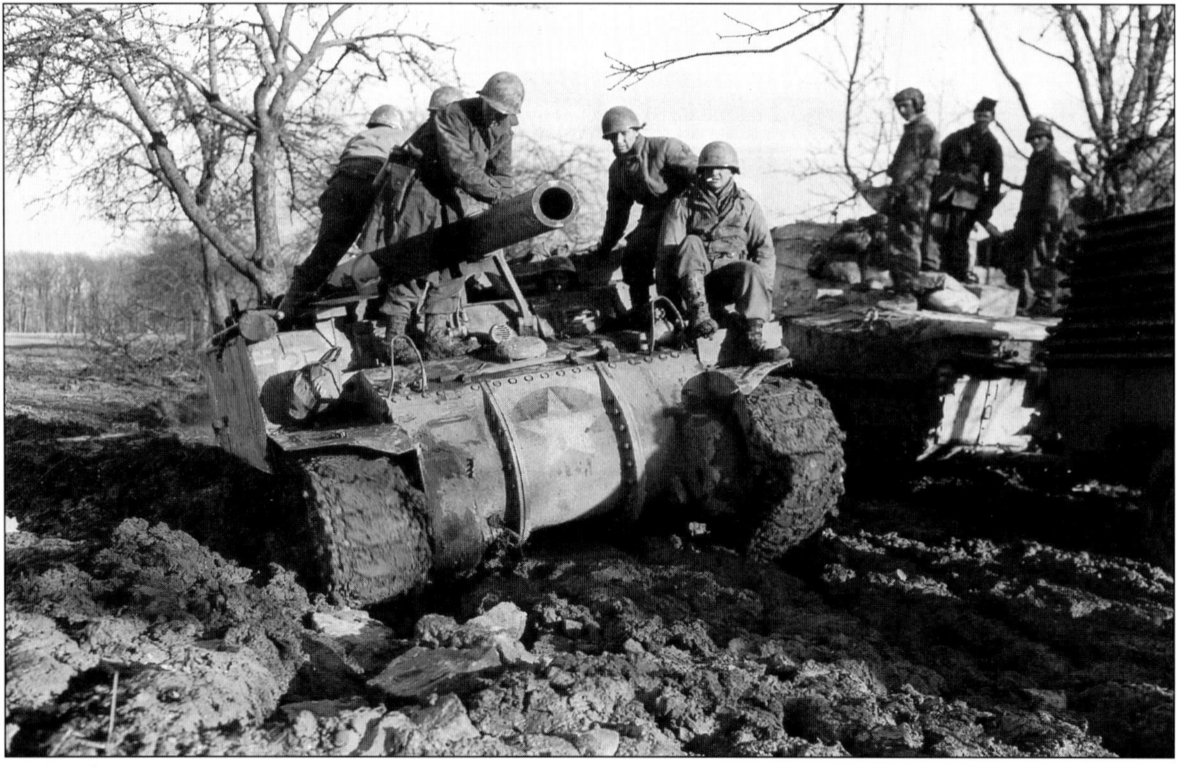

A M-12 155mm GMC wrestles with thick mud while supporting the 5th Infantry Division in Luxembourg on 9 February 1945. The M-12 was very popular in the battles along the German frontier for attacking German pillboxes and other reinforced positions of the Siegfried line.

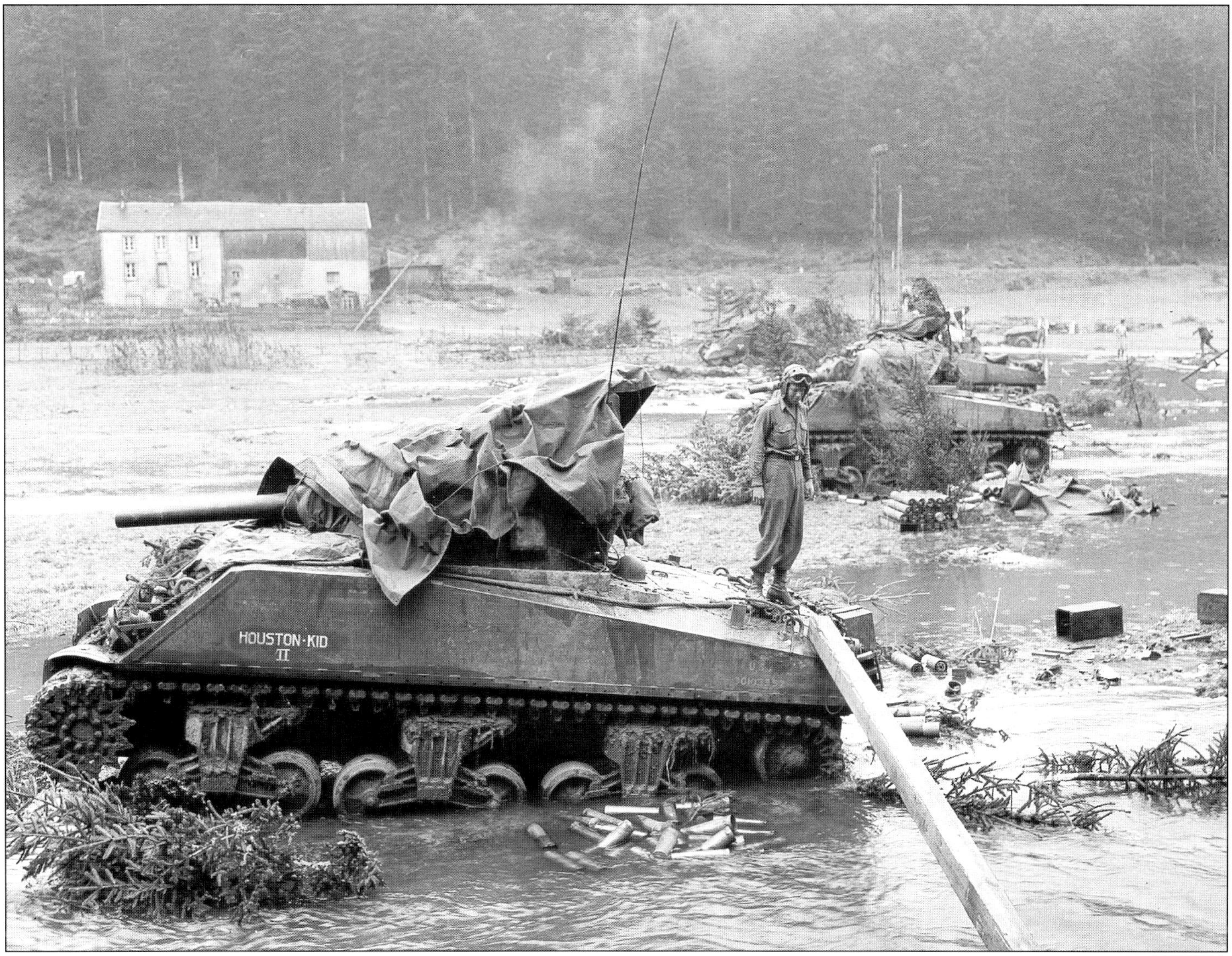

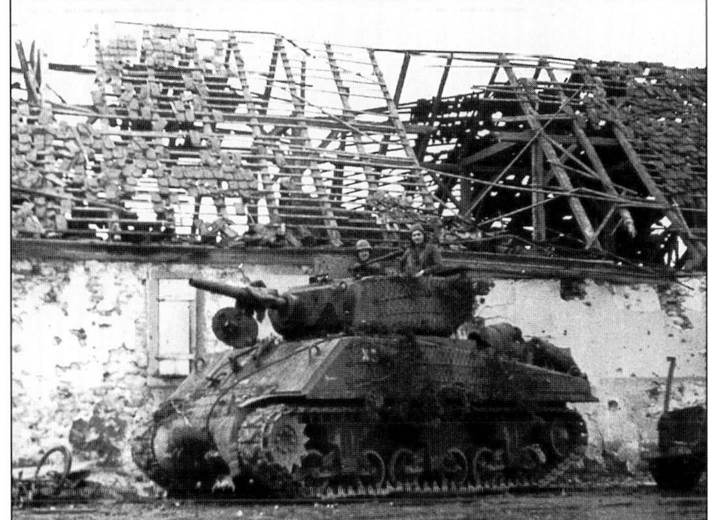

A pair of M4A3(105) howitzer tanks provide fire support from water-logged fields on the German border in February 1945. The ground nearby is littered with spent shell casings and packing tubes. The crew of Houston-Kid II has improvised a bridge over the water using a timber.

A rare view of a M4A3E2 Jumbo assault tank in action during the fighting in the Colmar area in February 1945. The M4A3E2 had additional armor and was intended to be used at the head of attacking tank columns. Most M4A3E2s were rearmed with the 76mm tank gun, but this one retains the original 75mm gun. The tank is covered with Sommerfield matting for attaching foliage camouflage.

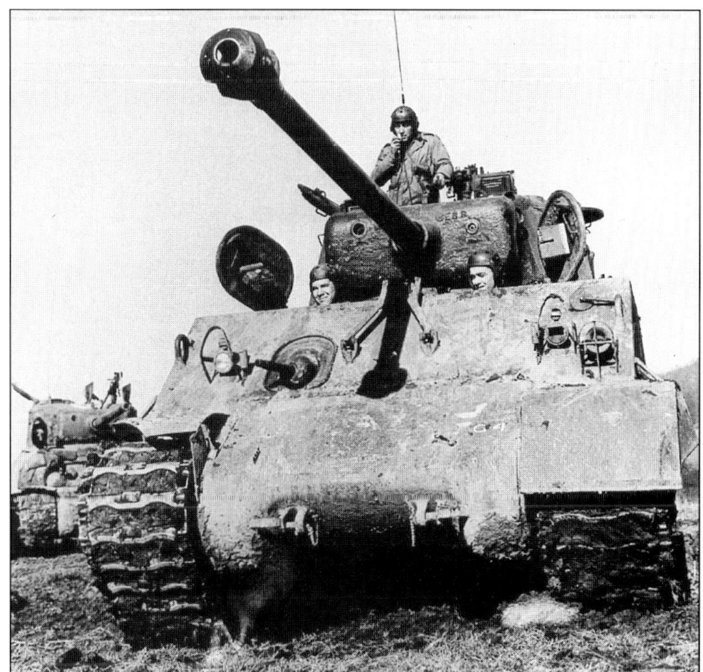

Crews from the 66th Armored Rgt., 2nd Armored Division take their new M4A3(76)W HVSS (aka M4A3E8) for a test spin after the division was reequipped near Tueven, the Netherlands for the final assault into Germany.

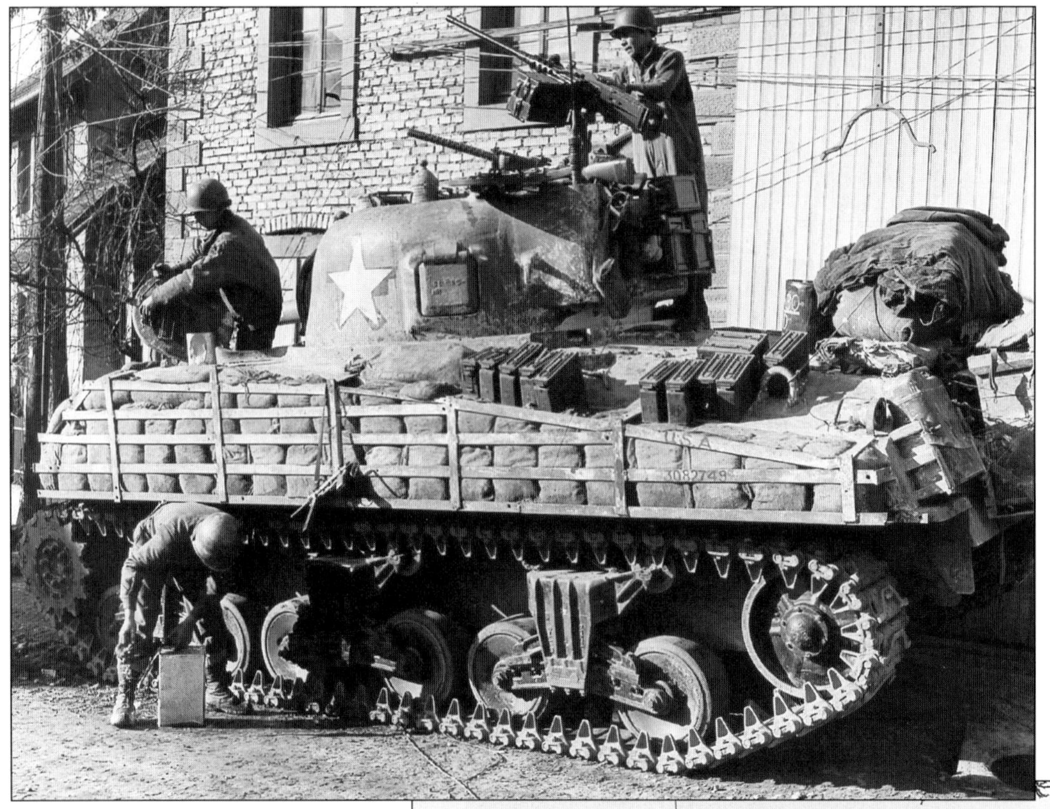

The Wehrmacht's defeat in the Battle of the Bulge exhausted the German reserve of tanks, and most tanks were then sent eastward in vain attempts to stem the Red Army's January 1945 offensive. As German tanks became less common, the main threat to the Sherman tank became German infantry panzerfaust and panzerschreks. Here, M4A3(75)W of the 25th Tank Bn., 14th Armored Div. displays a full arrray of sand-bag armor protection while the crew prepares the tank for action. This photo gives a clear view of the final style of VVS suspension with the raised trailing roller arm and concave disc wheel covers.

A M4A3(76)W of the 14th Armored Division during exercises near Huttendorf, France on 11 February 1944 prior to the assault on Germany. This tank has the side cage for sand-bags, but none have been fitted so far. Because the sand-bags covered the usual location of the divisional markings on the transmission cover, the 14th Armored Division moved these markings to the sides of the gun tube.

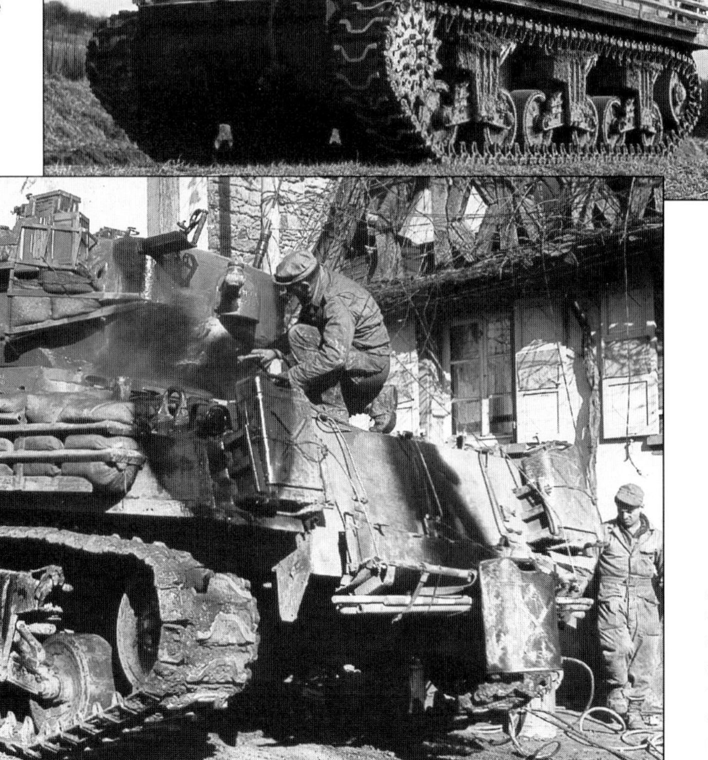

As a final touch, tanks of the 14th Armored Division were often camouflage painted. The crews simply sprayed black paint straight over the sand-bags and anything else in their way. This M4A3(76)W has a number of stowage changes such as the modification of the rear hull track block fittings to carry jerricans.

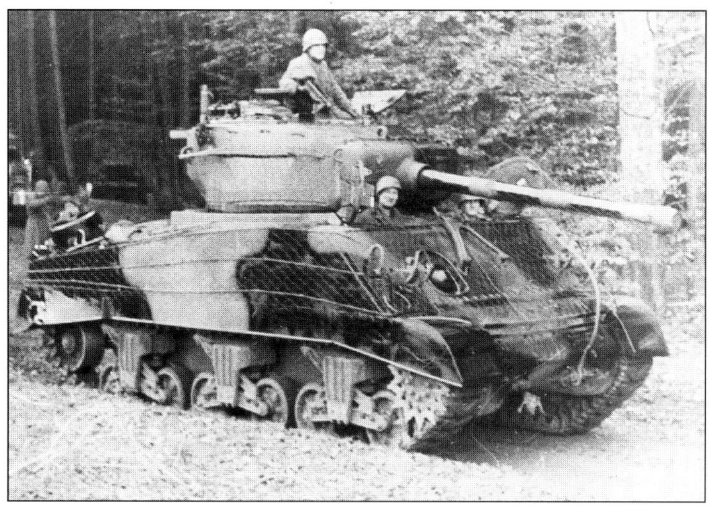

This photo shows an M4A3(76)W straight out of an engineer camouflage workshop, fitted with a full set of Sommerfield matting for attaching foliage camouflage, and a standard pattern painted camouflage of black and light green over the usual olive drab.

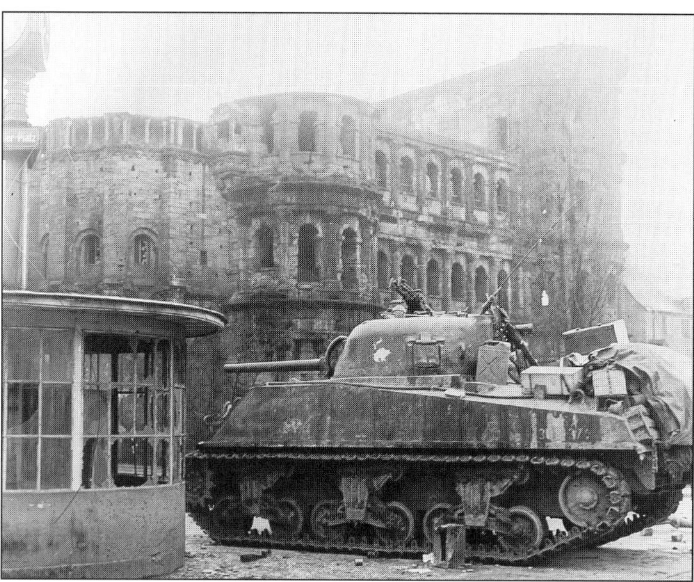

A M4A3(75)W of the 10th Armored Division covers the Adolf Hitler Platz in Trier, Germany following its capture by Patton's Third Army on 2 March 1945.

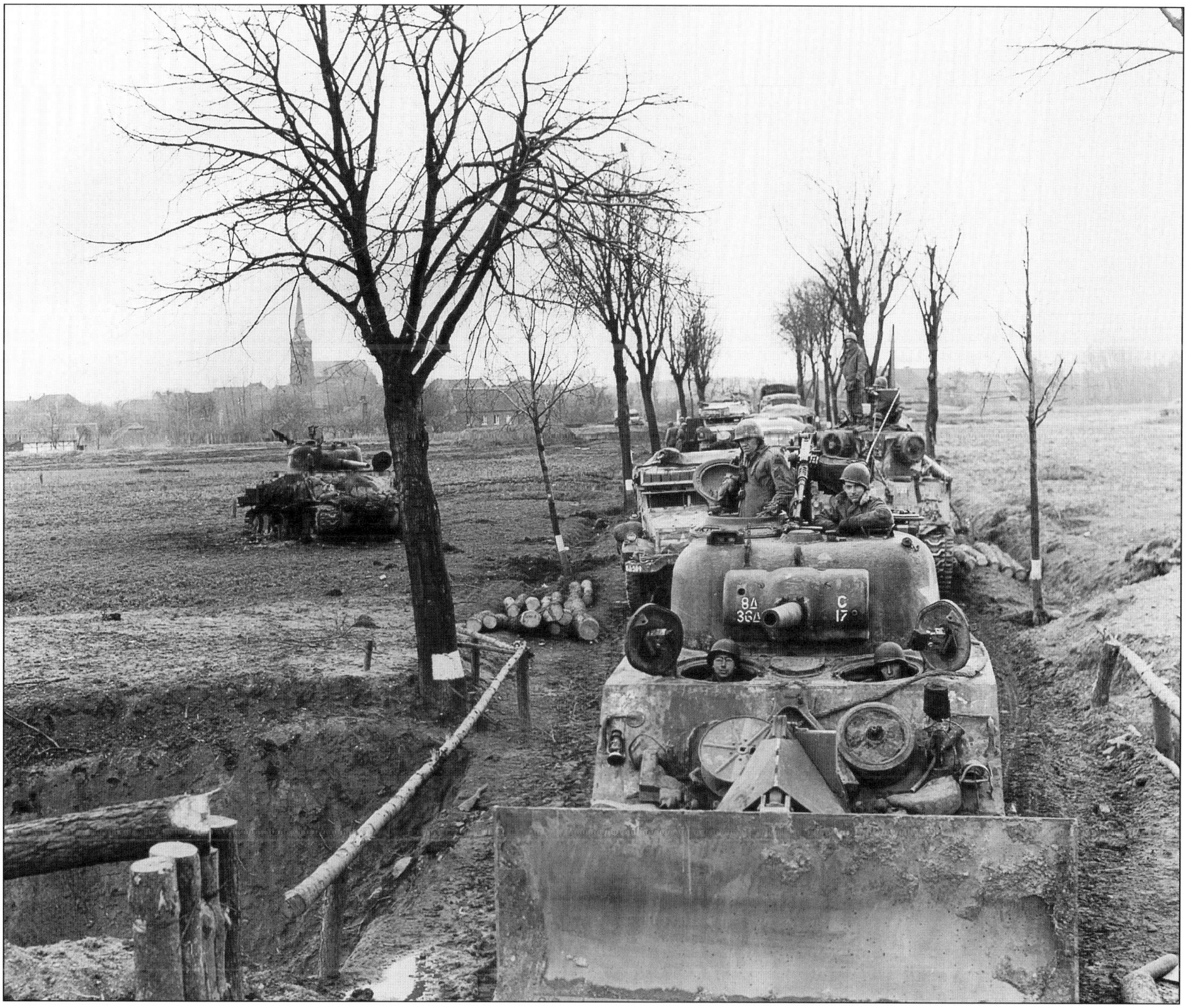

A M4A3(75)W with a M-1 bulldozer blade leads a column of vehicles including a M32 armored recovery vehicle from the 36th Tank Bn., 8th Armored Division near Merbeck, Germany on 2 March 1945. In the background is a knocked out and burned Sherman tank. This bulldozer tank has its unit identification codes painted on the M34A1 gun mount instead of the usual location on the transmission housing.

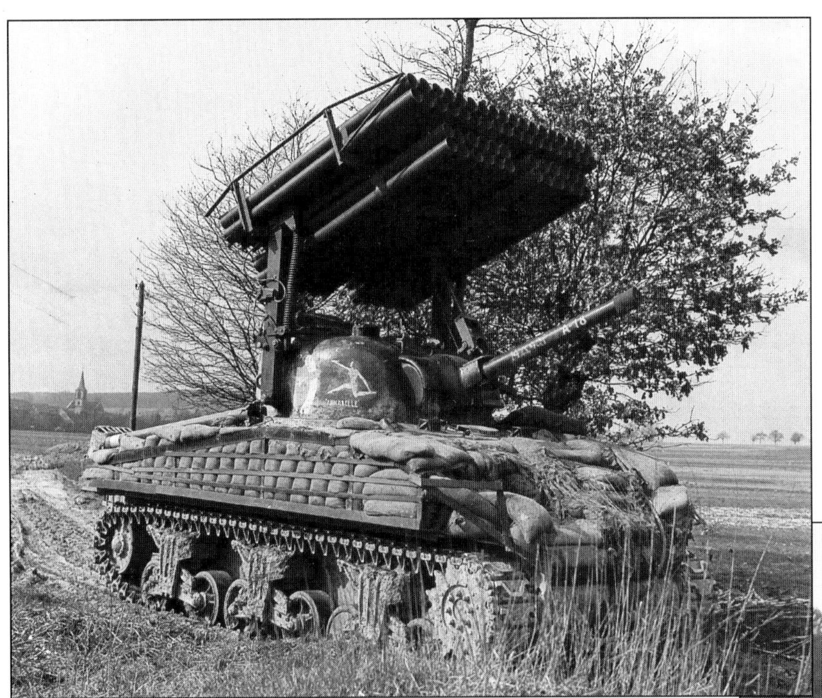

A M4A1 fitted with a T-34 Calliope multiple rocket launcher of the 40th Tank Bn., 14th Armored Division preparing to fire near Obermodern on 3 March 1945. These Calliope launchers could fire a salvo of sixty 4.5 inch artillery rockets.

A M4A1 medium tank of the 741st Tank Bn. covered with Sommerfield matting crosses a treadway bridge at Dumpelfeld, Germany on 9 March 1945. This was the only survivor of the original tanks that landed with the battalion at Normandy, and is still fitted with a Cullin hedgegrow cutter. For unexplained reasons, the tank commander is wearing a French-pattern tanker's helmet.

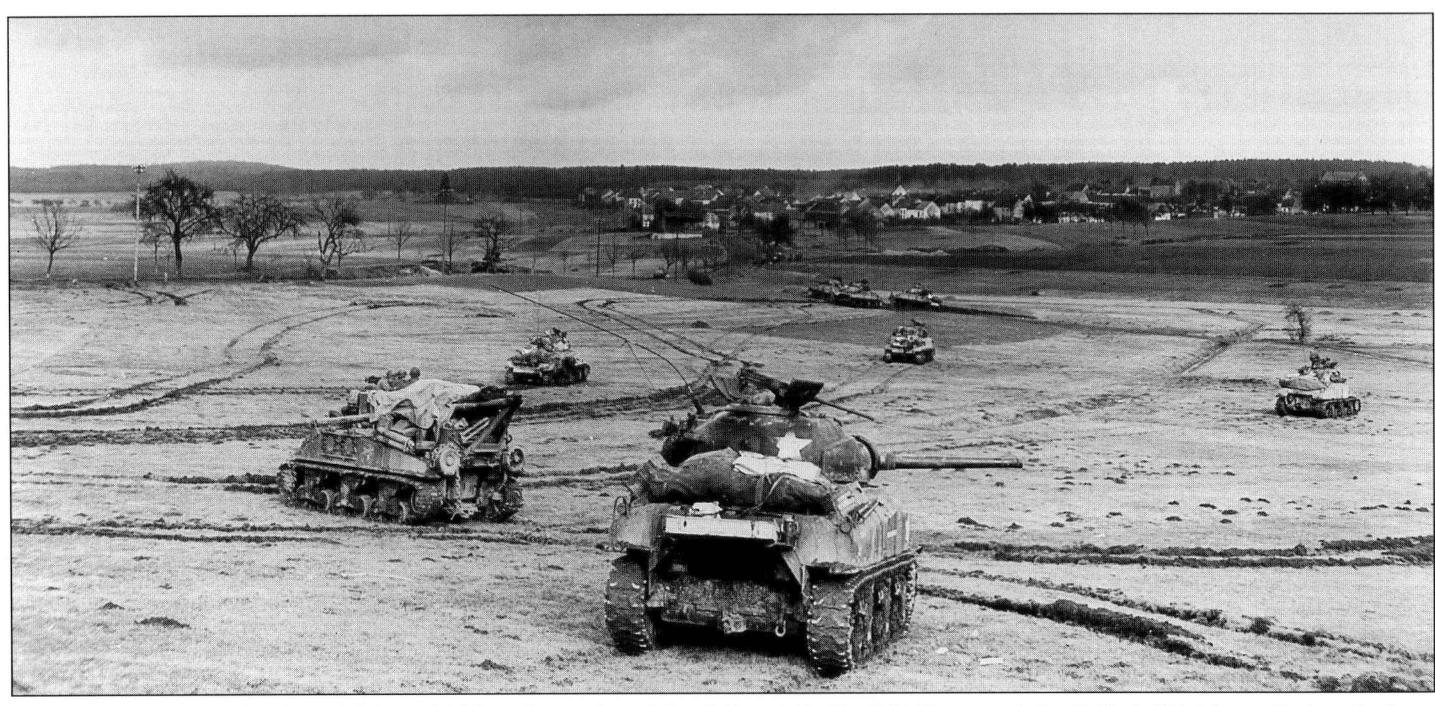

M4A1 tanks supporting the 76th Infantry Division advance through the fields outside Binsfield, Germany during Patton's Third Army attack on the town on 8 March 1945. To the left of the Sherman is a M32 armored recovery vehicle.

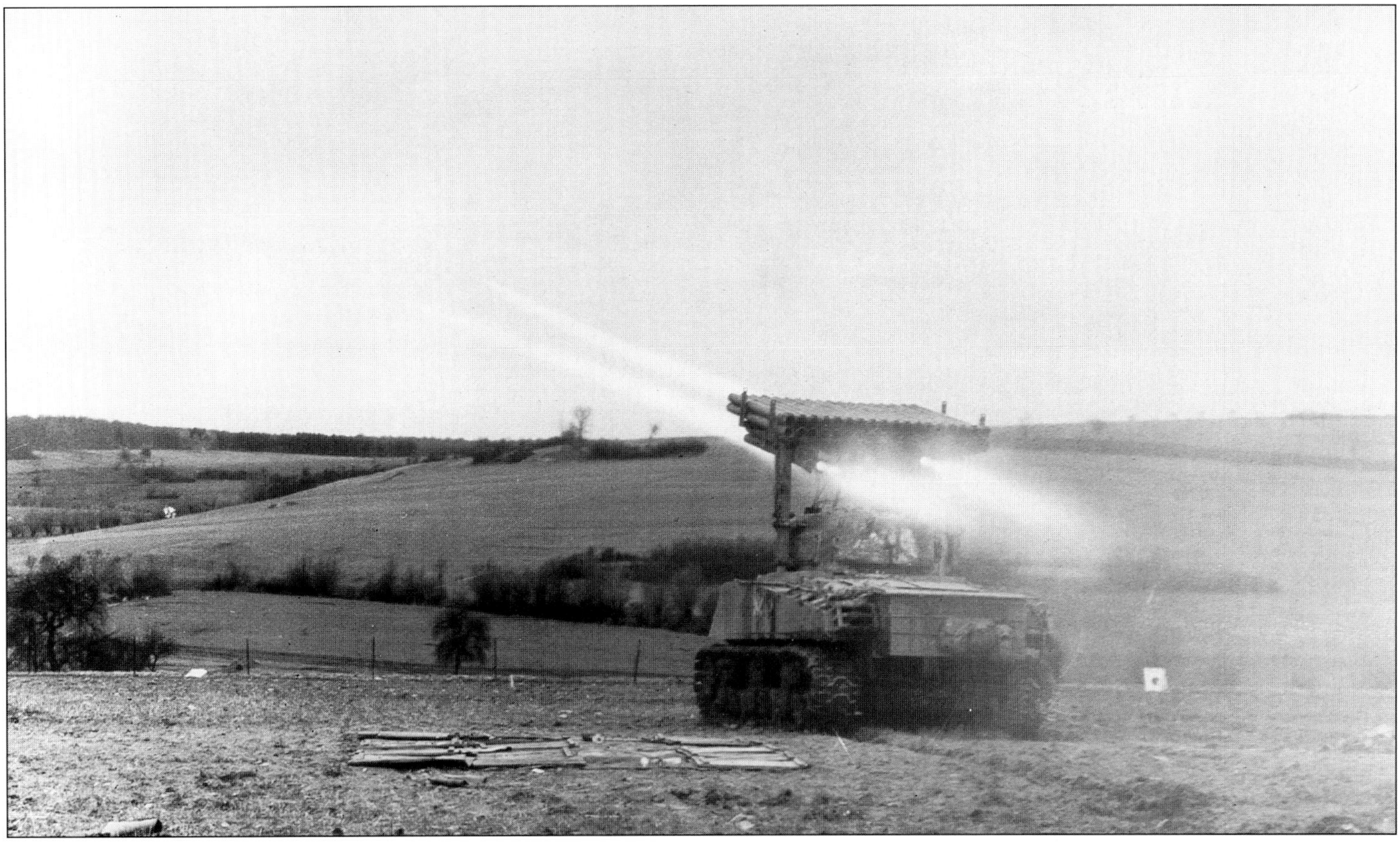

A M4A3 tank of the 14th Armored Division equipped with a T-34 Calliope rocket launcher gives a demonstrations of its firepower at Fletrange on 9 March 1945.

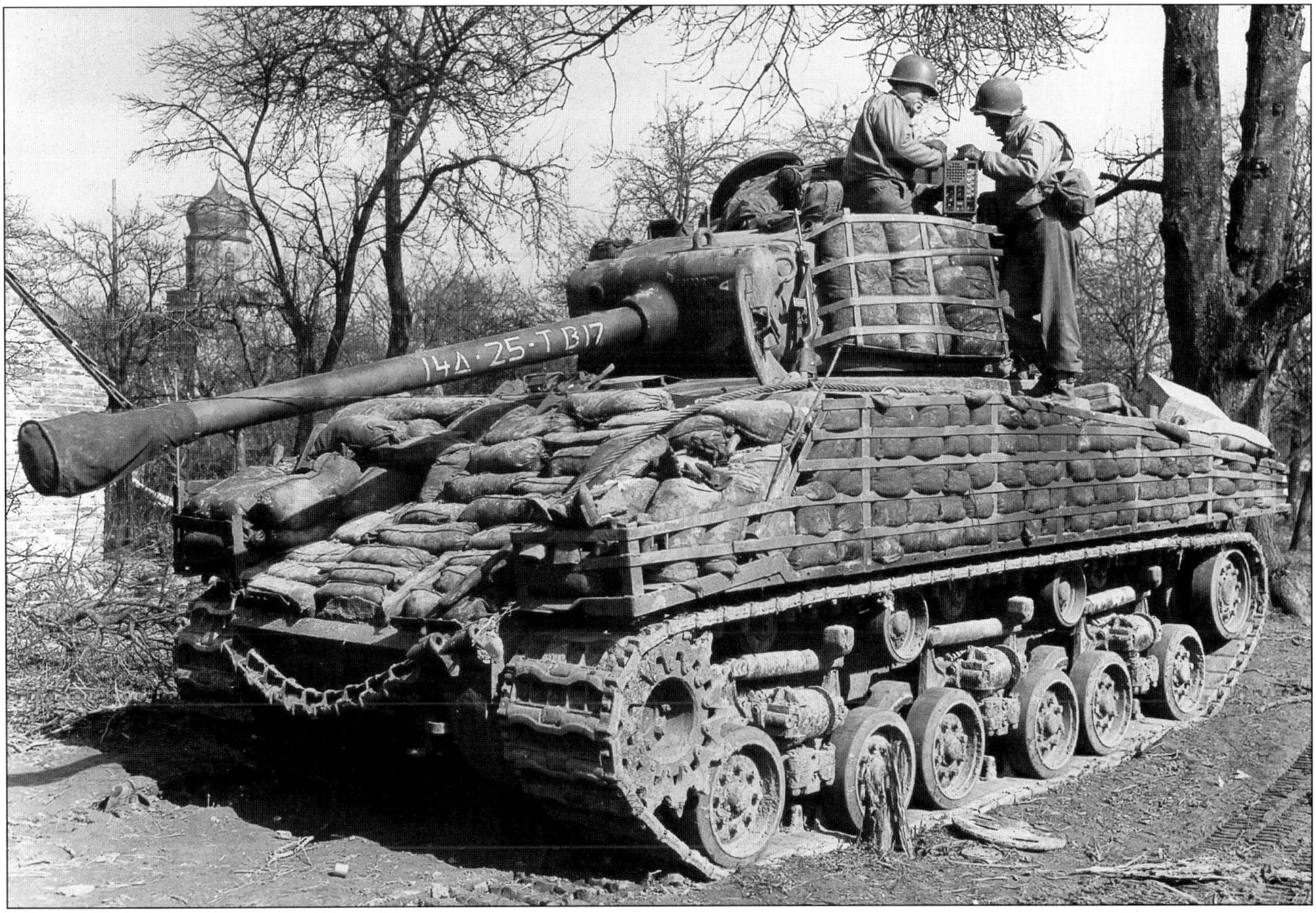

A good example of a thoroughly sand-bagged M4A3(76)W HVSS of the 14th Armroed Division undergoing a radio check near Ohlungen on 14 March 1945. Although this was permitted in the 7th Army, in some units, such as Patton's 3rd Army, it was officially discouraged.

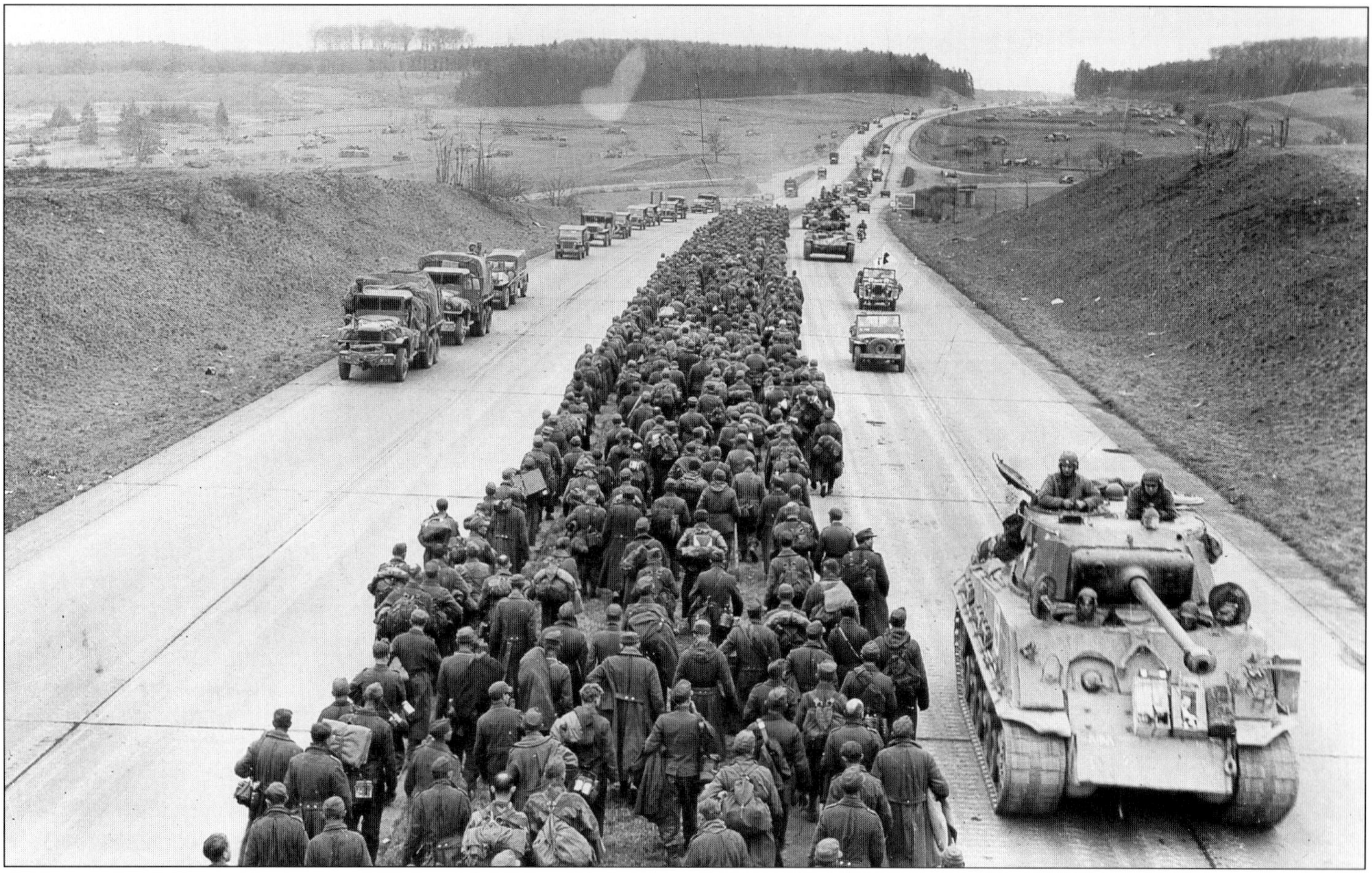

An enormous column of German prisoners walks westward along the median divider on the autobahn near Giesen, Germany as the 6th Armored Division moves to the front on 29 March 1945. The M4A3(76)W HVSS to the left is fitted with additional steel armor on the glacis plate, transmission cover and turret sides. Although kits were eventually fielded for this, many units improvised their own applique armor using knocked out American and German tank hulls.

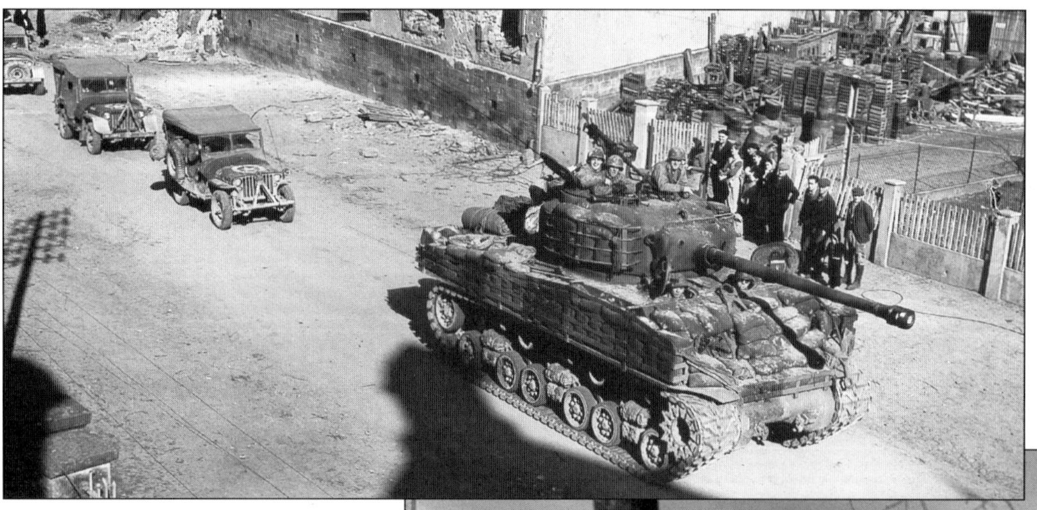

A well protected M4A3(76)W HVSS of the 781st Tank Battalion passes through Bitche following the long siege by the 100th Infantry Division which ended on 16 March 1945.

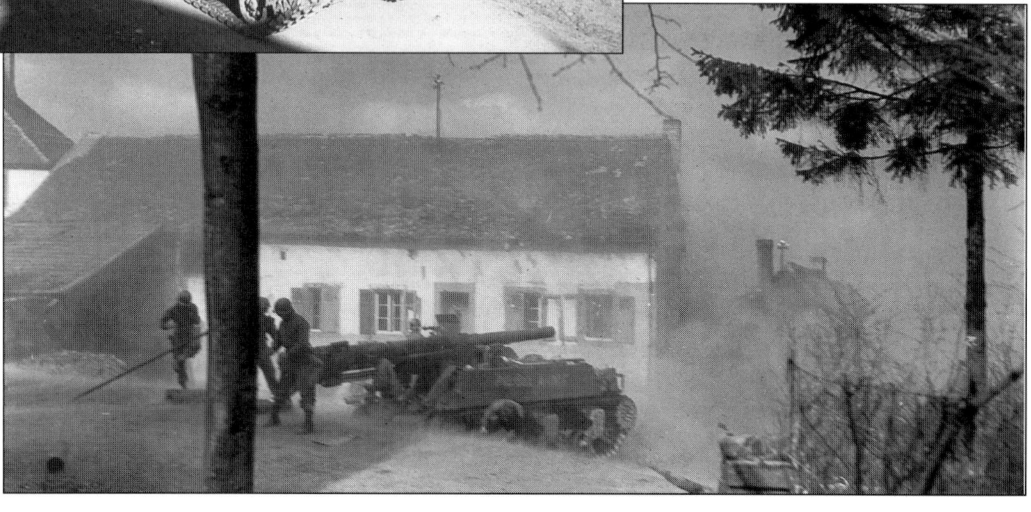

The ground shudders when a M-12 155mm GMC of the 989th FA Bn. fires point-blank at a German pillbox of the Siegfried line near Schelbach, Germany on 18 March 1945. The M-12's 155mm gun, derived from a World War I French gun, was one of the few weapons capable of penetrating the pillboxes along the Siegfried line.

The 37th Tank Bn., 4th Armored Division enters Alzey, Germany on 20 March 1945. The M4A3(76)W HVSS to the right is the battalion commander's tank (Creighton Abrams by now commanded one of the division's combat commands). The tank on the left is a M4A3E2 Jumbo assault tank which has been rearmed with a 76mm gun. The thickened side armor, glacis armor and thickened gun mantlet are evident in this view.

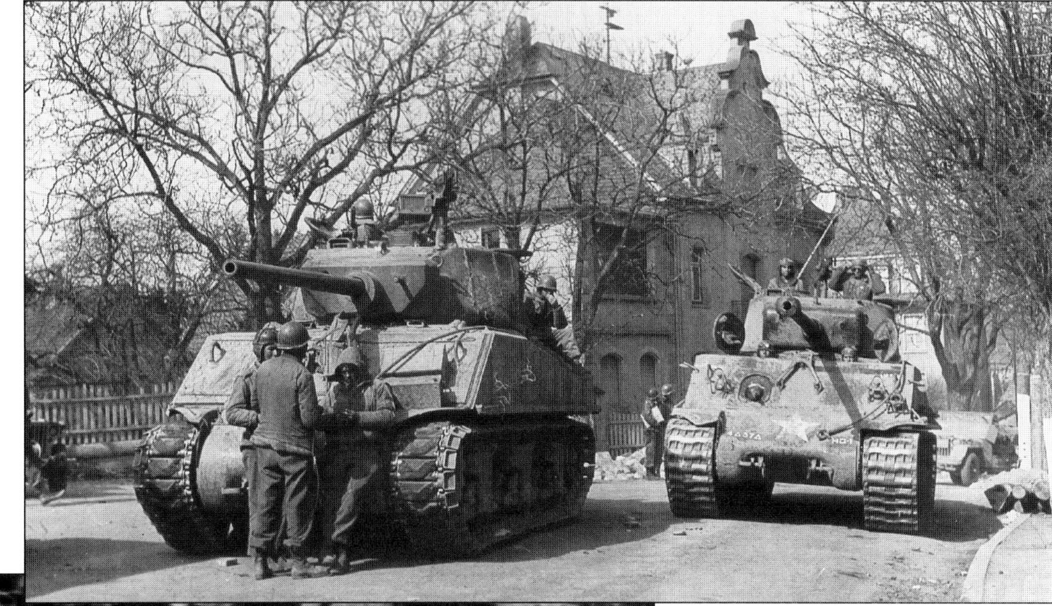

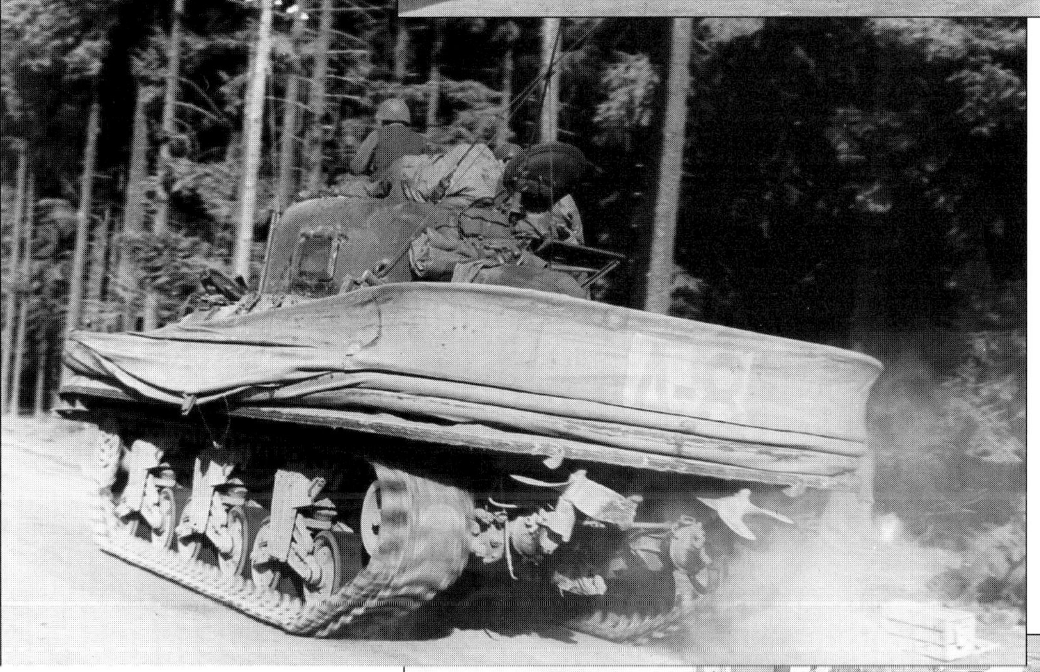

A long way from the Normandy beaches, this M4A1 Duplex Drive amphibious tank of Patton's 3rd Army races through Braunshorn, Germany on its way to the Rhine river. A number of DD tanks originally prepared for the D-Day invasion in 1944 were used during the 1945 Rhine river operation. This view clearly shows the folded canvas screen and twin propellors that characterized this version of the M4A1.

A M4A3(76)W HVSS of the 41st Tank Battalion, 11th Armored Division named Flat-Foot-Floosie which was the first tank from Patton's 3rd Army to reach the Rhine river in Germany during the 21 March 1945 breakthrough. Careful inspection of the hull front will reveal that the tank sports a layer of applique steel armor.

A M4A1(76)W of the 14th Armored Division moves past a roadside littered with debris from the retreating German forces near Silz, Germany on 23 March 1945. This tank is fitted with a .30 cal machine gun instead of the usual .50 cal Browning M2 HB.

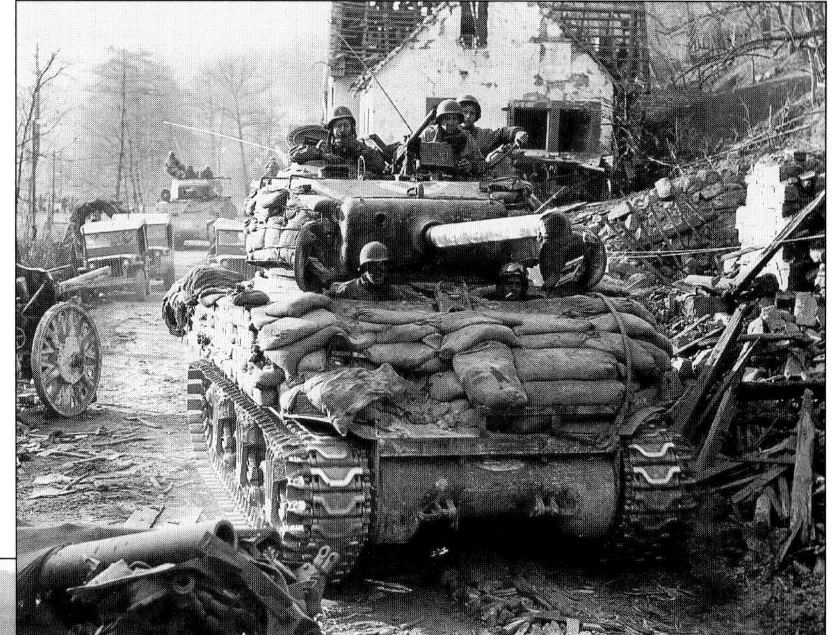

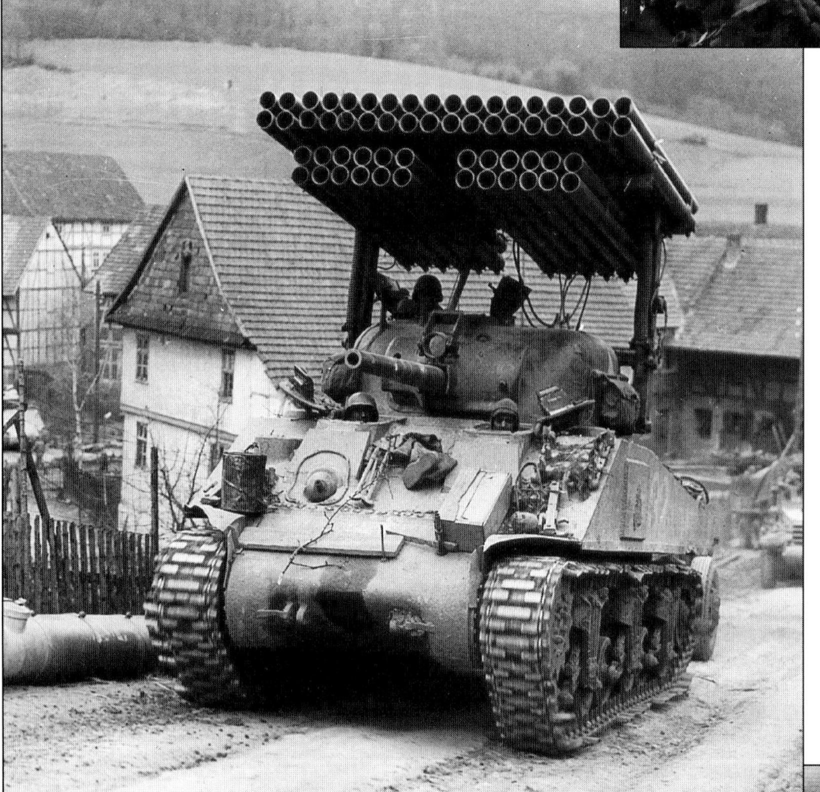

A M4 fitted with a T-34 Calliope multiple rocket launcher moves through the town of Wichte, Germany while in support of 6th Armored Division efforts to gain a bridge over the Fulda River on 1 April 1945. This tank still has some duckbill extended end connectors fitted, but many have been lost from hard driving.

Much of the fighting in the final weeks of the war was brutal house-to-house skirmishing in German towns. These two M4A3(76)W tanks of the 14th Armored Division were knocked out, in spite of their sand-bag armor, in the narrow streets of Lohr, Germany by panzerfausts.

This sequence of two photographs show infantry supported by a M4A3(76)W HVSS tank cautiously moving through Oberderla, Germany on 4 April 1945. In the foreground lies a US infantryman hit by a German sniper. A BAR gunner is at the right.

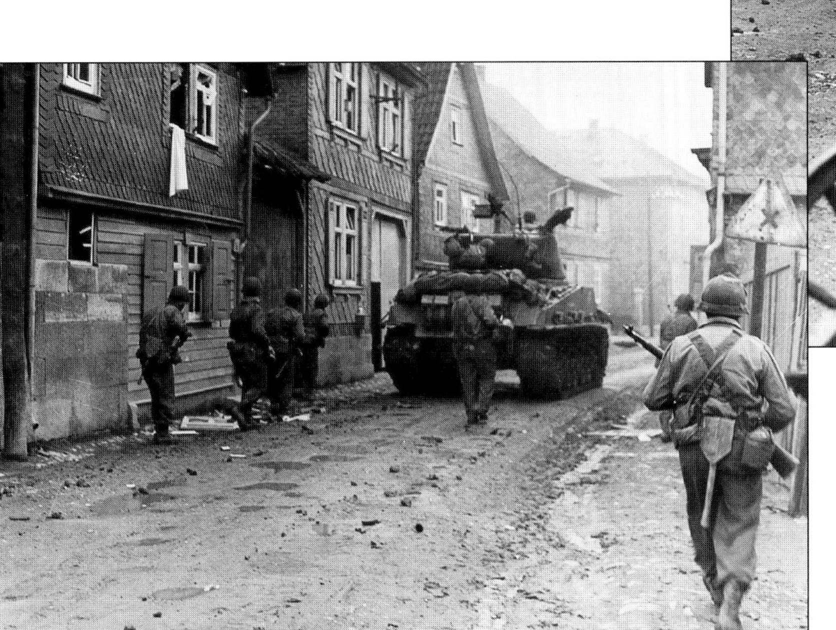

In the second photo of this sequence, the infantry from the 6th Armored Division move past a house flying a white flag while cautiously trying to rout out snipers. Although the stiffest German resistance had collapsed by April, there were still determined German soldiers who refused to surrender.

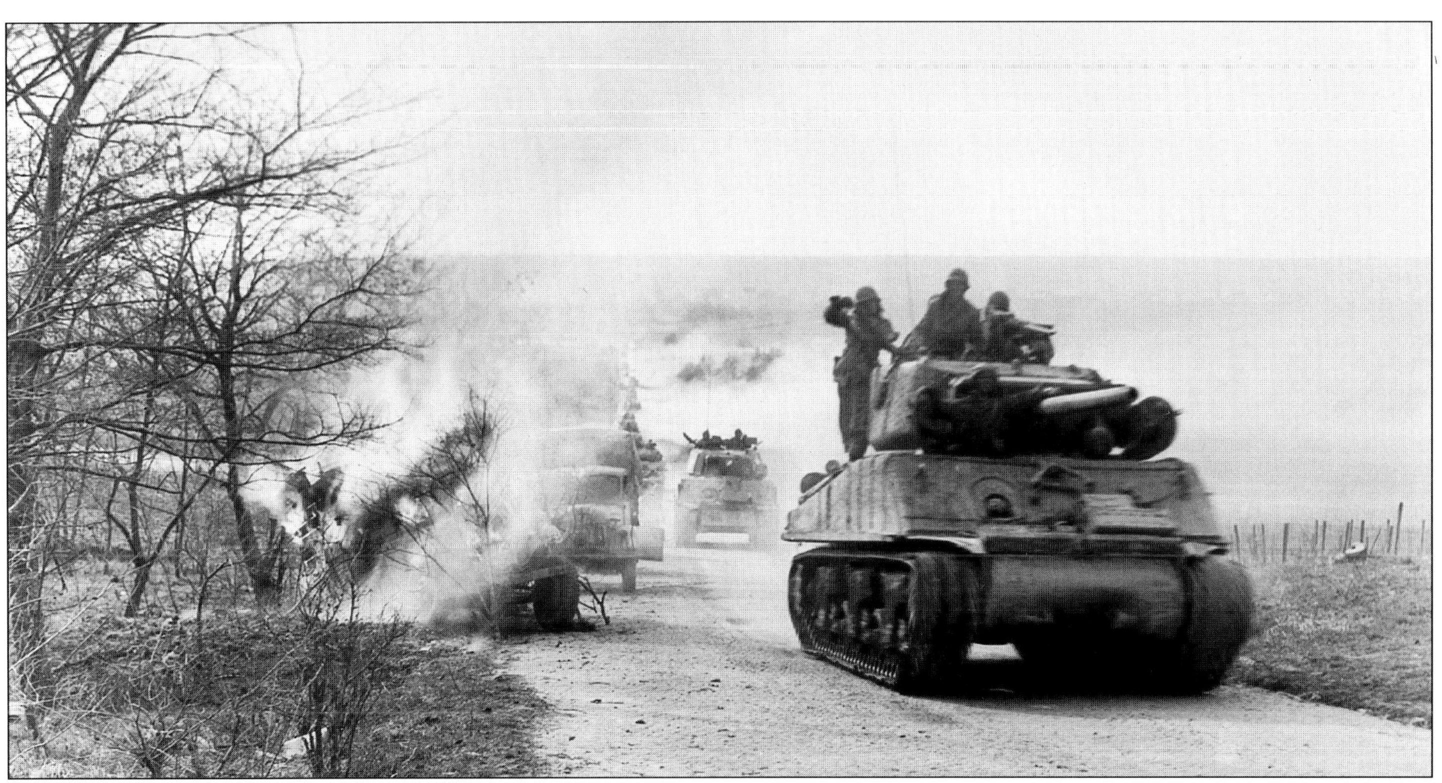

An armor column from the 6th Armored Division passes the smoking remains of a German column during the fighting in Germany in April 1945. The lead tank is one of the rare M4A3E2 Jumbo assault tanks.

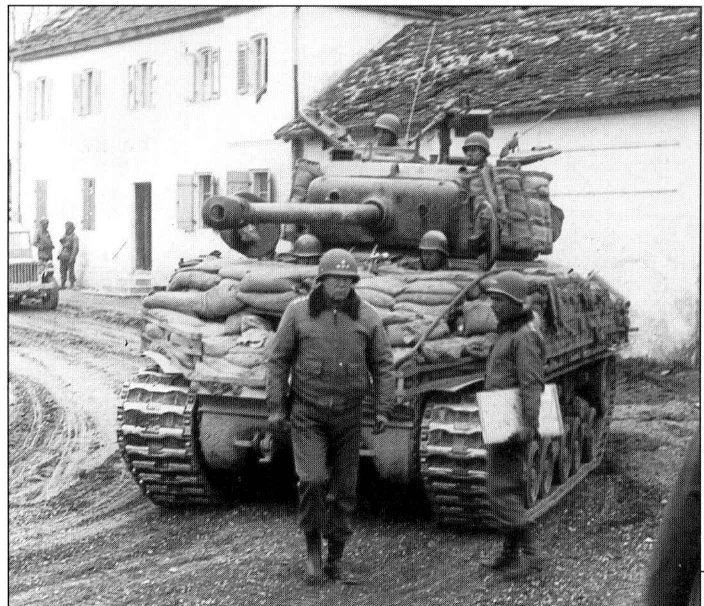

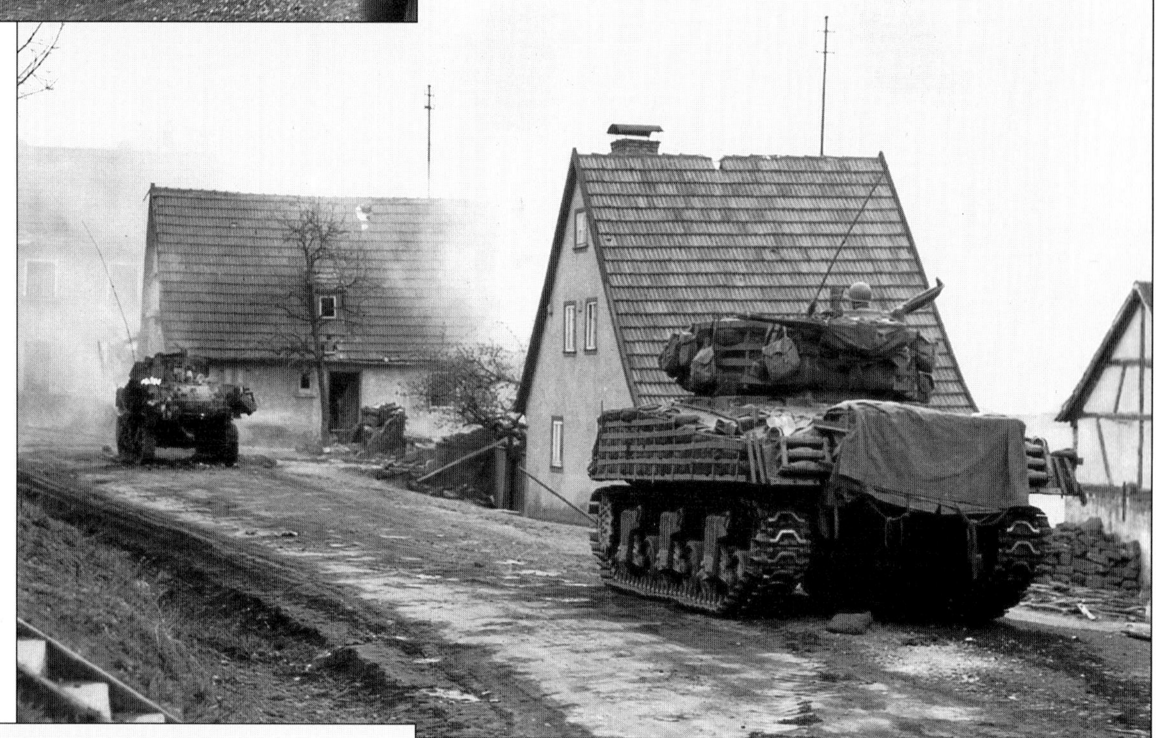

Gen. George S. Patton rebukes the crew of a M4A3(76)W for their use of sand-bag armor on their vehicle. Patton felt that the sand-bag armor wasn't effective and that the extra weight led to premature automotive breakdowns of the tanks. The tank crews felt otherwise, and his orders on this subject were widely ignored.

A M4A3(76)W cautiously moves up behind a burning M-5A1 light tank in the outskirts of Langenprozelten, Germany during an attack by the 47th Tank Bn., 14th Armored Division on 4 April 1945.

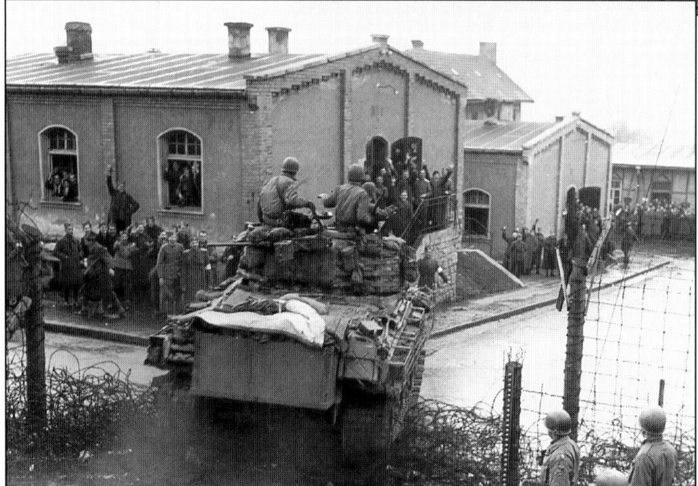

An M4A3(75)W from the 14th Armored Division crashes over the barbed wire into the Hammelburg POW camp on 6 April 1945. An earlier attempt by Task Force Baum of the 37th Tank Bn., 4th Armored Division was a bloody failure. The first attempt has been the source of controversy as it was suspected that Patton ordered the raid because his son-in-law was a prisoner in the camp.

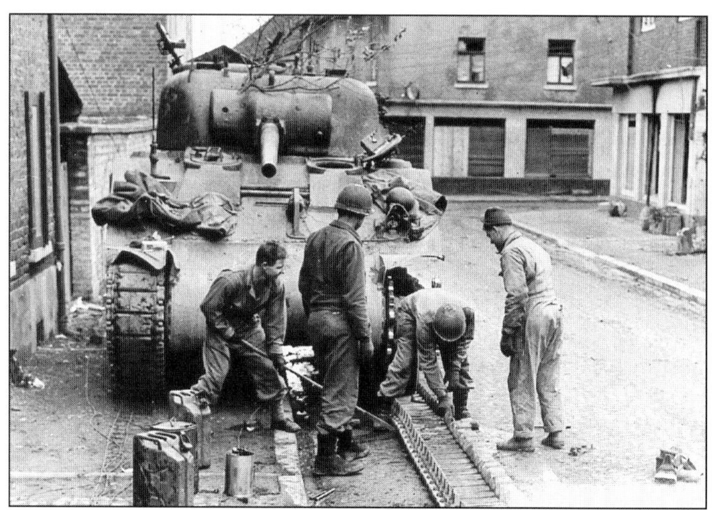

An old M4 of the HQ Co., 2nd Armored Division is serviced by its crew in Baesweiler, Germany on 12 April 1945. The crew is removing the extended end connectors which were not as necessary once the spring weather improved. There is a small stack of end-connectors to the right.

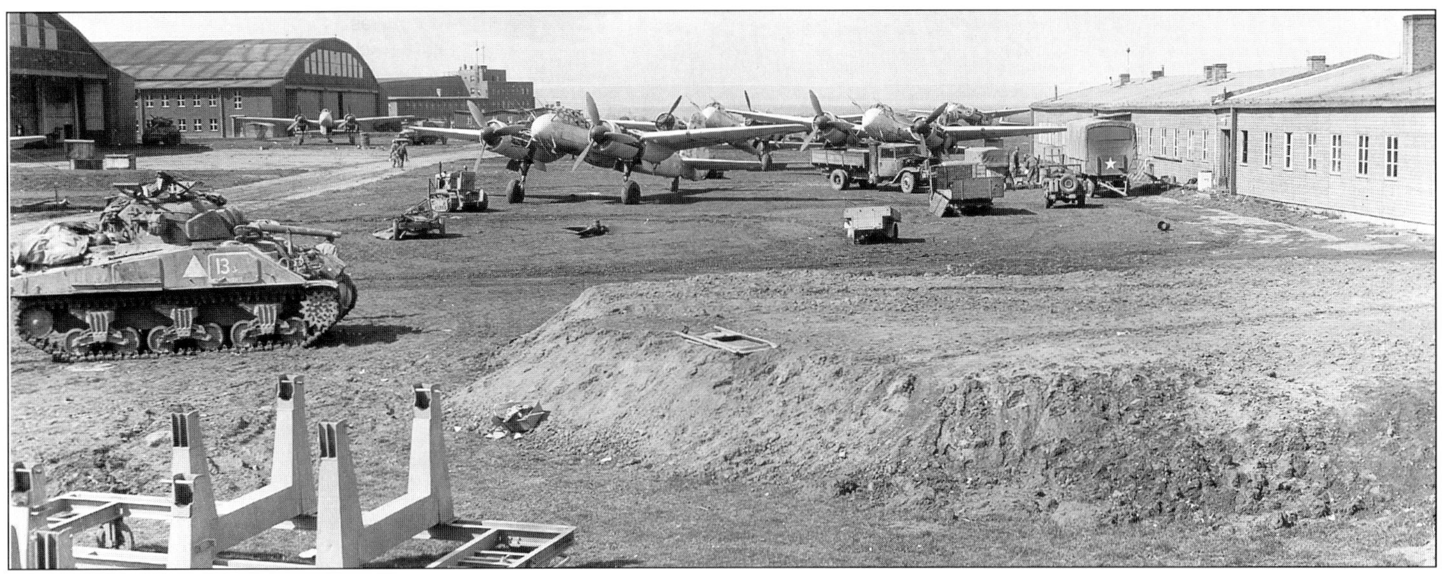

A M4 of the 15th Tank Bn., 6th Armored Division occupies Lanensalz airbase near Mulhausen on 6 April 1945. In the background some of the 32 German Junkers Ju-88 radar-equipped night fighters captured at the base.

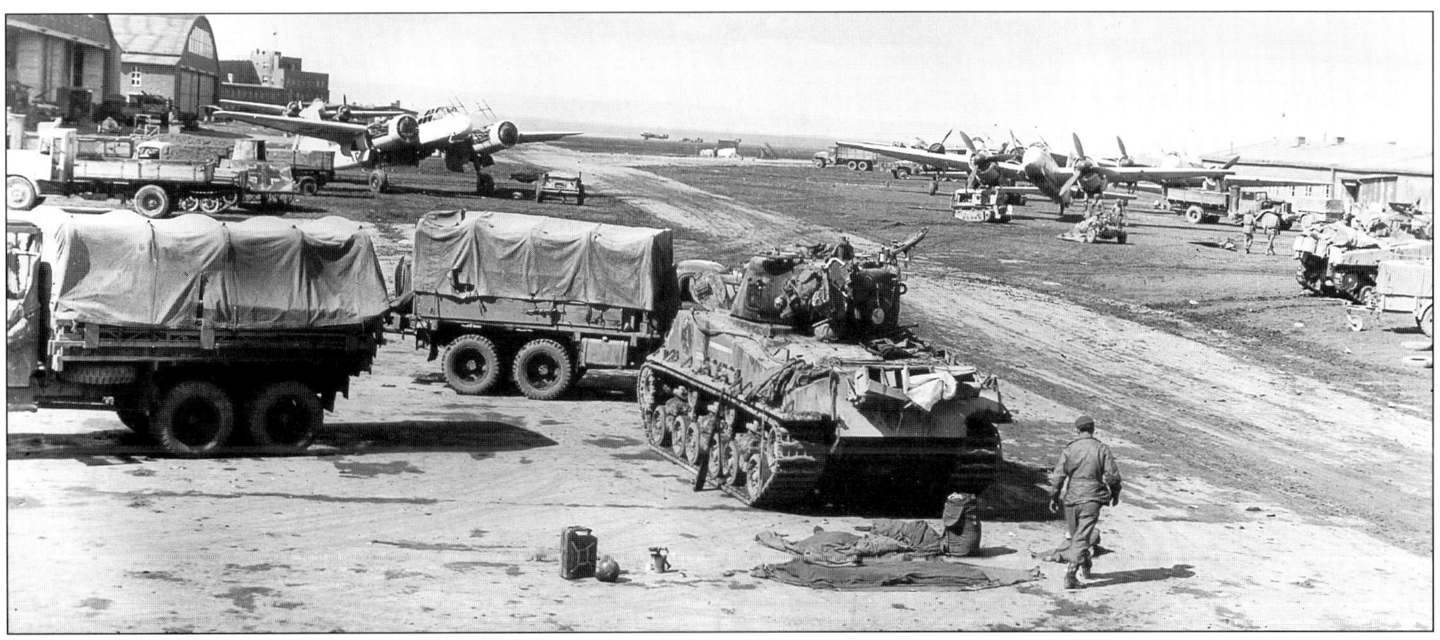

Another view of the German airfield with a new M4A3(76)W HVSS in the foreground.

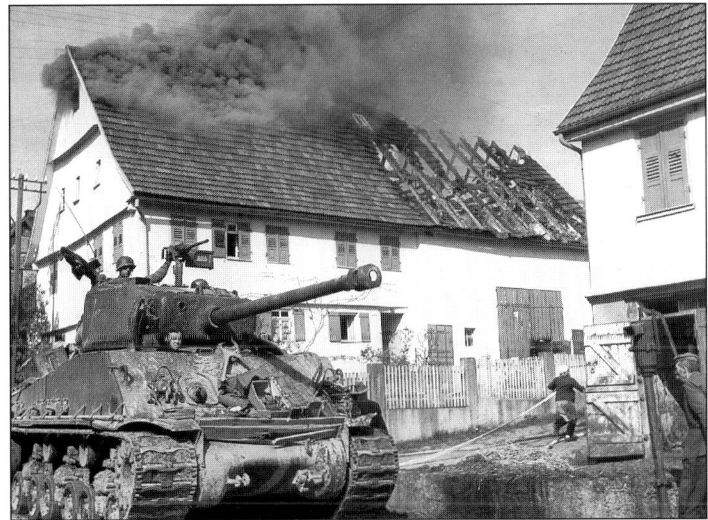

A M4A3(76)W HVSS of the 21st Tank Bn., 10th Armored Division passes by a burning German farm house on the outskirts of Rosewalden, Germany on 20 April 1945. The house had been set on fire after the tanks had shot at German snipers in the attic.

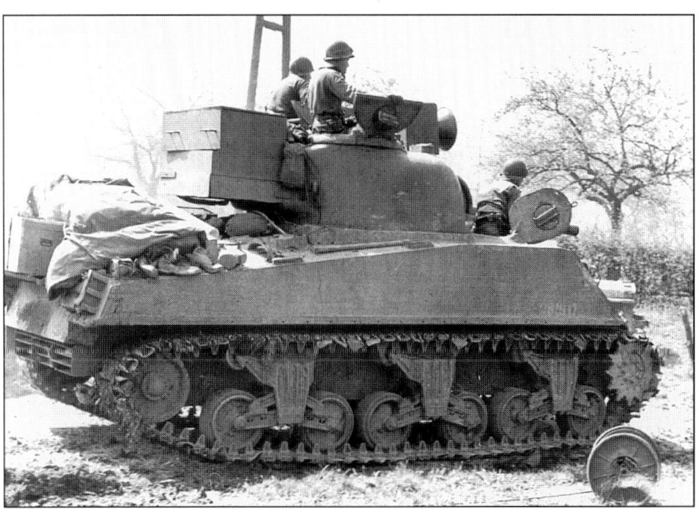

Some M4A3(75)W tanks were converted for special roles. This vehicle was modified by the addition of a loudspeaker system, including a power generator in a container at the turret rear. It was used by Task Force Griffiths of the 7th Armored Division in the hopes of getting German troops to surrender rather than fight.

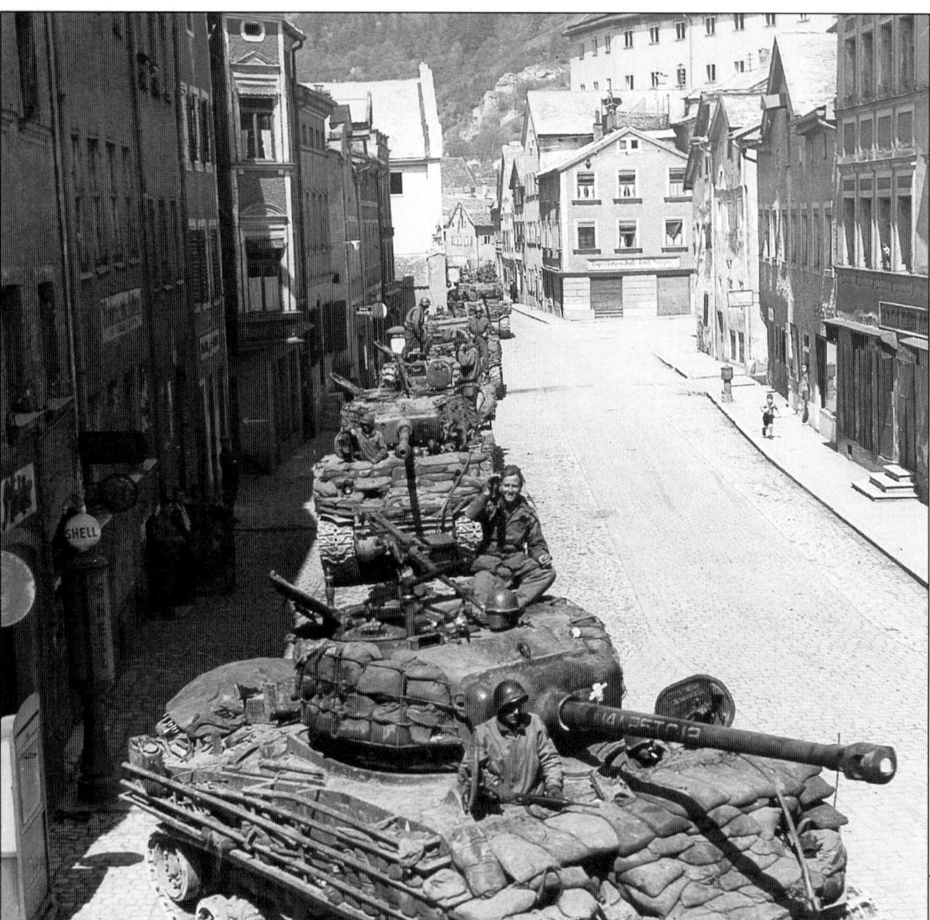

A column of M4A3(76)W HVSS tanks of the 25th Tank Bn., 14th Armored Division clank through the streets of Eichstadt in southern Germany on 25 April 1945.

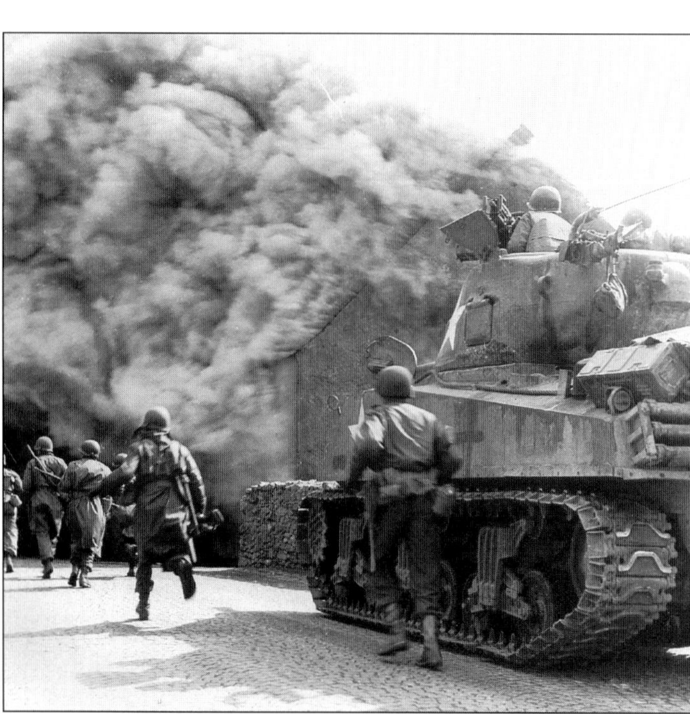

Soldiers of the 55th Armored Infantry Bn., advance past a M4A3(76)W of the 22nd Tank Bn, 11th Armored Division during fighting in Wernberg, Germany on 22 April 1945.

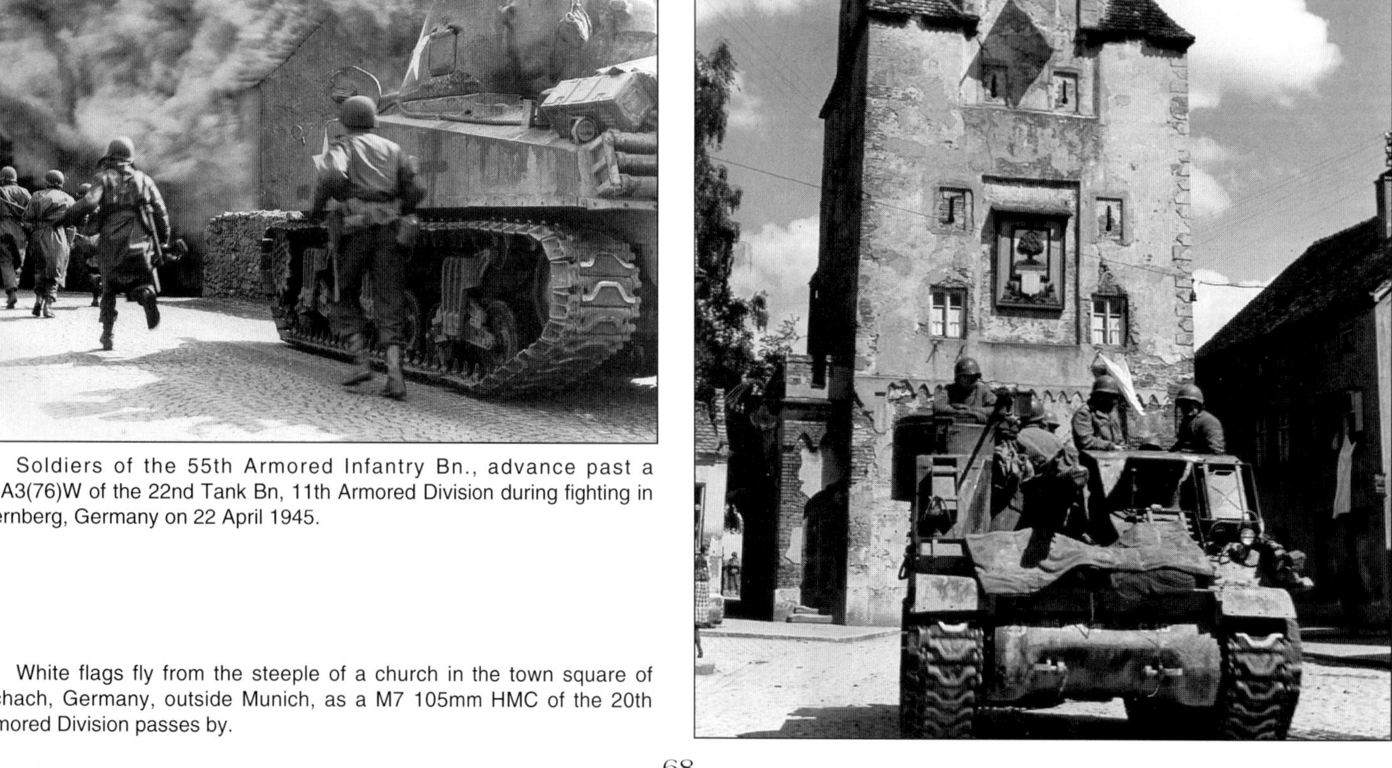

White flags fly from the steeple of a church in the town square of Aichach, Germany, outside Munich, as a M7 105mm HMC of the 20th Armored Division passes by.

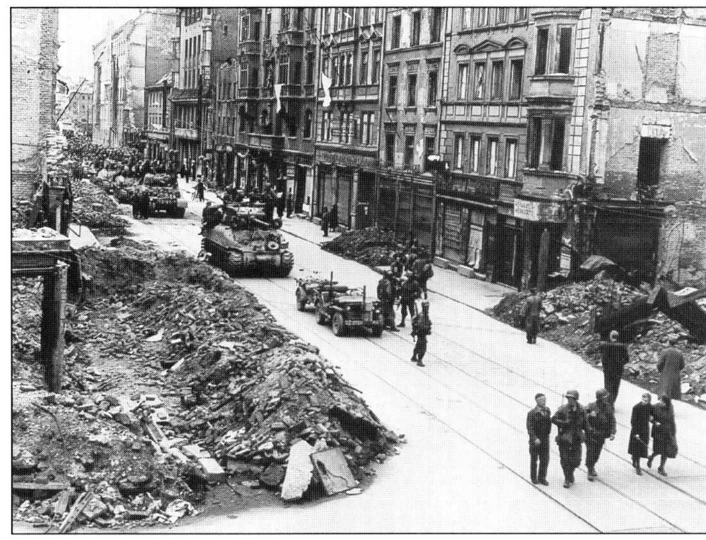

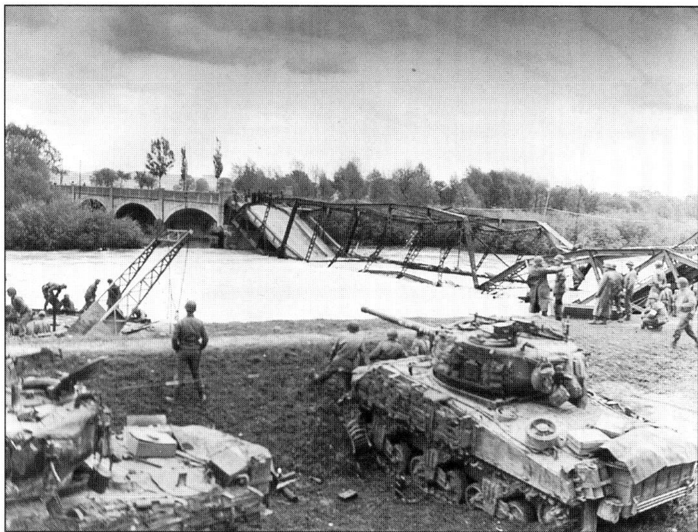

The main objective of the US 7th Army was the Bavarian capital of Munich. Here, a column of Shermans led by a M4A1(76)W form up in the outskirts of the city for a march into the city square on 30 April 1945. Munich had been heavily damaged by previous bomber raids as is evident in this view.

A combat engineer battalion begins work on a pontoon bridge over the Isar river in Bavaria to replace the Moosburg bridge demolished by the retreating Wehrmacht. In the foreground are a pair of M4A3(76)W tanks, the one on the right with some of its sand-bag armor knocked off.

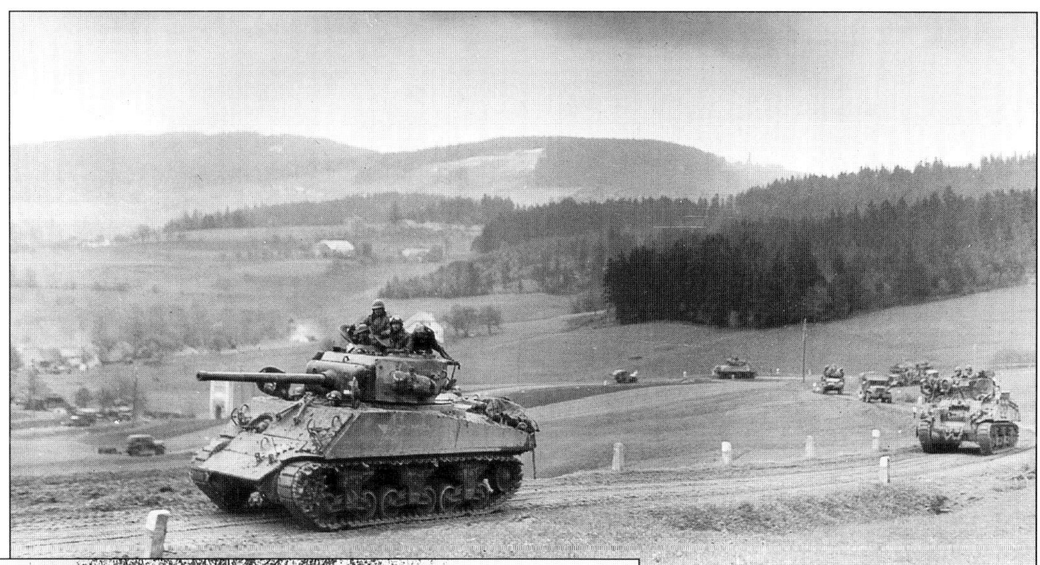

An armored column from Patton's 3rd Army advances into Austria near Lembach on 3 May 1945. The M4A3(76)W is fitted with applique armor on the turret and on the hull front.

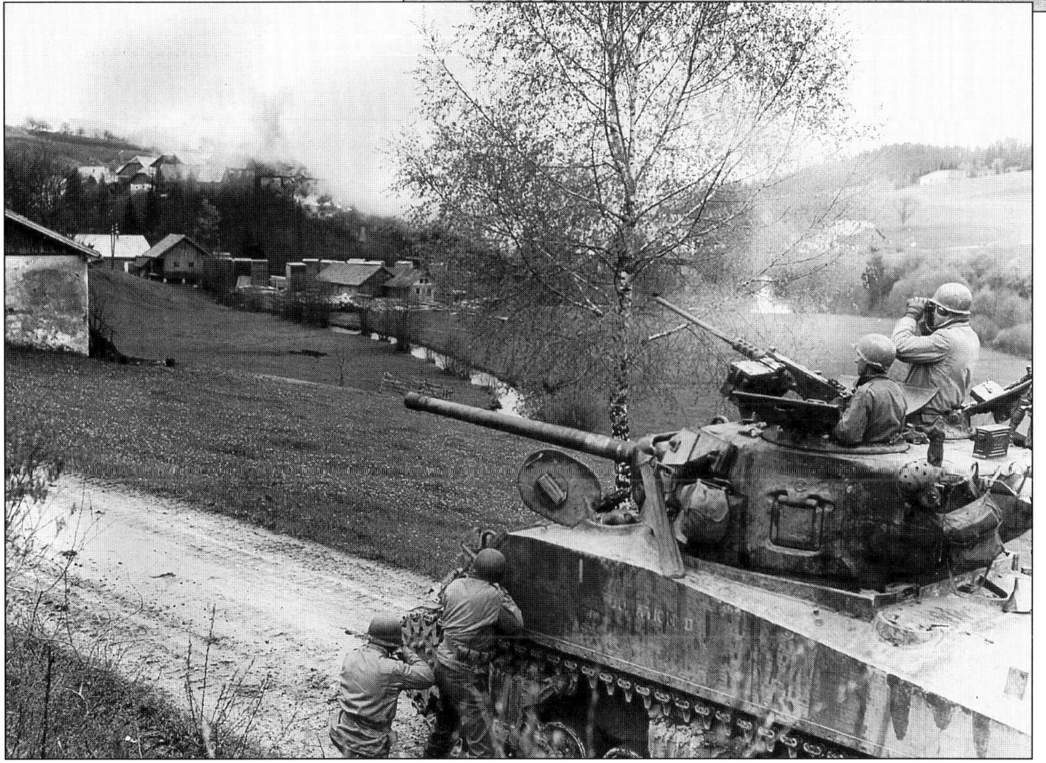

Troops of the 11th Armored Division fire on German positions in the town of Keppl, Austria on 4 May 1945. The M4A3(76)W in this picture is fitted with applique armor on the turret front, and probably the hull front as well.

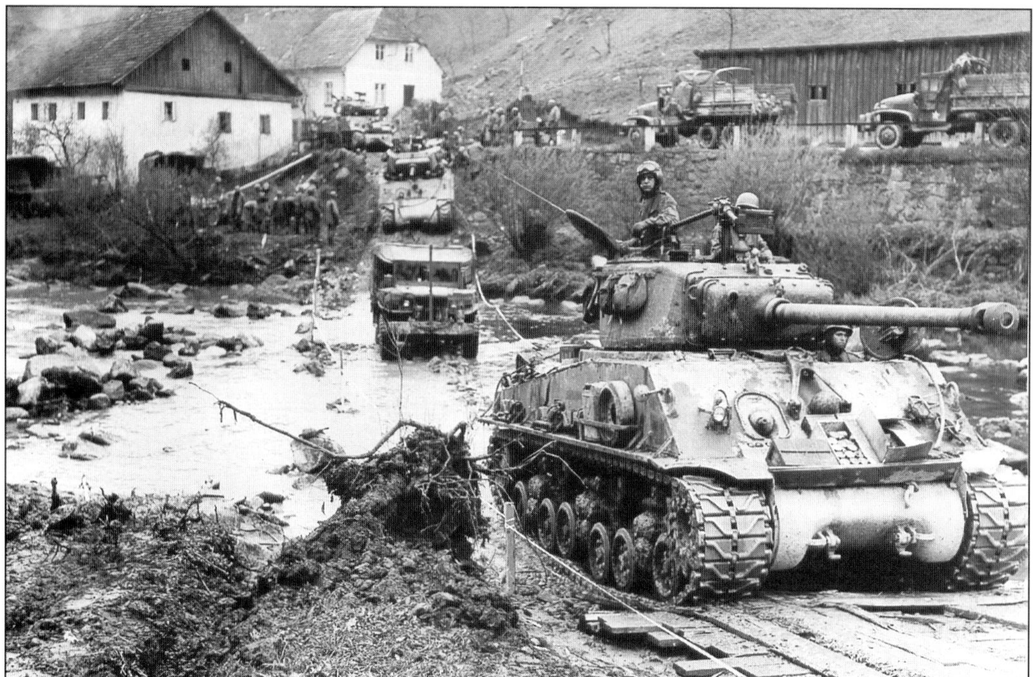

A M4A3(76)W HVSS of the 11th Armored Division fords the Muhl river at the head of a column advancing into Neufelden, Austria on 4 May 1945.

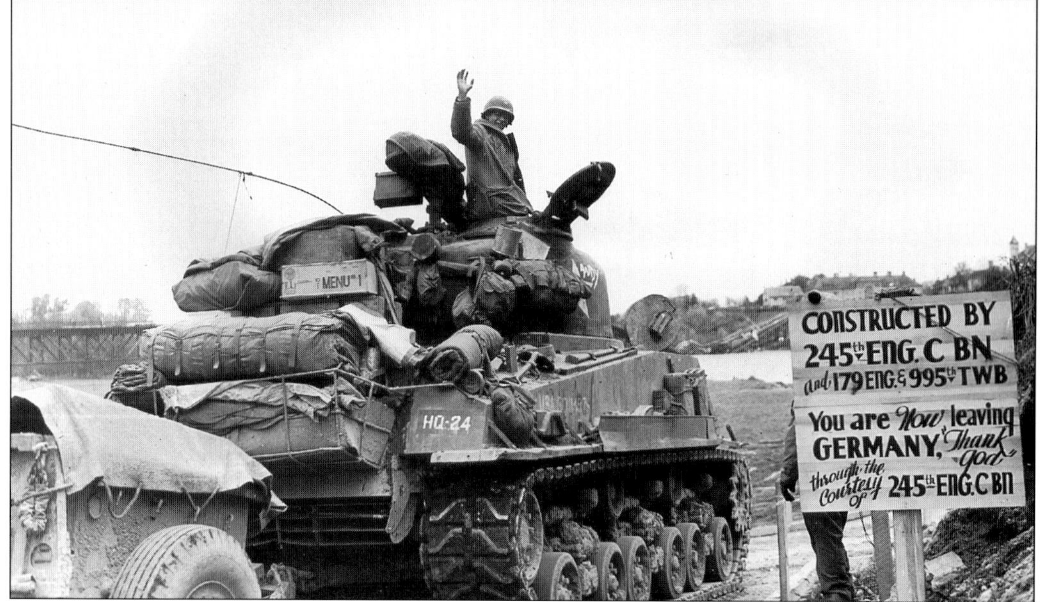

A M4A3 HVSS 105mm HMC howitzer tank of the 13th Armored Division crosses a pontoon bridge between Germany and Austria. The new version of the 105mm howitzer tank with HVSS suspension was not common until the final months of the war in Europe.

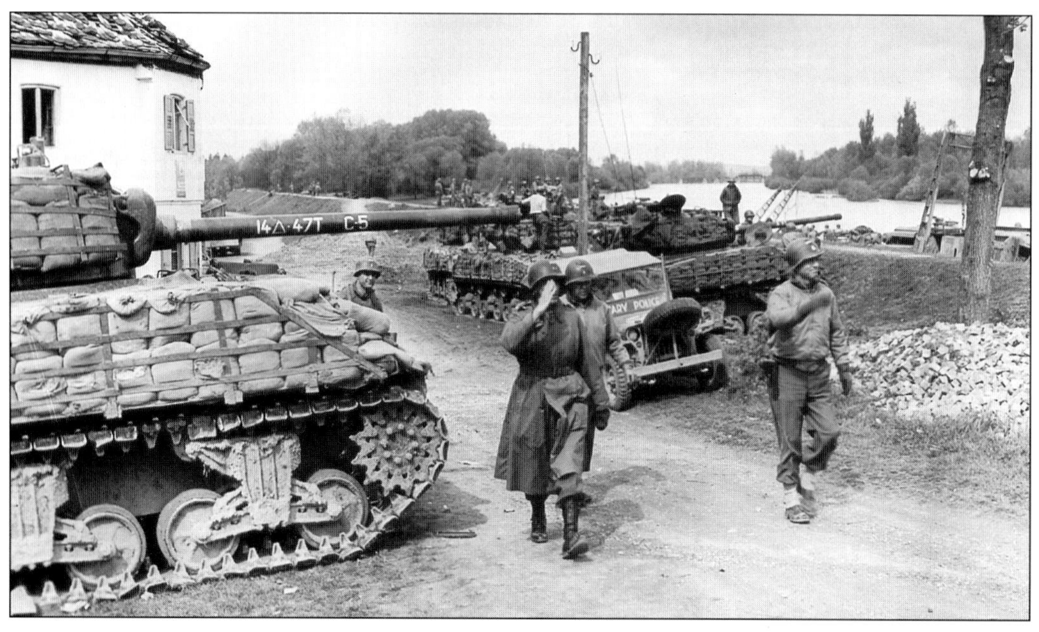

In a final review of the troops, Maj. Gen. A. C. Smith, commander of the 14th Armored Division, inspects his units along the Isar river near Moosburg on 30 May 1945 a few weeks after the end of the war. The M4A3s have a mixture of the old VVS and new HVSS suspensions.

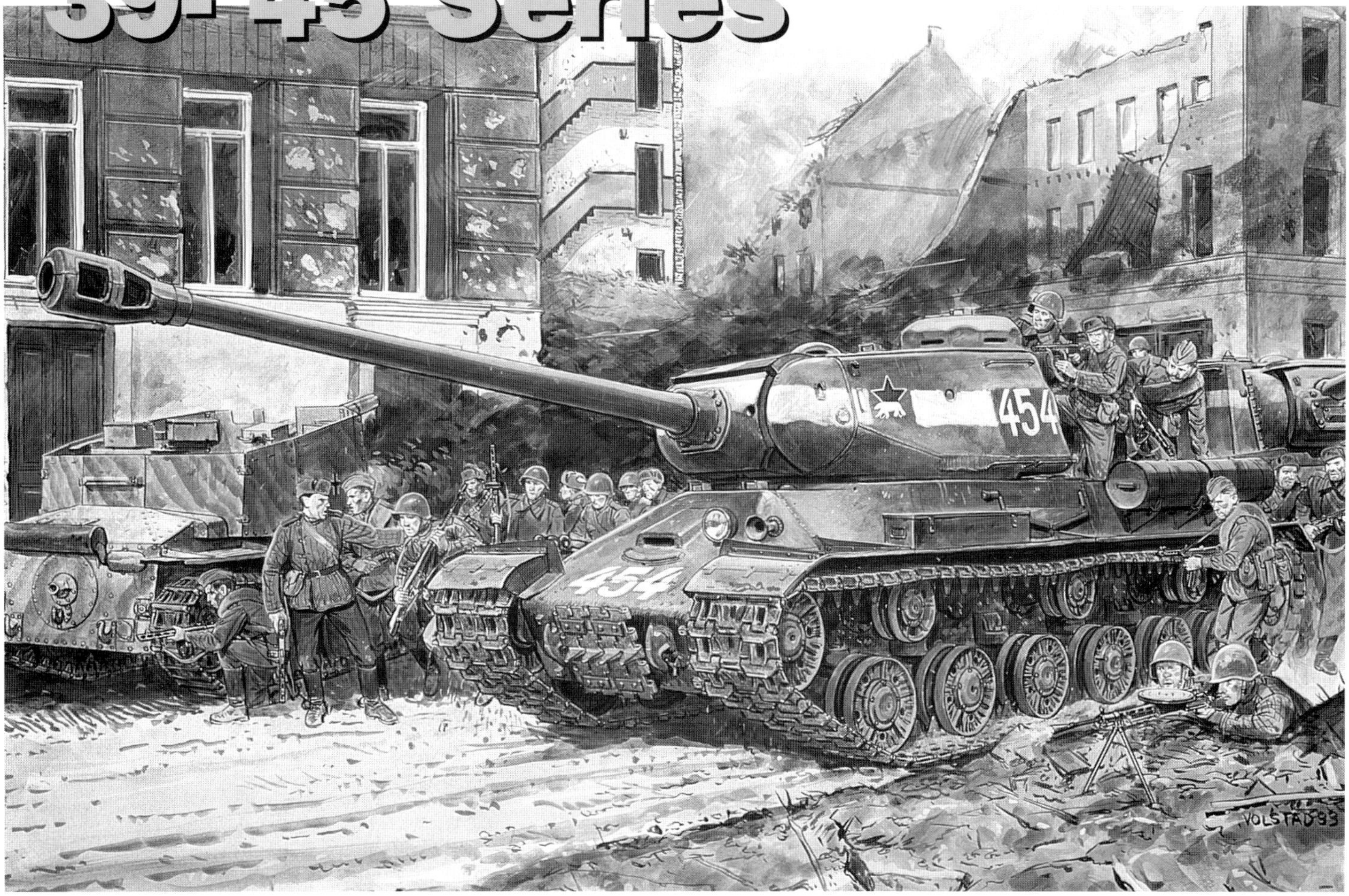

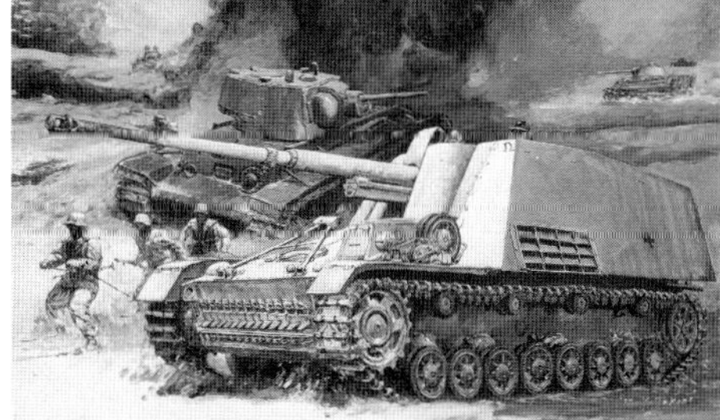

6018 JS-2m ChKZ PRODUCTION TYPE

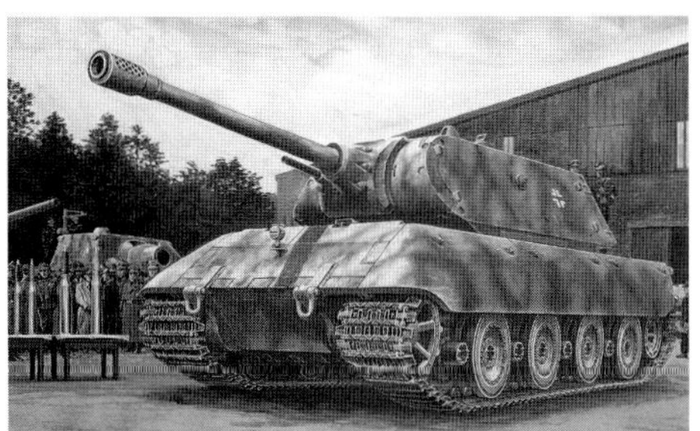

6001 NASHORN, Sd. Kfz. 164

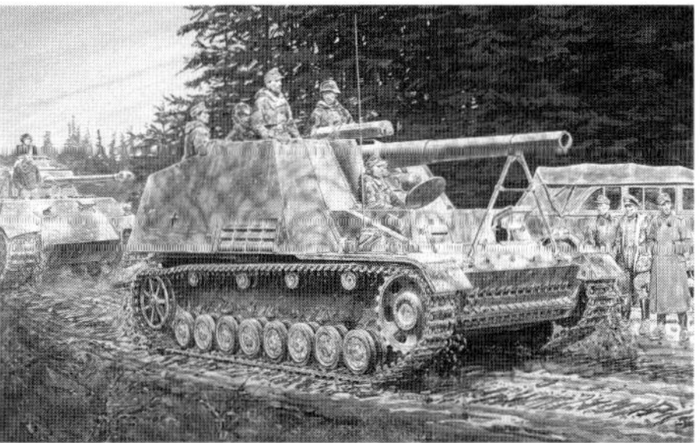

6004 HUMMEL, Sd. Kfz, 165

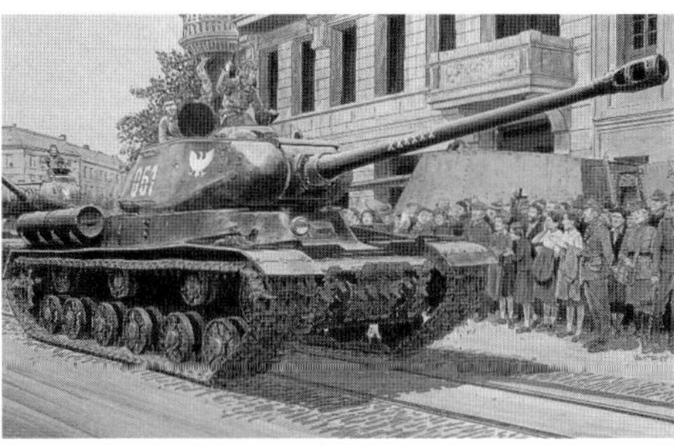

6007 GERMAN SUPER TANK 'MAUS'

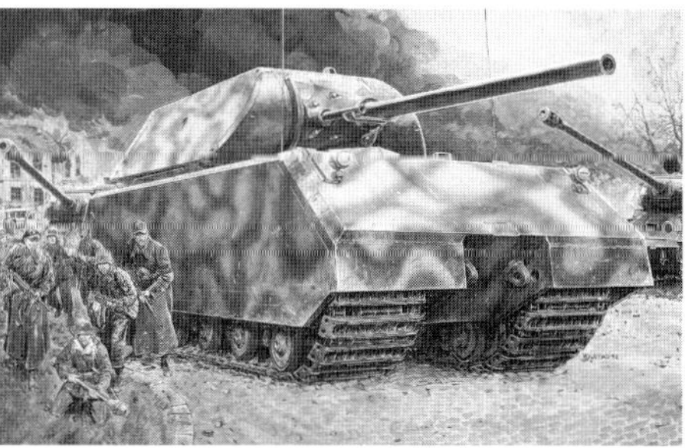

6011 GERMAN E-100 SUPER HEAVY TANK

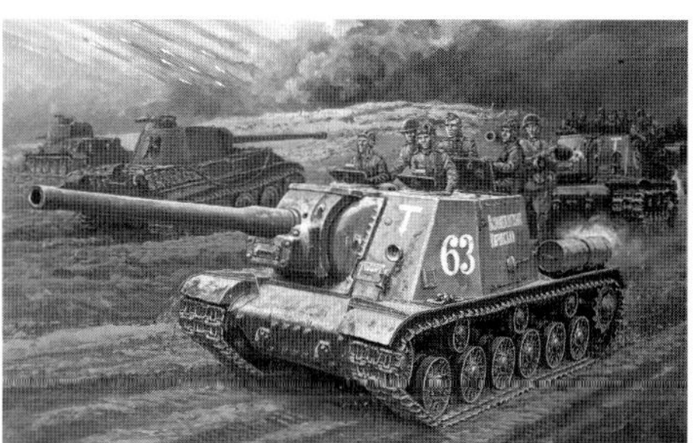

6012 JS-2 STALIN II

6013 JSU-122 TANK DESTROYER

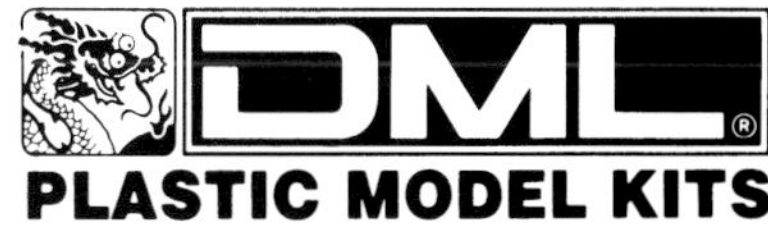

DML ®

PLASTIC MODEL KITS

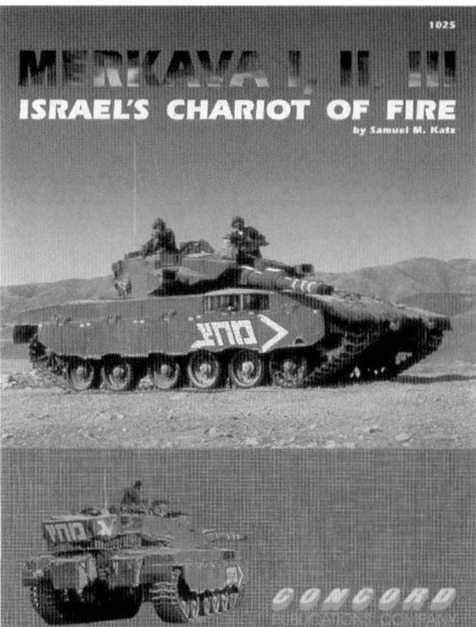

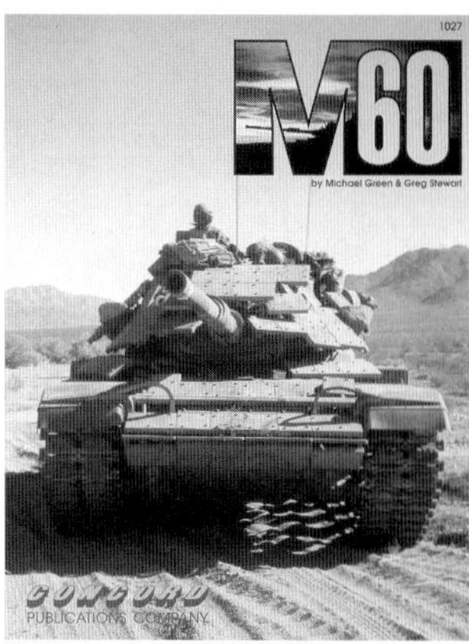

1025 Merkava: Israel's Chariot of Fire
Samuel M. Katz

1027 M60
Michael Green & Greg Stewart

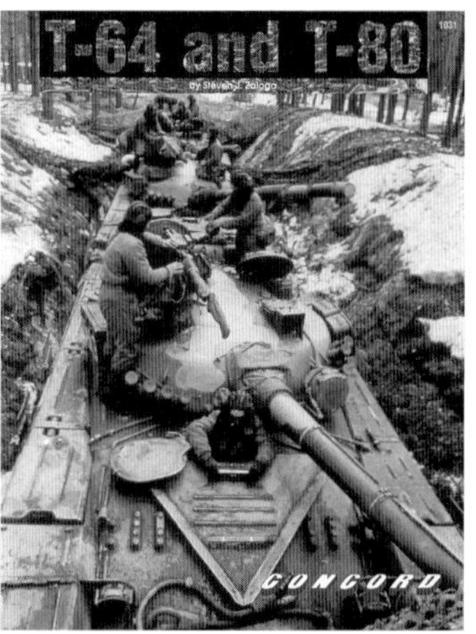

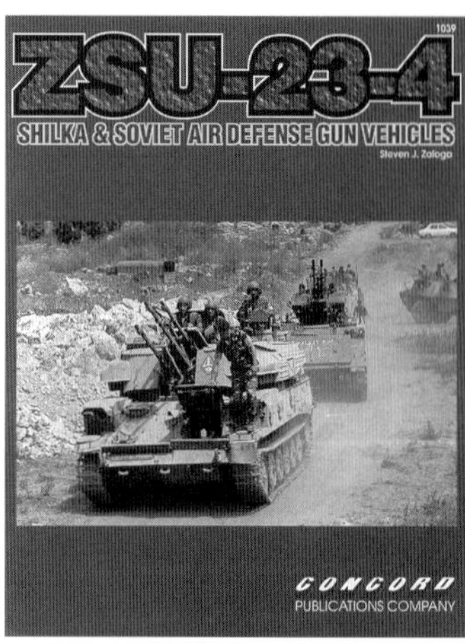

1031 T-64 and T-80
Steven J. Zaloga

1039 ZSU-23-4 Shilka & Soviet Air
Defense Gun Vehicles
Steven J. Zaloga

4004 Armor of the West:(1) NATO's AFNORTH & NORTHAG
Yves Debay

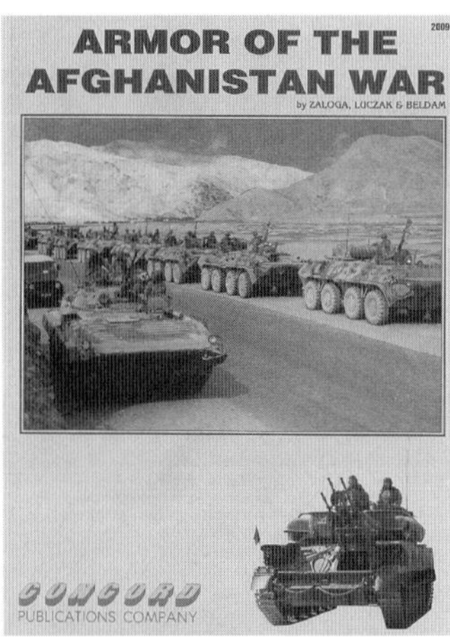

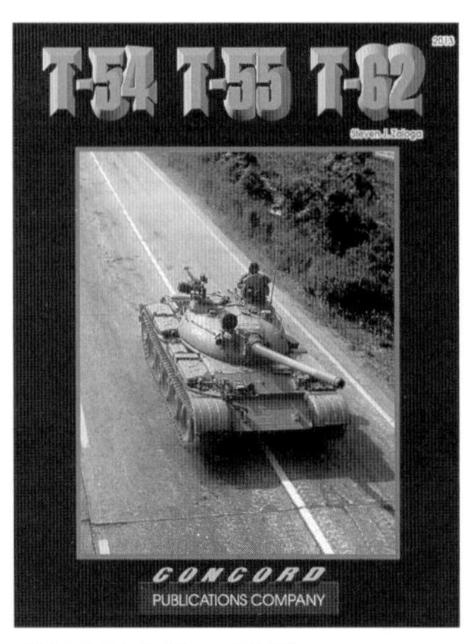

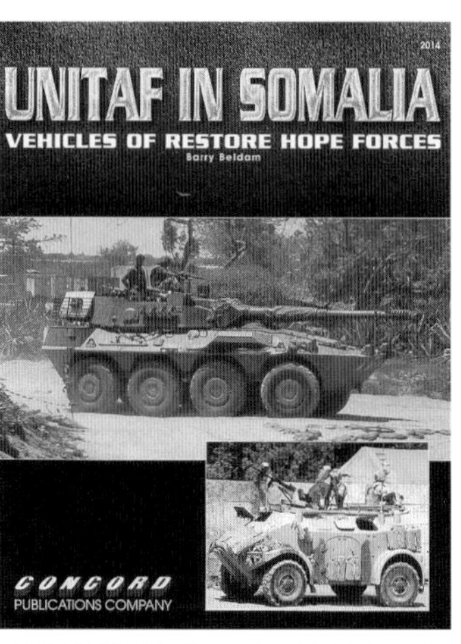

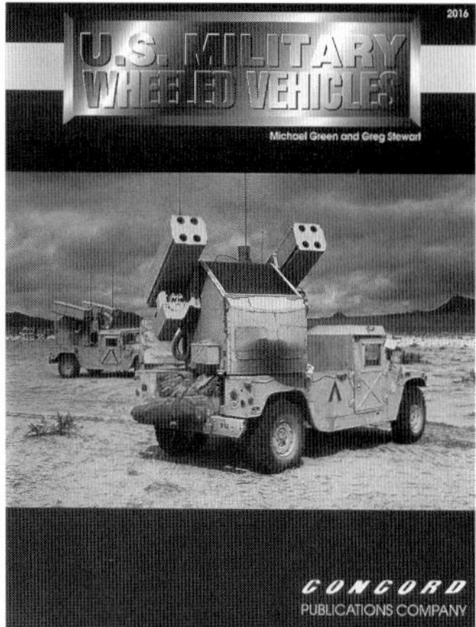

2009 Armor of the Afghanistan War
Steven J. Zaloga, Wojciech Luczak &
Barry Beldam

2013 T-54, T-55 and T-62
Steven J. Zaloga

2014 UNITAF in Somalia: Vehicles of
Restore Hope Forces
Barry Beldam

2016 U.S. Military Wheeled Vehicles
Michael Green & Greg Stewart